Institutional The
Political Science

INSTITUTIONAL THEORY IN POLITICAL SCIENCE

The New Institutionalism

Third Edition

B. Guy Peters

continuum

The Continuum International Publishing Group
80 Maiden Lane, New York, NY 10038
The Tower Building, 11 York Road, London SE1 7NX

www.continuumbooks.com

Library of Congress Cataloging-in-Publication Data
Peters, B. Guy.
Institutional theory in political science: the new institutionalism / B. Guy Peters. – 3rd ed.
p. cm.
Includes bibliographical references and index.
ISBN-13: 978-1-4411-9286-8 (hardcover: alk. paper)
ISBN-10: 1-4411-9286-7 (hardcover: alk. paper)
ISBN-13: 978-1-4411-3042-6 (pbk.: alk. paper)
ISBN-10: 1-4411-3042-X (pbk.: alk. paper) 1. Political science–Methodology.
2. Public institutions. I. Title.

JA71.P477 2011
320.01–dc23

2011032813

ISBN: HB: 978-1-4411-9286-8
PB: 978-1-4411-3042-6

Typeset by Newgen Imaging Systems Pvt Ltd, Chennai, India

Contents

Preface to the Third Edition vi

Chapter 1 Institutionalism Old and New 1

Chapter 2 Roots of the New Institutionalism: Normative Institutionalism 25

Chapter 3 Rational Choice Theory and Institutional Theory 47

Chapter 4 Legacy of the Past: Historical Institutionalism 70

Chapter 5 Empirical Institutionalism 90

Chapter 6 Ideas as the Foundation of Institutions: Discursive and Constructivist Institutionalism 112

Chapter 7 Sociological Institutionalism 127

Chapter 8 Institutions of Interest Representation 143

Chapter 9 International Institutionalism 159

Chapter 10 Conclusion: One Institutionalism or Many? 174

Bibliography 186

Index 213

Preface to the Third Edition

The continuing interest in institutional theory in political science has led to this third edition of *Institutional Theory in Political Science*. Not only have the various approaches to institutions contained in the earlier editions continued to develop and react to the criticisms that have been leveled against them, but there have also been new approaches. In particular, this edition has added a new chapter on discursive institutionalism. Like several of the other approaches in the book, this new approach depends upon ideas to define institutions, but unlike others depends more upon debate and discussion rather than on perpetuating one set of ideas.

The remarkable expansion of the literature on institutions makes doing justice to this literature difficult. The basic structure of the previous editions is still viable but I have attempted to include as much of the more recent literature as possible. At the same time, it was important to retain some of the earlier literature that functioned as the foundation of this field. This edition therefore attempts to integrate the developments in the field with the basics of the approach.

In preparing this third edition I have benefited from my continuing working relationship with Jon Pierre, and our continuing discussions on all matters institutional. Yesamin Irepoglu provided very useful feedback on the manuscript and carefully edited the chapters. I also appreciate the support from Marie-Claire Antoine and her colleagues at Continuum. The arguments here have also been tested before students and colleagues in Pittsburgh and in a number of other countries and have been improved by their questions and comments.

B. Guy Peters
Pittsburgh, PA
April 2011

CHAPTER 1

Institutionalism Old and New

The roots of political science are in the study of institutions. During much of the post-World War II period the discipline of political science, especially in the United States, has rejected those roots in favor of two theoretical approaches based more on individualistic assumptions: behavioralism and rational choice.[1] Both of these approaches assume that individuals act autonomously as individuals, based either on sociopsychological characteristics or rational calculation of their personal *utility*. In either theory, individuals were not seriously constrained by either formal or informal institutions, but would make their own choices; in both views preferences are exogenous to the political process. As well as altering the theoretical perspective of the discipline, this change in orientation also was associated with a growing concern for the appropriate use of rigorous research methods and an equally strong concern for more explicit construction of empirical political theory. Those methodological and theoretical concerns appeared incompatible with an institutional focus.

A successful counter-reformation, beginning in the 1980s, produced some return to the previous concern with formal (and informal) institutions of the public sector and the important role these structures play. Institutional explanations had remained somewhat popular in policy and governance studies, but the institutionalists also have revived their use for explaining individual level behavior.[2] The "New Institutionalism" reflects many features of the older version of this approach to understanding politics, but also is advancing the study of politics in a number of new theoretical and empirical directions. It utilizes many of the assumptions of older institutionalist thinking but enriches that thought with the research tools and the explicit concern for theory that had informed both behavioralism and rational choice analysis. For example, the old institutionalism argued that presidential systems are significantly different from parliamentary systems, based upon the formal structures and rules. The New Institutionalism goes further and tries to determine if these assumed differences do

---

[1] For an early and influential statement of the tenets of behavioralism in political science see Heinz Eulau (1963). For a similar statement on rational choice analysis see Riker and Ordeshook (1973).

[2] "Revived" may not be exactly the right word given that individual level behavior tended to be assumed by the older school of institutionalists, or ignored as largely irrelevant in a political world dominated by institutions.

indeed exist, and if so in what ways do those two alternative ways of organizing political life differ, and what difference does it make for the performance of the systems (Weaver and Rockman, 1993; Von Mettenheim, 1996).

The attempted reconquest of the discipline by the institutionalists has been far from complete, and there are still marked tensions between it and several other components of the discipline. At the same time, there is also some blending of the strands of theory and some softening of the borders separating the contending approaches (see Dowding, 1994). Indeed there should be that softening of those boundaries, given that the several approaches should be viewed more as complementary rather than competitive explanations for political phenomena.[3] None of these approaches can fully explain all political actions, and perhaps none should attempt to do so. Scholars can acquire greater analytic leverage on some questions employing one or the other approach, but the macro-level analysis of institutionalists should be informed by the analysis of individual behavior produced in other areas within the discipline. Likewise, behavioralists and the advocates of rational choice analysis consider individuals to be fully autonomous actors, and to be isolated from the constraints of institutions only at their peril and need to be aware of institutional influences and constraints on the behavior of those individuals.

Further, as we will explore in much greater detail below, the New Institutionalism is not a single animal but rather is a genus with a number of specific species within it. These approaches to institutions also should be seen as complementary (Ostrom, 1990), even if the partisans of one or the other may often claim pride of place. This internal differentiation of the institutionalist approach implies several additional things about contemporary theoretical developments. First, some components of the New Institutionalism are more compatible with the assumptions of the dominant individualistic approaches to the discipline than are others. This differentiation further implies that there may well be a need in many instances to blend several of the versions of the New Institutionalism if researchers want a more complete perspective on the structural characteristics of the political system and the influence of structure on public policies and the conduct of government. In short, we will be arguing throughout this exploration of the institutional approach that some eclecticism in the use of approaches is likely to pay greater intellectual dividends for political science than a strict adherence to a single approach.

Institutionalisms Old and New

The primary focus of this volume is the New Institutionalism in political science, and to some extent also in other social science disciplines. Philip Selznick (1996), for example, has discussed contrasts between the old and the new institutionalism in sociology,

[3] For a general epistemological statement on the need to utilize complementary approaches in the social sciences see Roth (1987).

pointing out that the new institutionalism has certain "deconstructionist" elements in it because of the focus on the mulitplicity and complexity of goals.[4] The use of the word "New" to describe contemporary development implies first that there was an "Old Institutionalism" and second that the new version is significantly different from that older version. Both of those implications can be easily substantiated. For all of the insight and descriptive richness of the older institutionalist literature, it does not appear to contemporary eyes to have the theoretical aspirations and motivations we have come to associate with the social sciences. Further, the methodology employed by the old institutionalism- is largely that of the intelligent observer attempting to describe and understand the political world seen by him or her in nonabstract terms.[5] A number of extraordinarily perceptive individuals—Carl Friedrich, James Bryce, Herman and Samuel Finer—were engaged in the old institutionalism and produced a number of works that bear reading today, but they were simply utilizing different techniques for different purposes as against most contemporary social scientists (Apter, 1991).[6] Further, despite the interest in structure much of the new institutionalism uses some ideas of methodological individualism coming especially from behavioral research.

The Old Institutionalism

Going back even to antiquity and the first systematic thinking about political life, the primary questions asked by scholars tended to concern the nature of governing institutions that could structure the behavior of individuals—both the governing and the governed—toward better ends. The mercurial and fickle nature of individual behavior, and the need to direct that behavior toward collective purposes, required forming political institutions. The first political philosophers began to identify and analyze the success of these institutions in governing and then to make recommendations for the design of other institutions based upon those observations (see Aristotle, *The Politics* [1996 edition]). Although these recommendations were phrased almost entirely in normative terms, they constituted the beginning of political science through the systematic analysis of institutions and their impacts on society.

The same tradition of institutional analysis continued with other political thinkers. Some, for example Althusius (John of Salisbury), attempted to characterize the role of governing institutions in larger society conceived in organic terms. Thomas Hobbes lived through the breakdown of political life during the English Civil War and hence argued for the necessity of strong institutions to save humankind from

[4] Much of Selznick's own work on institutions, for example *The Organizational Weapon* (1952), had focused on highly institutionalized and unified organizations/institutions.

[5] The "her" here is more than an attempt to be politically correct. Gwendolyn Carter (1962) was a significant figure in the description of political institutions during the 1960s and 1970s.

[6] The posthumous publication (1997) of Samuel Finer's three-volume study of the history of government is indicative of scholarly work in that older tradition of institutionalism.

its own worst instincts. John Locke developed a more contractarian conception of public institutions and began the path toward more democratic structures (see also Hooker, 1965). Montesquieu (1989) identified the need for balance in political structures that served as a foundation for the American separation of powers doctrine for the weakening of potentially autocratic governments (Fontana, 1994; Rohr, 1995). This list of great political thinkers could be extended but the fundamental point would remain the same—political thinking has its roots in the analysis and design of institutions.

If we now skip over several centuries and move to the latter part of the nineteenth century, we come to the period in which political science was beginning to differentiate itself as an academic discipline. Prior to that time political science was a component of history, or perhaps of "moral philosophy," reflecting the importance of both the lessons of the past and of normative ideals in understanding contemporary political phenomena.[7] As the discipline began to emerge, its principal questions remained institutional and normative. Political science was about the formal aspects of government, including law, and its attention was squarely on the machinery of the governing system. Further, many of its aims were normative—what institution will work best, given the goals of a political system—and political science was very much in the service of the State.

The Anglo-American political tradition assigned a less significant role to the State than the Continental tradition, but American institutionalists were still concerned with the formal institutions of government. For example, in the United States, Woodrow Wilson was one of the earliest presidents of the American Political Science Association during the 1880s, as well as later being president of Princeton University and then president of the United States. His academic work centered on the role of institutions both in the United States and comparatively. His famous 1887 essay on bureaucracy pointed to what American government could learn from European government, even if European governments appeared to lack the participatory ethos of the United States (Doig, 1983). Likewise, Wilson's *Congressional Government* (1956) was an attempt to have American political scientists consider the problems of "divided government" (Sundquist, 1988; Fiorina, 1996; Elgie, 2001) that already were beginning to affect the separation of powers system of government and to think about parliamentary government as an alternative.

During his life as a practical politician, Wilson was an intellectual leader of the Progressive Movement. Scholars and practitioners associated with that movement were engaged in a number of efforts to reform the institutions of American government, especially to remove what were considered to be the deleterious effects of partisanship (Hofstader, 1963; Hoogenboom and Hoogenboom, 1976; Rice, 1977) through independent regulatory organizations, non-partisan elections, and

---

[7] That remains true today, as can be seen in the school of "normative institutionalists" (Chapter 2) and the historical institutionalists (Chapter 4).

professional public management. Thus, Wilson was linking his scholarly concerns with the needs of the real world for improving government. This progressive tradition was later reflected in organizations such as the Public Administration Clearing House at the University of Chicago. This group had scholars such as Charles Merriam, Louis Brownlow, Leonard White, and later Herbert Simon, and was a crucial player in the spread of reform ideas such as professional city managers, as well as providing assistance for administering the New Deal (Dimock and Dimock, 1963).

Although American political thought and practice has been less State-centric than that of Continental Europe, we should also point out that two of the great works of American "old" institutionalism were works on the State. One was by (again) Woodrow Wilson, with the forgettable title of *The State: Elements of Historical and Practical Politics: A Sketch of Institutional History and Administration* (1898). The other was by T. D. Woolsey (also an Ivy League university president), entitled *Political Science, or The State Theoretically and Practically Considered.*[8] Clearly these major academic figures did consider political science as the study of the State and an exercise in formal-legal analysis. After that time, the State was largely pushed aside in American political science until Theca Skocpol and others helped to bring it back in (Skowronek, 1982; Evans et al., 1985).

These titles, and the content of the works, point to two important aspects of American intellectual life. The first is the influence of German universities on the development of American universities. Wilson's book was in many ways a comment on German legal and institutional theory of the time. The second, and more relevant for our discussion here, is that the State *could* be brought back into American political science—it was there at one time. The roots were there but had been largely abandoned by the rush to explain microlevel political behavior. Despite its later description as a "stateless society" (Stillman, 1991), major theorists in the United States apparently did have a conception of the State and its place in the society.

In Europe, the emerging nature of political science was little different from that in the United States. To the extent that there was a difference it was that political science remained more associated with other areas of study and was even slower to emerge as a separate area of inquiry. The study of political phenomena remained a component of other areas of inquiry, particularly law in most Continental European countries. While this characteristic may have retarded intellectual development in some ways, it certainly reinforced the institutional and formal nature of the inquiry that was done. In essence, government was about the formation and application of law through public institutions, with politics as it is usually conceptualized being a very minor part of the exercise.

---

[8] I am indebted to Harry Eckstein's introductory chapter in Eckstein and David Apter, *Comparative Politics* (1963) for bringing these scholars to my attention. This happened first during graduate school and then again much more recently.

The scholarly dependence upon analysis of law and formal institutions was reinforced by the less participative nature of most European governments at that time. While Wilson may have been fighting against the perceived negative effects of partisanship in the United States, mass political participation was only at the beginning stages in all but a few European countries at that time. For example, as of 1900 except for Britain suffrage remained limited by property and other restrictions in most European countries. Therefore, for European scholars, the very pronounced and continuing emphasis on formal government institutions and law should have been expected.

Further, although Americans frequently praise our self-described "government of laws and not of men," European government was, and remains, even more firmly bound to law than American government. An examination of the training and recruitment of civil servants, and even politicians, in most Continental European countries reveals what the Germans have more recently termed the *Justimonopol* enjoyed by lawyers in public life. The job of the public servant is clearly defined by law, and their task is largely to apply the law to specific situations. The role of the public bureaucrat appears more akin to that of a judge than of a public manager in many European political systems.[9] Further, in this conception of the State, law is very much a formal institution of governing, developing, and imposing a set of clearly articulated norms and values for the society.

In much of Continental Europe (especially those parts dominated by German thinking) the dominant concern with the formal institutions of governing also meant that political science studied "the State," and this tradition continues today as *Staatswissenschaft*. The State is virtually a metaphysical entity which embodies the law and the institutions of government, yet somehow also transcends those entities. Also, in this tradition the State is linked organically with society and society is significantly influenced by the nature of the State. For example, social structures receive their legitimacy by being recognized by the State, rather than as being manifestations of popular will or the ordinary workings of the market.

Proto-Theory in the Old Institutionalism

We have now established that there is a school of "old institutionalists" whose work constituted the basis of political science for much of the late nineteenth and first half of the twentieth centuries. Despite their being characterized, or even stereotyped, as being atheoretical and descriptive, it is still important to note that there were theories lurking in this research. Like Moliere's gentleman, they were speaking theory without necessarily knowing it. This was true despite the specific rejection of many of these scholars, especially those working in the British empirical tradition, of theory as their goal, or of theory being a respectable goal for social analysis.

[9] This conception is changing, even in the Germanic countries. See Reichard, 2001.

Legalism

The first defining characteristic which emerges from the old institutionalism is that it is concerned with law and the central role of law in governing. As discussed above briefly, law is the essential element of governance for most Continental countries, and certainly plays a significant role in Anglo-American thinking about the public sector. Law constitutes both the framework of the public sector itself and a major way in which government can affect the behavior of its citizens. Therefore, to be concerned with political institutions was (and is) to be concerned with law.

To say that that an institutionalist must be concerned with law is only to make a beginning of the analysis. I will not propose to undertake a treatise on the theory of law, which requires several volumes by itself and may be well beyond my capabilities. What I will be concerned with is the manner in which law figures in the accounts of "old institutionalist" scholars of politics, and therefore its foundation for a nascent theory of government (see Damaska, 1986). As might be expected, there has been a variety of different versions of just what that relationship should be, and those differences are to some degree a function of different national perspectives on both law and governing.

For example, a very clear school of legal institutionalists developed in France during the late nineteenth and early twentieth century (Broderick, 1970). This school was a reaction against the natural law orientation of much legal thinking in France at the time, and attempted to establish a more positivist approach to the law. Such an approach implies that law is the product of human agency but that it is also an empirical reality expressing choices made through institutional means. The law was thus an institution, and had some of the capacity to spread a logic of appropriateness that we can see in the normative institutionalists.

The ideas of positive law contained in the French analysis are in marked contrast to the concepts of common law and its role in governing as put forth by Anglo-Saxon scholars. For example, Oliver Wendell Holmes (1909) provided a detailed study of the background and operation of common law. Rather than being the outcome of a more or less rational, deliberative process designed to create a State as in France, law in this view was more evolutionary but yet was clearly institutional, and established a basis for the more empirical approach to the State in Anglo-American countries.

Finally, as implied above, the study of the law as a basis for political knowledge achieved its heights in the Prussian state and thereafter in Germany. Law was crucial for molding what was in essence a new State into an effective body, something which could never have been done by political science as it has come to be practiced. Further, it has been argued that this domination of law was important in socializing a new generation of the German elite into a way of life built in large part on civic responsibility and commitment to the State (Konig, 1993). Further, the persistence of some elements of law even under the Communist regime facilitated the reunification of Germany in the 1990s.

Structuralism

A second dominant assumption of the old institutionalism was that structure mattered, and indeed that structure determined behavior. This was one of the fundamental points against which the behavioralists railed in their attempts to reform the discipline. The structuralist approach left little or no room for the impact of individuals, except perhaps exceptional individuals—the "Great Men" of history—to influence the course of events within government. Thus, if an analyst could identify the salient aspects of structure, he or she could "predict" the behavior of the system. Predict is placed in quotation marks simply because prediction is a goal usually associated with the social scientific mode of research and thinking, rather than with the traditional research of the old institutionalists.

The structuralism characteristic of the old institutionalism tended to focus on the major institutional features of political systems, for example, whether they were presidential or parliamentary, federal or unitary, and so on. Further, the definitions of these terms in the old institutionalism tended to be constitutional and formal.[10] There was no attempt to develop concepts that might capture other structural aspects of a system, for example corporatism or consociationalism, that linked state and society (see Chapter 6). Thus, Wilson could look at the American constitution and see what he considered to be defects within the formal design of the system, and then propose changes. A century later other scholars might look at the same system and see some of the same faults, but would tend to see them in terms of the way in which they functioned rather than their formal status within the constitution (see, for example, Sundquist, 1992).

Despite these implicit critiques of the formal-legal approach to political institutions, scholars working in that tradition produced significant works that did indeed develop theories that undergirded their largely empirical analysis of government. For example, Carl Friedrich might ordinarily be classified as one of the old institutionalists but yet generated a number of statements about government, for example "the Law of Anticipated Reactions," that demonstrated more than a little concern with the development of generalizations and theory. These statements further indicated a willingness to think in other than formal terms about the way in which government functioned.

Woodrow Wilson's major foray into comparative politics, *The State* (1898), also had a number of statements that bordered on the oretical, in almost anyone's conception of the term. For example, when introducing the subject of comparative analysis Wilson asks (p. 41) what are the functions of government, a question that presages some of the later functionalism in comparative politics. Later, when discussing government in the Middle Ages, he provides (pp. 104–5) a mini-theory on the formation of government. The bulk of this book is descriptive, but there is clearly some theoretical thinking as well.

[10] This is, of course, closely related to the legalism discussed as a component of this approach to scholarship.

This concentration on the formal aspects of political systems was the source for another of the critiques from the more "modern" scholars of political science. These critics argued that this formalism first concealed important informal features of politics from the researchers, or made them assume that key functions of a government would have to be performed in this formally designated organization—parliaments make law and executives enforce it. Further, the formalism tended to make political science more ethnocentric than it had to be (Macridis, 1955). With these formalistic assumptions political science could not function very well in less developed countries, or countries that lacked the constitutional structures common in Western countries (Almond and Coleman, 1960). Therefore, to embrace a larger world, political science would have to learn to cope with other forms of analysis that were sufficiently general to apply to almost any political system.

Holism

The old institutionalists often were comparativists, at least comparativists of a sort. To some extent, their emphasis on formal-legal analysis required them to use other systems in order to obtain any variation.[11] When they did their comparative analysis, scholars working in this tradition tended to compare whole systems, rather than to examining individual institutions such as legislatures. This strategy was in contrast to the contemporary pattern which tends to describe and compare component institutions within systems, for example legislatures or bureaucracies. All these parts of the system had to fit together in order to make the system comprehensible.

The holism of this approach again was natural given the concern with constitutions and formal structures, but it had some effect on the manner in which scholarship developed. In particular, holism tended to direct analysis away from comparison in the manner in which it is now often practiced. Countries were not so much compared as described one after the other. "The Politics of X" was, and is, a manner in which to engage in the study of foreign countries (or even one's own) without a direct confrontation with the political reality of another setting. Using that research strategy it is difficult to make any generalizations—again not really the goal of the old institutionalists—because countries tended to be treated as *sui generis.*

The older institutionalism had the most positive consequence of forcing political scientists to attempt to confront the complex interconnections of the numerous political phenomena among themselves, and within the environment of politics. One component of the argument of the new institutionalism is that most political analysis informed rational choice assumptions, which tend to divorce political life from its cultural and socioeconomic roots. Political life then becomes only a compilation of

---

[11] Again, these scholars would hardly have used the language of variance, but the logic of comparison they were using is virtually identical to the more formalized methodologies now in use.

autonomous choices by the relevant political actors. Behavioral political science has tended to include social influences more explicitly, but still looks at the individual as a largely autonomous actor. Clearly, the guiding assumptions of the old institutionalists were those of embeddedness (Granovetter, 1985) and complexity, rather than those of autonomy.

One final consequence of the concentration on whole political systems in the old institutionalism was that it tended to make generalization, and therefore theory construction, more difficult. If scholars can only understand a political system in its entirety then it is difficult to compare, and comparison is the fundamental source for theory development in political science (Dogan and Pelassey, 1990; Peters, 1997a). There were certainly important attempts at comparison undertaken by the older institutionalists, and these scholars even undertook comparisons by functions of government rather than by country (especially of bureaucracies and political parties), but these were the exception rather than the rule. There was, however, relatively little of the "middle range" thinking (LaPalombara, 1968) that has been crucial for the subsequent development of comparative politics.

Historical

The old institutionalism also tended to have a pronounced historical foundation for their analysis. Their analysis was concerned with how (then) contemporary political systems were embedded in their historical development as well as in their socioeconomic and cultural present. Thus, the implicit argument was that to understand fully the manner in which politics was practiced in a particular country, the researcher had to understand the developmental patten which produced that system. Further, individual behavior (for the old institutionalists meaning mostly the behavior of political elites) was a function of their collective history and of their understanding of the meaning of their politics influenced by history.

This implicit developmental conception of politics also pointed to the interactions of politics and the socioeconomic environment. Whereas contemporary political science tends to see interactions running in only one direction—from society to politics—the older institutionalists tended to see a long-term pattern of mutual influence. The actions of the State influenced society as much as society shaped politics. For example, Bismarckian laws about works councils were crucial to the formation of a particular German pattern of industrial relations and therefore of a particular form of capitalism that persists into the 1990s, and early choices about State intervention shaped American capitalism as well as the nature of government itself (Hughes, 1993; Sbragia, 1996; Orren and Skowronek, 2004).

The argument in favor of an historical understanding of a country and its politics is hardly novel, and for most area-studies scholars it would hardly be controversial, but for some contemporary social scientists it would be very controversial. They might not be willing to accept Henry Ford's statement that "History is bunk" but they do contend that history is unnecessary for an understanding of contemporary political behavior. In the more individualistic framework, and especially in the frame of the rational choice approach, calculations of utility or psychological reactions to certain stimuli are the proximate causes of behavior, not some deep-rooted conception of national history (Bates, 1988).

Normative Analysis

Finally, the older institutionalists tended to have a strong normative element in their analysis. As noted above, political science emerged from distinctly normative roots, and the older institutionalists often linked their descriptive statements about politics with a concern for "good government." This was perhaps most clearly seen in the American progressives as a self-described good government movement, but also tended to be characteristic of most of the old institutionalists. This normative element was also a target of the disciplinary reformers of the 1950s and 1960s, who argued for the positivistic separation of fact and value and for a discipline that would be concerned primarily if not exclusively with the facts.

This normative element of their analysis was another of the particulars in the indictment of the institutionalists by the disciplinary reformers during the 1950s and 1960s. Almost by definition, the institutionalists' concern with norms and values meant that this work could not be scientific, at least not in the positivist meaning of that term (for a critique see Storing, 1962). For the old institutionalist the fact–value distinction on which such contemporary social science has been constructed was simply not acceptable as a characterization of social life. Those two dimensions of life were intertwined and constituted a whole for the interpretation and improvement of government (see Dewey, 1938, p. 499).

Summary and Conclusion

The old institutionalists developed a rich and important body of scholarship. It is easy to criticize their work from the advantage of the social sciences as they have developed over the past 50 years, but that criticism is unfair to the purposes and the contributions of the older institutionalist scholars. These scholars did point out many factors that now motivate contemporary institutionalist analysis, even if not in an explicitly theoretical manner. This presaging of institutionalism is true of the structural elements of government as well as of the historical and normative elements. The new institutionalism grew up not so much merely to reassert some of the virtues of the older form of analysis but more to make a statement about the perceived failings of what had come to be the conventional wisdom of political science. Therefore, to understand the new institutionalists, we need to understand not only the old institutionalists but the schools of thought that emerged in between the times at which the two flourished.

The Behavioral and the Rational Revolutions

It is quite common to talk of the behavioral revolution which occurred during the 1950s and 1960s as fundamentally transforming the discipline of political science, and to a lesser extent other social sciences like sociology. This "revolution" did constitute a very fundamental shift in the manner in which political science was studied in the leading departments in the country. Also, it served as the stalking horse for an even more fundamental shift in the assumptions guiding work for a significant, and increasingly influential, component of the discipline—the rational choice approach. Both of the movements have fundamentally transformed the discipline, and although they are very different from one another in some respects they also share some common features. These attributes include: Concern with Theory and Methodology, Anti-Normative Bias, Assumptions of Individualism, and "Inputism."

Theory and Methodology

One of the most important distinguishing features of the behavioral revolution was the explicit concern with theory development. The argument was that if political science was to be a true science then it had to develop theory. That is, it had to develop some general, internally consistent statements that could explain phenomena in a variety of settings. It would no longer be sufficient to describe politics in a number of countries and make interesting interpretations of those systems; the interpretations had to be fitted into a more general frame of theory.

As the behavioral revolution proceeded, a number of candidates for general theories were developed and "tested." For example, in comparative politics—the area most akin to the old institutionalism—structural-functionalism (Almond and Coleman, 1960; Almond and Powell, 1967) was a major candidate for theoretical domination. This approach argued that all political systems must perform certain requisite functions and comparison therefore consisted of comparing which structures[12] performed the tasks, and perhaps how well they were performed in various countries. Further, this approach contained a number of developmental assumptions (Wiarda, 1991), so that as political systems developed they became increasing differentiated structurally and increasingly secularized culturally.

In areas of the discipline such as voting behavior there was an ongoing struggle between those who ascribed behavior more to social factors (e.g., social class) impinging on the life of citizens (see Franklin, 1985), and those that ascribed the behavior more to psychological factors, most importantly partisan identification (Campbell et al., 1960). For both of these cases, as well as for students of the behavior

[12] One list of the requisite functions for the political system: recruitment, interest articulation, interest aggregation, rule making, rule application, rule adjudication, and political communication (Almond and Powell, 1966).

of legislators[13] (Wahlke et al., 1962), judges (Schubert, 1965), and administrators (Aberbach et al., 1981), political life tended to be a function of other characteristics of the individual, but still an individualistic phenomenon. If we are to understand the world of politics, we have to look at the people who inhabited that world and ask them why they did what they did.

Theoretical development certainly did occur as a part of the behavioral revolution in politics, and the drive to make general statements about political behavior became even more evident with growth of the rational choice approach to politics. In this approach, rather than reducing political behavior to social or psychological attributes, political behavior became a function of economic motivations and calculations. More specifically, political actors and political groups were assumed to be rational utility maximizers. For example, in one of the earliest statements on this approach, Anthony Downs (1957) assumed that politicians would maximize their utility by seeking to be reelected. In this view, party platforms and the policies of government were means to the end of being reelected, rather than being the ends of politics themselves (see also Fiorina, 1982).

Both the behavioral and the rational choice approaches to politics also required political science to invest heavily in methodology, and to think much more systematically about the collection of evidence. While the observations of a skilled and astute scholar would be sufficient for the old institutionalists, the newer approaches, especially behavioralism, required careful attention to developing data in ways that were "intersubjectively transmissible" and replicable (see King, G., 1995). Also, the hypotheses derived from the theories would have to be tested, and this required increasingly high levels of training in statistics and mathematics.

Anti-Normative Bias

The desire to eliminate the normative elements of political science research follows from the emphasis on developing science in political science. As noted, the old institutionalists had very clear normative concerns about making government perform better, according to their own definitions of "better," of course. Their concern with comparison reflected to some extent their collective desire to learn how other governments worked, and to see if there were lessons which might make their own function better. For example, when Woodrow Wilson was criticized for his willingness to learn from the imperial German bureaucracy about how best to manage a State and to translate those ideas into republican America, he argued that if one ". . . saw a murderous fellow sharpening a knife cleverly . . ." (1887, p. 220) one could still learn how to sharpen knives without having to adopt the sinister intentions of the

[13] One exception in the early days of behavioralism was the Wahlke, Eulau, Buchanan, and Fergueson study that focused on the roles of legislators, with those roles being determined in large part by the institutions themselves.

sharpener. In this view, therefore, efficiency was the central value to be pursued in government, and that goal could be pursued through comparative analysis.

Critics of the old institutionalists argued that there were some less clearly stated and less obvious normative implications of the old institutionalism, and that these implications were not as positive as the concern for good government. In particular, the criticism was argued that there was a very strong bias in favor of the industrialized democracies of the world as presenting a model, or actually the model, of how government should be run. To some extent the emphasis on formal legal institutions tended to exclude countries with less formalized arrangements as having government in any meaningful sense. What is perhaps most interesting about this argument is that critics of approaches such as structural functionalism and "The Civic Culture" (Almond and Verba, 1965) were quick to point out that the newer forms of analysis had many of the same biases, albeit dressed up in more complex language.

Methodological Individualism

One of the most fundamental tenets of behavioral and rational choice analysis is methodological individualism. This is the argument that only actors in political settings are individuals, and therefore the only appropriate foci for political inquiry are individuals and their behaviors. In behavioral analysis this individualism is relevant not only for methodological reasons but also because the focus of inquiry is often the individual, whether as a voter, a holder of opinions, or a member of the political elite. For rational choice analysis the assumptions of individual utility maximization tend to drive the entire approach, and to give its analytical power, whether discussing individuals or collections of individuals.

This approach can make a strong claim that individuals are the appropriate focus for social and political analysis. Social collectivities such as political parties, interest groups, legislatures, or whatever, do not make decisions. The people within these collectivities make the decisions, and there are then rules permitting the aggregation of individual behaviors.[14] The institutionalist answer, however, is that the very same people would make different choices depending upon the nature of the institution within which they were operating at the time. They might behave in a utility maximizing manner while at work during the week, but behave in a more altruistic manner while at church or synagogue on the weekend. If that is true, then is it the individual who matters or the setting?[15] Indeed, much of the

[14] The adage in Washington DC is that "buildings don't make telephone calls." This means simply that the White House didn't call, a member of the president's staff at the White House made the call.

[15] The logical "rational choice" answer is that both behaviors maximize individual utilities at the time, but if that is the answer then the theory may not really be falsifiable.

logic of designing institutions is to structure decisions and to eliminate random, individualistic elements.[16]

Inputism

The traditional institutionalists tended to concentrate on the formal institutions of government and the constitutions which produced those structures. The behavioral revolution in political science tended to reverse completely this emphasis and to concentrate on the inputs from society into the "political system" (Easton, 1953). What really mattered in this view of politics was voting, interest group activity, and even less legal forms of interest articulation, which were then processed into "outputs." In this conception of a political system, the formal institutions of government and the policy process were reduced to the "black box," where the conversion of inputs into outputs occurred, almost magically as it appeared to critics of the approach.[17]

This characteristic of political science at the time can be seen very clearly in a number of studies of policy choices which argued that "politics did not matter." These studies (Dye, 1966; Sharkansky, 1968) all argued that politics, and especially the politics that occurred within formal institutions, could not explain policy choices as well as indicators of the socioeconomic environment. Even this vein of scholarship and its findings were influenced by the "inputism" of the time. Rather than looking at the complex and largely determinative decision-making that occurs within the formal institutions making policy, this research used input measures (voting for parties, measures of openness) as the only measures for identifying the potential impact of politics.

While it can be readily argued that the old institutionalism did exclude many interesting and important features of mass political behavior, the behavioral revolution appeared to go to the other extreme. It tended to deny the importance of formal institutions for determining the outputs of government, even if they were to some extent interested in the behavior of the individuals within those institutions. It was the behavior, not the performance of government, that was the principal concern. Furthermore, the direction of causation was entirely in one direction—economy and society influenced politics and political institutions. Institutionalism, both old and new, argues that causation can go in both directions and that institutions shape social and economic orders. For example, most markets now are not the result of random interactions of buyers, but rather structures that have been systematically created by government through regulation and which inhibit autonomous or random actions by the participants (North, 1990; Whitley and Kristensen, 1997).

The rational choice approach potentially is somewhat more hospitable to institutionalism. Rational choice applies its models to both individual behavior and to

---

[16] This logic is seen most clearly in the design of bureaucracies in which the specialization of tasks and formalization of rules is intended to produce equitable treatment for all clients.

[17] For a more generous view using a wide variety of Easton's work see Kriek (1995).

collective decision-making, although always assuming that the institutions are little more than means to aggregate the preferences of the individuals who comprise them. In this view, institutions do possess some reality and some influence over the participants, even if for no other reason but that institutional or constitutional rules establish the parameters for individual behavior (Buchanan and Tullock, 1962). What the rational choice approach does tend to deny is that the institutions play any significant role in shaping preferences of the participants. These tend to be exogenous and determined prior to participation, something which would be denied vigorously by institutionalists.

Behavioralism and Rational Choice as the Background for the New Institutionalism

The success of these two disciplinary revolutions is the backdrop against which the new institutionalism came into existence. The initial advocates of the new institutionalism, especially James March and Johan Olsen who named the movement (1984), made positive statements about what they believed empirical political theory should be. In that process, however, they were also making several more critical statements about how they believed the discipline had been led astray. They did not argue for a complete return to the *status quo ante*, but they did point to a perceived need to reassert some of the features of the older institutional analysis. In particular, they argued that the behavioral and rational choice approaches were characterized by: Contextualism, Reductionism, Utilitarianism, Functionalism, and Instrumentalism. Several of these terms are similar to my own descriptions of the nature of the two approaches presented above, but obviously were presented with more pejorative connotations by March and Olsen.

The *Contextualism* discussed by March and Olsen is very similar to the idea of "inputism" advanced above. The argument that March and Olsen put forward is that contemporary political science, at the time of their writing at least, tended to subordinate political phenomena to contextual phenomena such as economic growth, class structure, and socioeconomic cleavages (1984, p. 735). Perhaps even more importantly, unlike the central role assigned to the State in traditional institutional thinking, politics in the contemporary political science described by March and Olsen depends upon society. This view is in contrast to society depending upon the State and law for defining its existence, or their existing in an organic condition of mutual dependence as in most Continental political theory (Dyson, 1980). Thus, scholars can talk about "bringing the State back in" (Evans et al., 1985; Almond, 1988) as constituting a major theoretical event and can do so convincingly.[18]

[18] Again, this is especially true in American political science. In European political science the State never really left.

Similarly, the *Reductionism* identified by March and Olsen refers to the tendency of both behavioral and rational choice approaches to politics to reduce collective behavior to individual behavior. Further, the properties of any collectivities tend to be derived from the choices of the individuals, rather than vice versa, or even having the individuals also influenced by the norms, rules, and values of the institutions. As they state (1989, p. 4):

> . . . the central faith is that outcomes at the collective level depend only on the intricacies of the interactions among the individual actors, that concepts suggesting autonomous behavior at the aggregate level are certainly superfluous and probably deleterious.

March and Olsen argue that this "central faith" decomposes all collective behavior into its smallest components and therefore leaves no room for any appreciable impact of the larger structures in society and the polity.

The *Utilitarianism* described by March and Olsen is concerned with the tendency to value decisions for what they produce for the individual, rather than as representing some intrinsic value of their own. Utilitarianism can be more clearly linked with rational choice analysis than with behavioralism. The fundamental assumption of rational choice is that people act to maximize their personal self-interest.[19] Thus, while for institutionalists acting within an institutional framework involves commitments to values other than personal values, and has a pronounced normative element, most contemporary science is based on personal values. Also, March and Olsen argue that decision-making is prospective and we cannot know what will be in our interest in the future—we do indeed operate under Rawls's "veil of ignorance" (1970). Therefore, it may be fully rational to rely more upon settled institutional criteria when making decisions than to attempt to maximize individual well-being.

Thinking about history plays a significant role for the new institutionalists, and *Functionalism* represents a critique of the way in which the behavioral and rational choice approaches have dealt with history. The argument from March and Olsen is that the dominant schools of political science assume that history is an efficient process moving toward some equilibrium. Thus, the structural functionalists in comparative politics assume that societies are moving from lower to higher forms of political organization. Similarly, students of political parties, for example Anthony Downs (1957) or Laver and Hunt (1992), assume that parties move toward some competitive equilibrium based upon conscious adjustments to the demands of the

---

[19] One major problem with rational choice as "science" is that this statement may not be falsifiable. Even if individuals act in what appears from the outside to be extremely irrational ways, it can always be claimed that in their own "felific calculus" the decision was the right one.

political marketplace.[20] Students of institutions, on the other hand, tend to assume much less functionality in history and to assume that political processes are much less smooth and untroubled than their colleagues in other theoretical camps appear to assume.

Finally, March and Olsen claimed that contemporary political science was characterized by *Instrumentalism* or the domination of outcomes over process, identity, and other important sociopolitical values. In other words, political life is analyzed as simply doing things through the public sector, rather than as a complex interaction of symbols, values, and even the emotive aspects of the political process. To the extent that political actors engage in symbolic actions, contemporary political analysis may see it as only more self-interested attempts to legitimate their policy decisions, rather than as an integral component of the art of governing. March and Olsen argue that ritual and ceremony, the parts that Bagehot (1928) once described as "the dignified parts of the Crown" are rendered largely meaningless by most contemporary political science.

On the basis of these criticisms of the political science of the time, and in fairness their characterizations of political science remain an accurate description in the late 1990s, March and Olsen argued for creating a "New Institutionalism." This new institutionalism would replace the five prevailing characteristics of political science with a conception that located collective action more at the center of the analysis. Rather than collective action being the major conundrum that it is for economists, collective action should become, they argued, the dominant approach to understanding political life.[21] Further, the relationship between political collectivities and their socioeconomic environment should be reciprocal, with politics having the option of shaping society as much as society does of shaping politics. Only with this more institutional and multifaceted conception of politics, it was argued, could political science really be able to understand and explain the complex phenomenon which we have chosen as our subject.

Varieties of Institutional Theory

We have been asserting that the new institutionalism itself contains a variety of different approaches to institutional phenomena (see Heclo, 2008). Even without

[20] This view could have some credibility in the two-party system of the United States (on which the arguments were based) but appears to fall apart when confronted with multi-party systems in which the parties have deep historical and ideological roots.

[21] Collective action is a problem for economists because of the difficulties of designing appropriate means of aggregating individual values—the basic problem of welfare economics. Kenneth Arrow's struggles with this problem helped win him the Nobel Prize, but did not solve the fundamental problems when one begins from an individualistic position.

spreading our net too widely, it is clear that at there are at least six versions of the new institutionalism in current use. Most of these refer to themselves by that term, or else allude to the existence of other forms of institutional thinking in doing their own research. This is a rich array of literature, but that very richness presents a problem of understanding. Is this really a single approach to political science, or are the assumptions and intentions of the various versions of the "New Institutionalism" too widely separate to be put under the same intellectual umbrella?

Institutionalism: What Are We Talking About?

As well as simply taking the proclamations of most of these approaches that they are institutional, it is crucial to ask ourselves just what criteria should we think about that might disqualify any approach attempting to crash the institutionalist party under false pretenses. What makes an approach to political and social activity peculiarly "institutional"? The details of the answer may vary in part depending upon which version is being discussed, but there should be some common core that binds all the approaches if there is to be anything worth discussing as a common corpus of scholarly work.

Perhaps the most important element of an institution is that these are in some way a structural feature of the society and/or polity. That structure may be formal (a legislature, an agency in the public bureaucracy, or a legal framework), or it may be informal (a network of interacting organizations, or a set of shared norms). As such, an institution transcends individuals to involve groups of individuals in some sort of patterned interactions that are predictable, based upon specified relationships among the actors. Institutions vary in the amount of predictability they require—universities appear to require predictability for course hours but little else, while prisons require rigid adherence to schedules—but all require some regularities.

A second feature would be the existence of some stability over time. Individuals may decide to meet for coffee one afternoon. That could be very pleasant, but it would not be an institution. If they decide to meet every Thursday afternoon at the same time and place, that would begin to take on the features of an institution. Further, if those people are all Senators then the meeting may be relevant for our concern with institutions in political science. Some versions of institutionalism argue that some features of institutions are extremely stable and then predict behavior on that basis, while others make institutions more mutable, but all require some degree of stability.

The third feature of an institution for our purposes is that it must affect individual behavior. If we continue with our trivial example of the coffee klatch above, it may not be an institution if the members do not assign some importance to the meeting and attempt to attend. In other words, an institution should in some way constrain the behavior of its members. Again, the constraints may be formal or they may be informal, but there must be constraints if there is to be an institution in place.

Finally, although this characteristic may be sung *sotto voce* in comparison to the others, there should be some sense of shared values and meaning among the members of the institution. This view is central to the normative institutionalism of March and Olsen, and also appears clearly in other versions such as the sociological and the international versions of institutionalism. Even in the rational choice version of institutionalism there must be some relatively common set of values or the incentives so central to their models would not function equally well for all participants in the institution.

Institutional Theories

The first of the approaches is that advanced by March and Olsen in their seminal article (1984) and then in a variety of other writings (1989; 1995). I will be referring to this as *Normative Institutionalism* in my discussions of this body of literature. This term was selected because of the very strong emphasis these authors place on the norms of institutions as a means of understanding how they function and how they determine, or at least shape, individual behavior. March and Olsen place a great deal of emphasis on the "logic of appropriateness" as a means of shaping the behavior of members of institutions.[22] These values may enter the frame of reference of individuals, but are difficult to place within a utility-maximizing framework.

The most stark contrast to the assumptions of the normative institutionalists is the school of *Rational Choice Institutionalists.* Rather than being guided by norms and values, scholars working within this framework argue that behaviors are a functions of rules and incentives. Institutions are, for this group, systems of rules and inducements to behavior in which individuals attempt to maximize their own utilities (Weingast, 1996). Further, institutions can answer one of the vexing problems of rational choice analysis—how to achieve equilibrium among a set of rational egoists. These models are explicitly functionalist, and argue that institutions do emerge to meet social and economic necessities (see Knight, 1992, p. 94).

The third approach to the role of structures in governance is *historical institutionalism.* For these scholars the basic point of analytic departure is the choices that are made early in the history of any policy, or indeed of any governmental system. These initial policy choices, and the institutionalized commitments that grow out of them, are argued to determine subsequent decisions. If we do not understand those initial decisions in the career of a policy then it becomes difficult to understand the logic of the development of that policy. As numerous scholars (see Krasner, 1984; Pierson and Skocpol, 2002) have argued, policies are "path dependent" and once launched

[22] They also discuss other factors (see pp. 30–1), but the normative elements appear central to their conception of institutions.

on that path they will persist in that pattern until some significant force intervenes to divert them from the established direction.

Old institutionalists are closer to the old institutionalism than any of the groups discussed here, except perhaps the normative institutionalists. The empirical institutionalists argue that the structure of government does make a difference in the way in which policies are processed and the choices which will be made by governments. Some use very conventional categories such as the difference between presidential and parliamentary government (Weaver and Rockman, 1993), while others use more analytic categories such as "decision points" (Immergut, 1992a) or "veto points" (Tsebelis, 1990). As we move into several of the latter areas of institutional theory, the direct connections to institutionalism may become more remote. Despite that, it is important to attempt to understand the structural and institutional aspects of these theoretical perspectives in order to have a more complete picture of the place assigned to institutions in the discipline. One of the less obvious forms of institutional theory is *international institutionalism*. By this I do not refer to the role of the United Nations or the International Monetary Fund but rather to the theoretical place assigned to structure in explaining the behavior of States and individuals. One of the clearest examples is international regime theory (Krasner, 1983; Keohane, 1989; Rittberger, 1993) which assumes the existence of structured interactions to be very much as would be expected within State-level institutions.

Finally, we come to "societal institutionalism," an infelicitous phrase to describe the structuring of relationships between State and society. The pluralist model of State–society relationships common in the United States assumes a very loosely coupled and largely uninstitutionalized pattern of interactions between interest groups and the State. European conceptualizations of these relationships, including corporatism (Schmitter, 1974) and corporate pluralism (Rokkan, 1966), imply a more structured interaction between official and unofficial actors in the governance process, and hence they approach institutional status (see Chapter 7). Similarly, more recent network analysis of these relationships (Knoke and Laumann, 1987; Sorenson and Torfing, 2002; but see Jordan, 1990) also imply a significant degree of structuring of interactions, and can be extended to cover relationships within government as well as between government and society. Thus, applying an institutionalist characterization to this body of literature does not appear to violate its basic pattern of thought, although these patterned relationships may not correspond closely to other patterns of institutional theory.

A Note on Other Disciplines

The discussion thus far has centered on political science. This is my own area of interest and expertise, and this is also the discipline within which most of the serious discussions and debate of these theoretical issues has taken place. The central position of this debate in political science is in part because my discipline has been more eclectic than most in borrowing the approaches of others while, as argued above, institutionalism represents a return to the original foundations of the discipline. Despite their concentration in the one discipline, many of the same debates are being carried out on other disciplines in the social sciences. The fundamental methodological and theoretical issues of how to explain aggregate behavior apply in almost any human science (see Giddens, 1984). Can we reduce collective behavior to merely the aggregate of individual behavior? If simple aggregation is inadequate, do we not run the risk of reifying collectivities and giving them the human properties of volition and decision that may not be appropriate?

The discussion over these issues has also been somewhat heated in economics, with the revival of a once-strong strand of institutional economics[23] by scholars such as Nobel Laureate Douglass North (1990), and the increasing importance of rational choice models of political and social institutions (Shepsle, 1989; Ostrom, 1990) bridging political science and economics. As in political science there has been some reaction against the individualistic assumptions of contemporary microeconomic theory and a desire by some major scholars to understand the effects that larger, seemingly amorphous, structures exert over the behavior of presumably autonomous, rational individuals. Indeed, some of the most important concepts in economics—the market most notably—appear to possess some collective properties that extend beyond the mere aggregation of individual decisions, and which are often referred to in institutional terms (Williamson, 1985).

Sociology also has had a substantial revival of interest in institutional analysis. The conflict in sociology over this issue has not been as great perhaps as in the other disciplines, in part because the two strands of thinking have tended to coexist somewhat better in that discipline than in others. There is a strong tradition of institutional analysis going back to monumental figures in the field such as Marx, Weber, and Durkheim. Historical sociology also has placed a strong emphasis on the role of institutions in shaping behavior (Wittfogel, 1957; Eisenstadt, 1963; see also Finer, 1997). More recently, the tradition of organizational sociology has tended to keep interest in non-individual behavior alive and thriving (Scott, 1995a; Jessop, 2003). At the same time, sociology also has had a thriving tradition of microlevel analysis, including substantial attention to political sociology, and with that some attention to interactions across levels of analysis (Achen and Shively, 1995).

Although perhaps less controversial than in political science, there has been some revival of explicit institutional theorizing in sociology. DiMaggio and Powell (1991, p. 13) provide an extensive examination of the differences between old and new institutional thinking in sociology. In particular, they argue that although the two sets of literature share many points, especially the rejection of rationalistic analysis of organizations, they differ in the sources of the irrationality they identify

[23] Scholars such as Thorsten Veblen, Rexford G. Tugwell, and John R. Commons are commonly cited as the leaders of this vein of theory in economics.

in institutions. They also differ in the relationship of institutions to their environments and the role assigned to politics in shaping the institutions. The impetus for this shift in sociological theory appears to be a reaction to the rapid spread of arguments about the individuation of societies (Cerny, 1990; Zürn, 1993), and the analogous strengthening of methodological individualism in other social science disciplines, especially economics (Scott, 1995b). Sociology also has been drawn into several of its own internal cultural wars over the extent to which globalization and homogenization of society is merely spreading Western, Weberian thinking, as well as conflicts between Parsonian and other conceptions of social action (see Campbell and Pedersen, 2001). These theses are all somewhat familiar in social thinking, and for sociology the new institutionalism has been as much or more of a return to its intellectual roots as has the revival of institutionalism in political science.

Plan of the Book

Having now identified seven institutionalists' perspectives that exist within political science, I will proceed to discuss these six *ad seriatem*. As well as providing a more complete description than the one provided above for each version of institutional theory, I will ask a series of questions to explore each of the assumptions:

(1) What constitutes an institution in this approach? What criteria can be utilized to determine whether an institution exists or not?
(2) How are institutions formed? What is the process of institutionalization, and is it mirrored by a process of deinstitutionalization with the same dynamics (Eisenstadt, 1959)?
(3) How do institutions change? How do they change intentionally and how do they evolve without the conscious actions of designers? How much change is acceptable before one must say that the institution has changed into another?
(4) How do individuals and institutions interact? If institutions are assumed to mold human behavior, how is that influence exerted in practice? Is it exerted in the same way in all political institutions?
(5) How does this approach explain behavior and can that explanation be falsified? Is there any way of differentiating individual and collective influences over behavior? Are there ways of generating testable hypotheses from this approach? Can those hypotheses be differentiated from those arising from other views of institutionalism?
(6) What are the limits of explanation using this approach? What can it do, and what can it not do? Does it make empirical and theoretical claims that cannot be substantiated?
(7) What does this approach have to say about the design of institutions? Can institutions be designed purposefully, or are they an organic outgrowth of human processes that escapes design?
(8) How does the institution work? What are the fundamental social and political processes through which the institution maintains itself and achieves its purposes?
(9) Last, but certainly not the least, is the deontological question: What is a good institution, and what normative criteria are embedded in the theory, whether explicitly or implicitly?

These questions will address the scientific status of the theory, as well as its utility for the actual description of political behavior. As is so often the case in social science research, theoretical approaches that perform well on some criteria appear to perform poorly on others, so that the researcher wishing to choose one of these approaches to institutions will be forced to choose very wisely, and must know precisely what he or she wants to know about institutions.

CHAPTER 2

Roots of the New Institutionalism: Normative Institutionalism

The phrase "new institutionalism," and much of the impetus toward redirecting the focus of contemporary political science, is derived from the work of James G. March and Johan P. Olsen (1984; 1989; 1996; see also Olsen, 2006). These scholars argue that political science as well as the other social sciences, to some extent, have been directing far too much of its theoretical and conceptual energies in directions that would diminish the centrality of political values and collective choice. March and Olsen argued that the centrality of values in political analysis was being replaced with individualistic, and largely utilitarian, assumptions and methodologies. Further, these individualistic assumptions were argued to be inherently incapable of addressing the most important questions of political life, given that they could not integrate individual action with fundamental normative premises, or with the collective nature of most of the important political activities.

March and Olsen further argue that organizations and institutions are central for understanding the role of values and collective choices in politics. The individualistic approaches to political life assume that individuals are either rational utility maximizers or have many of their political values formed by sociological or psychological processes. In this institutional framework, however, individuals are assumed to gain most of their political values through their membership in institutions, formal or informal. Thus, becoming a political animal means learning, and continuing to learn what values are important as well as how to be a participant in the political process.

Although they were appealing for a return of the discipline to its intellectual roots, there have been a number of criticisms of March and Olsen's solutions to the theoretical problems they identified (Jordan, 1990; Pedersen, 1991; Searing, 1991; Sened, 1991). These responses include several critiques that argue that they fundamentally misinterpreted rational choice theory (Dowding, 1994) and therefore successfully demolished a straw person. Despite these critiques, March and Olsen and their theoretical perspectives have fundamentally reshaped the nature of discourse on contemporary political science, and have forced substantial rethinking of the intellectual direction of the discipline.[1] Whereas at one time institutions and

[1] Almond's (1988) characterization of a "discipline divided" is even more apt because of the continuing, and growing, influence of institutionalism.

institutional analysis were almost always written out of the discipline, they have now made a major comeback and have become a central part of the discourse on political science.

We will be referring to this particular version of the new institutionalism as "normative institutionalism." This title reflects the central role assigned to norms and values within organizations in explaining behavior in this approach. Another apt characterization—coming from the sociological tradition—has been "mythic" institutionalism, reflecting the importance of organizational myths and stories in defining acceptable behavior of members of organizations (Meyer and Rowan, 1977; see also Lowndes, 1996). Narrative institutionalism argues that rather than being atomistic individuals reflecting only their socialization and psychological make-up, or acting to maximize their personal utility, political actors reflect more closely the values of the institutions with which they are associated. These individuals have had their values, and therefore their behaviors, shaped by their membership in institutions and hence are changed because of that membership.

In this view individuals are not atomistic but rather are embedded in a complex series of relationships with other individuals and with collectivities (Granovetter, 1985). For most individuals, this complexity of interactions with multiple institutions in their environments means that they may have to choose among competing institutional loyalties as they act. They are, however, assumed to be always influenced by their full range of organizational attachments and hence cannot be the autonomous, utility-maximizing, and fully rational individuals assumed by rational choice theories. Importantly, however, neither are they the automata responding only to socialization that the inhabitants of behavioral theories of politics sometimes appear to be. Rather, the individuals must pick and choose among influences and interpret the meaning of their institutional commitments.

Although the importance of these multiple institutional commitments is central in this version of the new institutionalism, it is not always clear exactly how the individual copes with his or her multiple memberships. One answer is that the individual selects a number of different roles and plays those appropriate for the institution that is most relevant at the moment (Searing, 1991; Beyers, 2005). Another might be to utilize the bounded rationality logic that has constituted at least part of the foundation of this approach to institutions and consider that individuals will search for some reconciliation among the memberships that is "good enough."

Another way to understand the differences that March and Olsen posit between their approach to politics and the dominant (in their perception) "exchange" conception of politics is in the difference between exogenous and endogenous preference formation (March and Olsen, 1996). For exchange theories (meaning largely rational choice) the preferences of political actors are exogenous to the political process, and are shaped by forces beyond the concern of the immediate choice situation. The assumption is that individuals bring their preferences—notably utility maximization—with them when they join an organization.

For normative institutional theories, on the other hand, individual preferences are shaped to a large extent by their involvement with institutions (see also Wildavsky, 1987). Institutions thus to a great extent mold their own participants, and supply systems of meaning for participants in politics, and in social life taken more broadly. Some institutions will do this overtly through training, especially with the military or fire services when they expect individuals to perform dangerous acts. Other institutions may allow institutional socialization to occur through more natural processes.

Although this approach is labeled as a part of the "new" institutionalism in political science, in many ways it reflects a traditional format for institutionalism encountered in sociology and organization theory. The roots of this approach are especially evident in the work of Philip Selznick (1949; 1957), but they go back even further to the work of major scholars such as Emile Durkheim (1922; 1986) and Max Weber (Gerth and Mills, 1946; Bendix, 1960). Weber, for example, identified the manner in which cultural rules tended to constitute the basis for collective action in a variety of settings including both market and political behavior. Also, Durkheim (1992) emphasized the critical importance of symbols in structuring human behavior, inside and outside of formal institutions. From its earliest days, sociology emphasized the importance of values in defining the nature of institutions and organizations and individual behavior within those structures, and that pattern of thought continues to be seen in the normative approach to institutions.

Selznick (1949, pp. 25ff.) differentiated between organizations as the structural expression of rational action and organizations as more adaptive and normative structures. These two models are mirrored in the distinction made by March and Olsen (1989, pp. 118ff.) between aggregative and integrative political processes. The former is in essence a contractual form for organizations in which individuals participate largely for personal gain.[2] The latter form of organization comes closer to the idea of an institution as expressing a "logic of appropriateness," a central concept in the normative version of the new institutionalism. Participation in integrative institutions is undertaken on the basis of commitment to the goals of the organization, or at least an acceptance of the legitimate claims of the organization (or institution) for individual commitment—again, preference formation is endogenous to the institution.

These distinctions between integrative and aggregative organizations are also mirrored in Etzioni's earlier approach to organizations and individual involvement. Etzioni (1975) argued that organizations had three types of power that they could manipulate over members, or perhaps three types of incentives—coercive, remunerative, and normative. Individual members of organizations had three types of involvement in those structures—alienative, calculative, and moral. Organizations

---

[2] In terms of Etzioni's scheme of organizational analysis this would be a "calculative" involvement of the individual with the organization.

that used remunerative power and attracted individuals with calculative reasons for involvement would be stable examples of aggregative institutions. Likewise, organizations using normative power that had individuals who were there for moral reasons would be stable integrative institutions. Either of these types (along with the coercive-alienative match) could work, but March and Olsen would see the normative basis more appropriate for political action than the calculative basis.

The focus of the March and Olsen treatment of institutions is thus on the *integrative* approach to understanding organizations and institutions. As noted, much of the reason that these two scholars developed and advocated their "new institutional" perspective on politics was the belief that political science was becoming dominated by assumptions that structures were aggregative, and individuals were only involved in politics for personal, material gain (see, for example, Downs, 1957; 1967). Their development of the concept of aggregative organizational structures does, however, point to the way in which institutions presumably dominated by individualistic and instrumental concerns also can, and perhaps must, contain important normative elements. Even the advocates of free markets as solutions to socioeconomic problems invest that institution with powerful normative values, for example "freedom" and "choice" (Hayek, 1973), and those institutions (and all others) cannot be understood adequately, it is argued, without including those normative statements embedded within the explanatory statements.

The work of Chester Barnard (1938; see Scott, 1995a; Williamson, 1996) in organization theory and management should be seen as another earlier root of the normative perspective on organizations and institutions. Barnard was a practical executive in the American telephone industry but he also realized that the creation of a positive organizational culture was perhaps the best way to create effective organizations. Barnard argued from the perspective of the executive attempting to make an organization perform better, but in the process created the foundations of a theory of organizational behavior that concentrated on symbols and the role of managers in manipulating those symbols to motivate employees.[3]

As well as reflecting the institutionalist tradition within sociology and organizational analysis, normative institutionalism reflects an influence from the traditional forms of institutionalism in political science (see above, pp. 2–7). That tradition in political science first argued that institutions mattered more than did individual characteristics in determining behavior. In addition, institutions were conceptualized traditionally as embodying normative as well as structural elements that could be used almost equally well to explain the behavior of their individual members. For example, although using some behavioral methods and assumptions, Donald Matthews's study of the U.S. Senate (1973) demonstrated

[3] Like other versions of "human relations management" this approach has the potential to be manipulative, but is perhaps still more normative and humane than traditional hierarchical management.

rather clearly the existence of a number of values within that institution that shaped the behavior of its members, and severely constrained the legislative roles they might play. As I will point out in more detail below, the *roles* that institutions provide for their members help to shape behavior and define the expectations for members of the institution.

Normative institutionalism rejects the full rationality of the autonomous individual assumed to exist in much of contemporary political science. Rather, this approach to institutions reflects the development of bounded rationality that has grown out of the work of Herbert Simon (1947; Cohen et al., 1972; Hood, 1999). The assumption of bounded rationality is that individuals can not really meet the conditions for full rationality and therefore utilize a variety of mechanisms to facilitate making decisions. In this context, the logic of appropriateness created by membership in the institution—along with the routines, standard operating procedures, and symbols that help to define the institution—provide the context of behavior of the members.

In this chapter, as well as in subsequent chapters on other versions of the new institutionalism, we will be answering a series of questions about the approach. These questions are both descriptive and evaluative. What does the approach argue about certain key features of institutional life, and are these arguments internally consistent as well as persuasive? Are we dealing with genuine theories here, or are we only dealing with rather vague approaches to social life that, although they do provide some assistance for understanding, are not integrated explanations and descriptions of social action? Few, if any, approaches to social behavior are unassailable as theories (Kaplan, 1965), but we still need to assess these approaches individually to understand just how far they can take the discipline in explanation, and what work is yet to be done to provide more complete and satisfying explanations of these phenomena.

What Is an Institution?

The first and most fundamental question about each approach will be regarding how does it define an institution. This word is used loosely in political science to mean everything from a formal structure like a parliament to very amorphous entities like social class, with other components of the sociopolitical universe such as law and markets also being described as being institutions (Teubner, 1986; Smith, 1988; Robinson, 1991). The term is also used somewhat loosely in sociology, often seeming to mean the same thing as an organization (see Scott, 1995a). While there is some validity in describing each of the above structures or constraints on behavior as institutions, if this form of analysis is to make a contribution to the development of the discipline that is intended then there is a need for somewhat greater specificity.

For March and Olsen, an institution is not necessarily a formal structure but rather is better understood as a collection of norms, rules, understandings, and perhaps most importantly routines (1989, pp. 21–6). They provide a stipulative definition of political institutions as:

> collections of interrelated rules and routines that define appropriate actions in terms of relations between roles and situations. The process involves determining what the situation is, what role is being fulfilled, and what obligation of that role in that situation is.

They also define institutions in terms of the characteristics that they display, and that their members display. First:

> Political institutions are collections of interrelated rules and routines that define appropriate action in terms of relations between roles and situations.

They go on to say that ". . . institutions have a repertoire of procedures and they use rules to select among them" (1989, pp. 21–2). Also, institutions are defined by their durability and their capacity to influence behavior of individuals for generations (1995, p. 99). Likewise, institutions are argued to possess an almost inherent legitimacy that commits their members to behave in ways that may even violate their own self-interest (1989, pp. 22–3).

The numerous definitional statements taken from this one version of the new institutionalism may still leave unanswered some questions, for example the boundary conditions of "appropriate" and what sort of interrelationships among rules and routines are being spoken about. Despite the multiple definitions offered in their several writings, it is clear what is meant by "institution" in their approach to the subject. It is a collection of values and rules, largely normative rather than cognitive in the way in which they impact institutional members, as well as the routines that are developed to implement and enforce those values. Thus, institutions in this view are rather amorphous "virtual" entities, although they may well have more tangible embodiments in formal structures and organizations.[4]

Perhaps the most important feature of the March and Olsen conceptualization is that institutions are argued to have a "logic of appropriateness" that influences behavior more than a "logic of consequentiality" that also might shape individual action. That is, if an institution is effective in influencing the behavior of its members, those members will think more about whether an action conforms to the norms of the organization than about what the consequences will be for him- or herself. Perhaps the extreme example would be the behavior of soldiers who face almost certain death but still behave "appropriately" (MacDonald, 1983), or firemen who willingly enter blazing buildings because that is the role they have accepted as a function of their

[4] This logic corresponds to the structuration approach associated with Giddens (1984) and Sewell (1992).

occupational choice and their training in the fire service. Even in less extreme situations, however, "no study of human behavior can ignore the adaptability of humans to the institutions that they create and modify" (Jones, 2001, p. 22).

This "appropriate" behavior can be contrasted to that assumed by economic models, in which individuals are expected to think first what the objective pay-off will be for them.[5] As March and Olsen (1989, p. 161) argue, behaviors will be "intentional but not willful," when individuals are motivated by the values of their institutions. That is, individuals will make conscious choices, but those choices will remain within the parameters established by the dominant institutional values. Those choices also will require that each individual make an interpretation of just what the dominant institutional values are; even the most thoroughly developed institutions will leave many areas of behavior open to interpretation by individual members.[6] This will, in turn, require some means of monitoring behaviors and reinforcing dominant views about appropriateness.

The logic of appropriateness also operates in less extreme situations than the ones outlined above. In most cases the logic of appropriateness in public institutions may be manifested through rather ordinary activities such as serving the client as well as possible, or not engaging in corruption on the job (Heidenheimer et al., 1989). These are very routine standards of proper behavior, but in this normative conception of institutions it is the routine and the mundane that appear most important. As Mills (1940, p. 908) put it, enacting a logic of appropriateness "... will often induce a man to become what at first he merely sought to appear."

No institution will be so well developed, nor have such an unambiguous logic of appropriateness, that anomalous situations will not arise. Therefore, there will have to be enforcement mechanisms to deal with inevitable cases of deviance, but for most decisions at most times routines will be sufficient to generate "appropriate" performance. Perhaps as important is the simple fact that the presence of routines may help to identify what the exceptional, and therefore the important, cases for any organization are. These exceptional cases may create the common law within organizations that define what is really appropriate and what is not, and just what constitutes the boundaries of acceptable behavior.

Although finding the limits of appropriate behavior is important in understanding the operations of the logic of appropriateness, it may be important for many organizations not to have too precise a definition, and some ambiguity may be functional for an institution (see Christensen and Rovik, 1999). While for some institutions, for example the Army or the Church, clear standards for behavior may be

[5] Rational choice theorists might explain the behavior of the soldiers as a willingness to trade probable death for certain death if they refuse orders, or as placing a very high value on not showing cowardice. Thus, their behavior becomes "rational," once the operative set of rewards and sanctions is understood.

[6] The possible exception would be "total institutions," but even then the inmates are able to define some spheres of personal choice (Goffman, 1961).

crucial, for many other institutions having greater latitude for action helps maintain commitment while permitting some individuality.

The operation of the logic of appropriateness can be conceptualized as a version of role theory. The institution defines a set of behavioral expectations for individuals occupying positions within the institution and then reinforces behavior that is appropriate for the role and sanctions behavior that is inappropriate. Some aspects of the role may apply to all members of the institution, while other expectations will be specific to the position held by an individual. Further, like organizational culture (see p. 28), there may be several versions of the role among which a role occupant can pick and choose—think of the different roles or styles of prime ministers (Helms, 2000). Despite the somewhat amorphous nature of a role, the concept does provide a means of linking individual behavior and the institution.

Role theory can be seen as a more general element in the study of political institutions (Searing, 1991; Beyers, 2005). In any version of institutional theory, there must be a means of linking the macro-behavior and constraints of the institution with the micro-behavior of the individual who operates within that institution. For rational choice institutionalism (see below, pp. 52ff.) that mechanism is conceptualized as incentives and rules, but for the other approaches the roles offered to individuals by the institution appears to be the most appropriate conceptualization. The linkage is clearest perhaps in the normative institutionalism, but this is a defensible means of thinking about the linkages in the other approaches as well.

As with any conceptualization in the social sciences, this one appears to contain some problematic elements. Perhaps the most fundamental issue in this approach to institutions is with the concept of a "logic of appropriateness." Critics of the approach have argued that "appropriateness" is too vague to provide stable, effective predictions about behavior (see Goldman, 2005). Further, in many contexts, it may be difficult to distinguish appropriateness from consequentiality when examining individual decision-making. Likewise, some critics argue that the term has greater normative appeal than it has analytic capacity (Sending, 2002).

Another potential problem with this approach to institutions is the degree of uniformity assumed to exist within an institution. We know, for example, that even in well-developed and long-standing institutions different people will read cultural signals differently and will define "appropriate" in very different ways.[7] Studies of organizational culture point to the existence of multiple cultures within a single organization, some of which appear "orthogonal" to the dominant culture and which may undermine that dominant culture (Martin and Siehl, 1983; Ott, 1989).

[7] For example, the large literature on "informal organization" existing within formal organizations points out just how important norms that may be at odds with the formal norms are in explaining behavior.

Therefore, we need to ask how much uniformity is required before we can say that an institution exists. Further, that question may differ for different social situations, depending upon the formality of rules required and the degree of variation among the "raw material"—people—within the institution.

Christensen and Rovik (1999) have discussed appropriateness as a very ambiguous concept. While much of the analysis included in the March and Olsen discussion of appropriateness assumes that this concept is operational within an institution, and relatively uniform throughout the institution, Christensen demonstrates rather clearly that these assumptions are not necessarily true, and institutional constraints on behavior are often rather vague. Further, the ambiguity may be beneficial to the institution, allowing it to operate with personnel who may have somewhat different ideas about what is indeed appropriate, and also having some greater openness for change in the logic of appropriateness. That may create generalized compliance within the institution, until there is a need for greater specificity in the decision-making of the institution.

Another potentially problematic element of the definition arises from definitions of components of the overall definition of an institution. What is a rule and what is a routine? March and Olsen do address these questions. First, they attempt to differentiate organizational routines from the stereotypical, bureaucratic adherence to conventional behavior and precedents. In this context a routine is simply a stable pattern of behavior, without the sense that it is unchangeable, dysfunctional, or even enforceable. Very much like variables conventionally used to describe (bureaucratic) organizations, such as differentiation and specialization (March and Simon, 1957), routines are assumed to make the behavior of an organization more predictable and more rational. It may be difficult, however, to determine when that predictability ends and inertia begins.

March and Olsen also address the question of rules. Unlike for many other institutional theorists, rules do not form the central component of their approach, but yet must still be addressed as a part of the control of behavior within institutions and organizations. First, these scholars are concerned with rules as constitutive, that is as means of structuring the macro-level behavior of political systems (March and Olsen, 1995, pp. 21–5). Second, rules are to some extent the formalization of "logics of appropriateness." They serve as guides for newcomers to an organization, or to attempt to create more uniform understandings of what those logics are. Even then, March and Olsen do note that rules will also be interpreted differently and hence acted upon differently.

The final basic question that appears unanswered in normative versions of the new institutionalism is the difference between an institution and an organization. This version of institutionalism has very strong roots in organization theory, including the various sociological theories of organizations mentioned above. Further, Olsen (1988; 1996; 2006) in particular has continued to advocate the importance of organization theory for understanding politics. What are the relevant differences between institutions and organizations? Again, there appears to be no definitive answer so that the division between the two types of structure remains fluid.[8] The distinction may be somewhat easier to make if we add the adjective "formal" in front of organization and thus apply a very strict definition for organizations and a loose, more culturally based definition to institutions.

Even with the addition of a concept of formalism in organizations the line between the two concepts remains indistinct. We may question, however, if that is a fatal flaw in the approach; numerous concepts and measures used in the social sciences share a "family resemblance" to other concepts (Collier and Mahon, 1993). On the one hand it is—why do we need two labels for a single phenomenon, and if they are the same thing why are we talking about institutions at all? That having been said, however, even in stricter attempts to separate the two concepts—organization and institution—(Habermas, 1984) there would be a certain amount of shared variance if we were to attempt to measure the two terms by more objective instruments.

The Formation of Institutions

The second question which we have proposed for the description and evaluation of the several institutional theories is where do institutions come from? Knowing how institutions are argued to be formed within each theory will convey a great deal about the power of the theory to explain a range of behaviors, as well as the general political dynamics assumed to be operating within each. So, for example, for March and Olsen, norms were assumed to be central to the nature of institutions. Where do the rules and norms that are argued to shape institutions and to govern behavior within those institutions come from?

The first answer to this question is that institutions derive a good deal of their structure of meaning, and their logic of appropriateness, from the society from which they are formed (March and Olsen, 1989, pp. 17–20). Thus, when individuals are inducted into an institution, he or she will in most instances have been pre-socialized by their membership in the society. Some common norms—reciprocity, honesty, cooperation—that are important for public actors are learned as a part of the general socialization process. Just as people starting a new mass-based organization will usually settle on 1/2 + 1 of all members voting as the standard for making a decision so too are a variety of social norms appropriate and useful for establishing political institutions.[9]

---

8 As we will note later this tends to be true for all manifestations of institutionalism coming from the sociological tradition. Pedersen (1991, pp. 132–4) provides a thorough discussion of this question.

9 Rational choice institutionalists might argue, however, that this voting standard is rational rather than merely traditional (Buchanan and Tullock, 1962). It simply is a means for minimizing total costs within an organization.

Routines appear to arise rather naturally once people begin to interact in a protoinstitutional setting. Routines are means through which individual members of an institution can minimize their transaction and decision-making costs during participation. Further, they are means through which the institution can enhance its own efficiency and enable it to cope with the normal demands placed upon it (see Sharkansky, 1997). As March and Olsen (1989, pp. 26ff.) point out, all organizations develop routines and then employ those routines as the means of monitoring and reacting to changes within their task environments. In some way the routines define the nature of the organization—police departments will have different routines than do fire departments, although both are in the "public safety" business (see McCubbins and Schwartz, 1984). As routines become more established and have some greater meaning attached to them, the degree of institutionalization within the structure is increased.

The above are partial answers to the question of the origins of institutions, but only partial ones. For example, while individuals may bring with them a variety of values when they join most institutions, the answer does not appear very satisfying for institutions that have rules and values which are quite different from those found in the surrounding society, but which yet perform important services for that society. Again, the military or quasi-military organizations appear to be the best examples here. Even within more "normal" political institutions the personal ambition of politicians may not correspond very well to societal norms about the role of the public official as a servant of the people. One sociological definition (Eisenstadt, 1959) of institutions, and especially bureaucracies, stresses the extent to which they are set apart from the remainder of society. If that is indeed the case then institutions seemingly cannot rely upon generalized social norms but must develop their own.

The Eisenstadt conception of the formation of an institution is similar to the idea of institutionalization developed by Selznick (1957). Selznick argues that institutions are created when an organization is "infused with values" greater than would be necessary simply to achieve their formal purposes of the organization. Thus, an institution is created when a formal structure has meaning for the members, and when those members begin to believe that the structure is something more than a means to an end. The institution will, therefore, be able to motivate the members—through its logic of appropriateness—to a greater extent than would a simple, mechanical organization.

A second worrying point about the March and Olsen definition is the question of how do individuals decide to interact to create routines in the first instance? It is very easy to accept the emergence of routines once an organization or institution has been brought together and begins to function, but the initial decision to institutionalize still seems to require somewhat clearer treatment in the theory. In some ways the process of institutionalization appears to be a two-step process. First, there must be some conscious decision to create an organization or institution for a specified purpose. The second stage appears to be then to fashion the institution over time, and to imbue it with certain values.

There is the possibility of substantial deviation in values as the original founders must implement their ideas within the context of a developing organizational structure. This implementation process requires interactions with other individuals, and hence some value drift may be expected unless there are clear means of control over the members. No matter how careful the selection of those individual members of the organization may be, there are almost certain to be some differences in values and perceptions. Those differences will influence the way in which institutional values are interpreted, and will generate a political process that will tend to result in some modifications of the initial constellation of institutional values.

Institutional Change

March and Olsen and their associates are clearer about the patterns of change within institutions once they are formed (1989; Brunsson and Olsen, 1993) than they are about the initial formation processes. The logic of change in institutions is, in fact, one of the strongest and most persuasive component of their argument (see particularly Brunsson and Olsen, 1993). The March and Olsen arguments about change and adaptation build on their earlier work, including the famous "garbage can" approach to decision-making (Cohen et al., 1972). The garbage-can approach conceptualizes solutions looking for problems, with the institution having a repertoire of stock responses available when there is a perceived need to adjust policies. The argument of the "garbage can" is that institutions have a set of routinized responses to problems, and will attempt to use the familiar responses before searching for alternatives that are further away from core values. The institutional changes that are implemented thus conform to the logic of appropriateness, and those institutional values serve the useful function of limiting the range of search for policy alternatives ("bounded rationality") for the institution (see also Cyert and March, 1963). The logic of the garbage can is also that change is rarely a planned event, but rather is the product of the confluence of several streams of activity and opportunities for action within the institution.[10]

The normative institutionalist literature points to the existence of several stimuli for change, but focuses on processes of learning as a principal means for adaptation (see also Olsen and Peters, 1996). The basic argument is that institutions identify and then adapt to changing circumstances in their environment through a process of learning. Changes in that environment constitute a set of opportunities for the institution, as well as a threat to its established pattern of behavior. Also, this perspective on change points to the almost random nature of change in public organizations, in contrast to the highly purposive reform programs assumed by other approaches to institutions, especially the rational choice approaches (see below, pp. 54ff.).

---

[10] Kingdon (2003) has a rather similar idea about the convergence of streams for agenda formation.

Finally, in this view, institutional change is not necessarily functional, but rather public institutions can misread the signals from society and can respond in dysfunctional manners. Given the adaptive model proposed, however, they will have repeated opportunities to adjust their behavior. The normative basis of the institution is an important source of guidance for which changes are appropriate and which are not, so that there is not the need to calculate outcomes extensively, as might be the case of the "logic of consequentiality." Although the logic of change is well explained, there does appear to be some tendency toward reification of institutions, and toward ascribing to the collectivity the capacity for choice. For example, there is a tendency to discuss organizations as resolving their conflicts, rather than focusing on the actors involved and their role in the decisions.

In a subsequent work Olsen along with Nils Brunsson (1993) addressed the question of reform in organizations and institutions directly. They, as might be expected from the general framework, focus on the role of values in organizational change (see also Brunsson, 1989; Brunsson et al., 1989). In particular, Brunsson and Olsen argue that the greater the degree of disjuncture between the values professed by an institution and its actual behavior, and the values held by surrounding society and the behavior of the institution, the more likely will change be. Further, in this view, change is rarely the rational, planned exercise found in strategic plans but rather tends to be emergent and more organic.

Institutional crises are another means of conceptualizing the roots of change (Boin and 't Hart, 2000). As well as the more manifest crises that may confront an institution, crises also arise from a growing mismatch between environmental conditions and demands, and the normative orientations of the institution. From this perspective the principal task facing the leaders of an institution is the effective management of a crisis and the reformulation of the institution (changing norms and expectations) so that more successful coping with the external demands can be made.

In summary, despite its descriptive powers, the normative institutionalist perspective does appear to have some difficulty in explaining where institutions come from. This is not a trivial question. If the institutionalist perspective is to provide a useful alternative to more individualistic and purposive explanations of political life, then it must be able to say how the institutions that are so central to the theory come into being in the first instance. Further, once the institutions are created there needs to be a clear logic for change. Again, this approach describes the change process well but tends to reify the institution as the dynamic element in the changes.

Individuals and Institutions

The next major question is how do individuals relate to institutions. Although institutional explanations are conceived of as alternatives to individualistic explanations of political events, they must contain some mechanism for relating with individual behavior. This is true for both directions. That is, there must be a mechanism through which the institution shapes the behavior of individuals, and there must be a mechanism through which individuals are able to form and reform institutions. Unless that linkage can be made clear, institutions will remain only abstract entities and will have little relationship with political behavior.

This question is another statement of the familiar structure–agency question in social theory (Dessler, 1989). That is, can we explain the behavior of individuals by the structures in which they function or do we look to individual action to explain the behavior of structures? Again, it is also evident that these interactions need not be unidirectional. Giddens (1981; 1984; see also Sewell, 1992) has argued that these relationships are "dual," meaning there is reciprocal causation of agent and structure. This in turn implies a continuing dynamic process linking these two basic components of social theory, as well as a sense that institutions cannot really escape a means of linking individuals with the more formal elements of social life.

It is clear how institutions affect individual behavior in normative institutionalism. Institutions have their "logics of appropriateness" that define what behavior is appropriate for members of the institution and which behavior is not. Some institutions, for example markets (Eggertsson, 1990), may also have a logic of consequentiality that will supplement, although not replace, the logic of appropriateness. For example, in even the most cutthroat markets, there are rules and accepted practices, and some practices that would not be acceptable. Members of that institution violate those norms only at their peril, even though profit is presumed to be the dominant concern in this consequentialist arrangement. A trader who violates the rules of the market risks being excluded from subsequent deals, just as a member of parliament who violates norms about party loyalty may "have the whip withdrawn," and essentially be expelled from the parliamentary party.

In order for this logic of appropriateness to be effective there must be some form of enforcement. As noted above, most institutions do have those means of enforcement, even if they have no formalized means for adjudication or sanction. There are always informal means through which members can be pressured to conform. Part of the argument for positing a normative basis for institutions is that in effective institutions the sanctioning and enforcement processes are built into the structures themselves through socialization, rather than requiring an external enforcement mechanism. In the extreme, this might be seen as a part of the self-criticism of the Red Guards during the Cultural Revolution in China (Lin, 1991; see also White, 1989), or at a somewhat lesser extreme in confession in religious communities, and in honor codes in military schools (Committee on Armed Services, 1976; 1994).[11] Numerous studies of informal organizations operating less

---

[11] These values have notably been breaking down at the U.S. Naval Academy, and perhaps in other places within the military. This breakdown can be considered as a process of deinstitutionalization, especially within a normative framework.

in extremis also point to the existence of means of quietly but effectively producing conformity with group norms.

The separateness of institutions from the remainder of society appears to be an important element in defining the institutions and is also important in their capacity to enforce their standards. Membership in an institution tends to be a valuable commodity for those who do belong. This is certainly the case for aggregative institutions when the members depend upon membership for their livelihood. It can also be the case for many integrative institutions such as churches and even social groups from which individuals derive a good deal of their personal meaning in life. Even organizations within the public bureaucracy, popularly considered perhaps the least exciting place in which to spend one's time, tend to mean a great deal to their members so that deprivation of association would impose definite costs.

Although it is clear that institutions can shape the behavior of individuals, the reciprocal process is not nearly as clear. In the extreme the leader of an institution, especially a small and hierarchical institution, can produce apparent change in the behavior of the institution. Even then, however, the compliance may be only for aggregative, instrumental reasons rather than a reflection of any real changes in the values that undergird behavior. If that is so, then in institutionalist terms there may not have been any meaningful change. It is important to note here the extent to which some contemporary "management gurus," most notably Peters and Waterman (1982) assume that the best way to change behavior of firms in the private sector is to change their values; they further assume that those changes are relatively easy to bring about.

What is more interesting and important is how individuals not in formal positions of control can initiate enduring changes within an institution. The organizational culture literature also points out that cultures within organizations or institutions are unlikely to be uniform. As noted above orthogonal cultures within any organization can be a source of alternative views and alternative "logics of appropriateness," and these cultures may be associated with individuals as well as with ideas and interests. For example, military organizations attempt to suppress internal dissent but often cannot keep down "orthogonal" leaders such as Charles de Gaulle and his interests in armor (Doughty, 1985), or Billy Mitchell and his interest in air power (Gauvreau and Cohen, 1942). These multiple cultures may present challenges to the leadership in any institution and hence normal interorganizational politics may produce changes within the institution.

Since institutions in this view[12] are to a great extent based on compliance and conformity one source of change is nonconformity. Perhaps the most interesting accounts of producing institutional change through this method are the campaigns of nonviolent resistance of Mahatma Gandhi in India (Borman, 1986), and

[12] This importance of compliance is also true for some versions of the rational choice perspectives in institutions, for example those based on rules (see p. 32).

Dr Martin Luther King in the American South (Branch, 1988). In both instances, fundamental transformations of social and legal institutions were achieved through simply not complying with many rules of the existing political order. That resistance was reinforced with moral/religious claims and further legitimated through the nonviolent manner in which resistance was carried out. These are the extreme cases, but change within more mundane situations has also been achieved simply by members not going along with the status quo.

Nonconformity in institutions as discussed to this point assumes that the standards of appropriateness are clear and hence readily enforceable. In many social institutions, however, there is a good deal of latitude available to members (Haveman and Rao, 1997). In universities, for example, a very wide range of behavior is considered acceptable or even "normal." Other institutions such as the military, however, may be threatened by more diverse patterns of behavior and will attempt to enforce such standards as exist. Thus, change in the former type of institution may be more gradual and evolutionary than in the latter type of institution.

Leadership constitutes a somewhat analogous manner in which to generate change within an institution through the efforts of individuals. In this case we refer to the capacity of an individual either in a nominal role of leadership (especially within a large institution) or one possessing exceptional personal capabilities to create institutional change. Few officials have been able to reshape an institution the way in which Mrs Thatcher reshaped British government (Marsh and Rhodes, 1992a; Gamble, 1994). She did have the formal position as prime minister, but most prime ministers have not been able to produce the type of enduring change in institutional values that she did.

Finally, linkage between the institution and individuals can be achieved through change in the individuals being recruited into the institutions. For example, military organizations around the world have been forced to react to changes in the values of their young recruits from the 1970s onward. The traditional manner of command and authority within the military simply was not effective in motivating and controlling a new cohort of young people raised possessing more participative and democratic values (Inglehart and Abramson, 1994). The military soon found that they could generate the desired levels of performance from their troops by using very different forms of military management (Clotfelter and Peters, 1976). In this case the institution gradually changed rather than attempting to change the social patterns becoming ingrained into their "raw material."[13] In a (perhaps) less extreme situation the Congress of the United States has had to change significantly to accommodate the behavior of the 1994 freshmen who were generally unwilling to accept

---

[13] A similar change has occurred after the American military began to integrate women into the combat arms, rather than confining them to traditional positions such as nurses and clerk/typists. The women brought different values about organizations and even about violence that had to be accommodated within the existing organizations.

conventional practices within the legislature (Aldrich and Rohde, 1997). The norm that junior legislators, especially senators, should be seen but not heard has been challenged severely,[14] and in general the style of interaction within Congress has been altered.

A final point about the interactions of individual and institutions in the context of normative institutionalism is that institutions will attempt to reproduce themselves so that over time the institutions may harden their profile of values. For example, in the United States there are two organizations concerned with anti-trust policy—the Federal Trade Commission (FTC) and the Anti-Trust Division (ATD) of the Department of Justice. Although administering many of the same laws these two organizations have to some extent diverged over time. Thinking within the FTC has tended to become dominated by economists and economic arguments, while the ATD has recruited mostly lawyers, in part as a function of being located within a larger legal organization. The recruitment patterns of these organizations, and the values that the recruits bring with them from their academic training, solidify the patterns of thinking and acting within each organization.[15]

The Operation of the Institution

We also need to inquire how institutions work. That is, if indeed these structures are to influence and even determine the behavior of the members, how does that occur? The answer for the normative institutionalism is to some extent contained in the section above. That is, the creation and diffusion of a set of norms for individual behavior may be the crucial element in defining the manner in which constraints are imposed. To a great extent, these constraints are enforced by self-policing, given that the individuals who have become members have for the most part done so willingly, and may have accepted the values of the institution even prior to having joined.

Normative compliance, therefore, is central to the functioning of institutions from this theoretical perspective. The source of compliance then is derived from a normative commitment to the institution and its purposes. It may also, however, become habitualized and routinized so that conscious commitment and conscious decision-making are minimized. Individuals continue to respond in the ways expected, and needed, by the institution because they have become accustomed to

---

14 This was not the first time. When Shirley Chisholm was elected to Congress in the 1960s she refused to accept her committee assignment (Agriculture) and challenged the system of committee distribution. Agriculture was a prestigious assignment for a freshman, but was largely irrelevant for Chisholm's constituents in Harlem.

15 The argument is that redundancy may be functional rather than dysfunctional (Landau, 1969; Bendor, 1985) for the policy area. By having the alternative perceptions of the issues there can be greater certainty that all cases of monopolistic behavior will be prosecuted.

doing so, and the various normative stances, as well as myths and stories associated, with the institution, help to reinforce that routinization.

Institutional Design

If there is a well-developed conception of change in the normative perspective on institutions, the capacity of that version of institutionalism to comprehend and guide the design of institutions appears extremely weak. This deficiency is perhaps to be expected, given the more evolutionary and adaptive nature of the theory. While the instrumentalism inherent in rational choice approaches to institutions (see below, pp. 51–2) makes design relatively straightforward, the value basis of institutions hypothesized within this perspective makes design more difficult and less certain. Designing institutions from a normative perspective involves application of some sort of template or prescriptive model to the institution. We pointed out above when discussing the initial formation of institutions that although there may be a design format in the consciousness of the founders, the nature of institutions in the March and Olsen model implies that this format may not actually be implemented. Even if attempts were made to implement that template, it actually may be implemented in a significantly modified manner because of the almost inherently evolutionary nature of institutions in this theory. Thus, design (whether at the initial stage or a redesign) may not produce what the formulators desired.

This difficulty in implementing a clear organizational design is probably true to some degree for all perspectives on organizational and institutional design, but the normative version of the theory appears to make this disappointing result almost inevitable.[16] Few political institutions are capable of molding behavior of their members in quite the way that might be hoped by the formulators of an institution. Over time the process of matching individuals and institutions actually may become easier, given that there will be a certain amount of anticipatory socialization. That is, the nature of an institution will become known and prospective members will know what to expect and will not join unless they agree with the "logic" of the institution.

The Limits of the Theory

Not surprisingly, this version of the new institutionalism has been subjected to a great deal of criticism. A good deal of that criticism has come from the natural adversaries of the approach, for example rational choice theorists (Sened, 1991; Dowding, 1994). The critics argue that, unlike their own more explicit assumptions about human behavior, there is little if any explicit argumentation about human behavior in the

[16] This realism may be in fact a strength of the approach rather than a failing.

normative version of institutionalism. Their methodological individualism in turn leads them to think that an approach without such a foundation cannot be useful for explaining behavior.

Criticism has, however, also been made by scholars who might be expected to be more sympathetic with the general purposes of the theory, but who believe that the theory as presented has some inherent flaws as a means of explaining political phenomena. A good number of the critiques of value-based new institutionalism focus on the internal logic of the theory, while several others focus attention on its capacity to explain political phenomena in a way that goes beyond the individual understandings of the scholars responsible for creating the theory and in propagating its use.

The most fundamental criticism of the approach is that it is, in essence, not falsifiable. That is, the criteria for the existence of a "logic of appropriateness" within an institution are sufficiently vague that it would be difficult to say that they did not exist and that they did not influence the behavior of the members of the organization. Just as rational choice theory may not be falsifiable—the individuals in question are acting rationally, outsiders just do not understand their premises—so too it can be said that members of an institution were merely acting in accordance with their own interpretation of the institutional values. Further, as we have pointed out, most institutions have multiple sets of values and an individual may be able to pick and choose as well as to interpret, so that apparent discrepancies can be explained away.

Another strand of criticism is that by placing so much emphasis on the role of institutions and "the logic of appropriateness" March and Olsen have removed human decision-making completely from the process (Dowding, 1994, p. 111). The argument is that even if institutions do constrain choice there will be some opportunity in practice, if not in the theory, to violate norms, or to interpret institutional values differently, or otherwise to exercise individual judgment. March and Olsen argued that rational choice analysis made individuals too autonomous, but their critics argue that they removed human agency too entirely from political decision-making.[17]

Keith Dowding's critique is somewhat too simple an interpretation of the argument being made by March and Olsen, but even a sympathetic critic must wonder about the autonomy of individuals as well as the autonomy of institutions in this analysis. This concern is especially apparent when the logic of appropriateness of an institution conflicts with individual or professional values. For example, traditional medical values of putting the interest of the patient first come into conflict with the clearly articulated financial "logics of appropriateness" in managed care organizations (Mechanic, 1996). Individual physicians must then make judgments about which set of values to follow.

---

[17] If we return to role theory then it can be argued that different people will interpret the roles being sent to them by the institution differently. While this is a means of coping with the autonomy critique it may make the falsifiability critique more difficult to refute.

The Good Institution

We finally come to the question of what constitutes a "good institution" in the normative conception of new institutionalism. Given the explicit normative basis of this approach to institutional questions that appears an apt question, but in some ways it is not one for which there is a ready answer. The focus of institutions from a normative basis is very much the use of internal norms to define the institution in its *own* terms, rather than the use of external norms to evaluate its performance or to evaluate those internal standards. Thus, in many ways, the utilitarian versions of political science so heavily criticized by the new institutionalists does provide a clearer, if perhaps inadequate, normative evaluation of institutions. Further, in some institutions values that externally might be considered quite unacceptable are indeed "appropriate" for defining behavior within the structure.

The above having been said, we can tease out an evaluative model existing within the normative version of the new institutionalism. In the first place, the emphasis on normative integration and the creation of collective values within an institution or organization does provide a way of judging the success of that institution. The problem is that this model of evaluation is very central to the conceptualization and definition of an institution in the normative model. Therefore, this evaluative criterion could evolve into a simple dichotomy of success or failure, with little possibility of measuring degrees of success. Or this criterion could evolve into a simple tautology—an institution. That is, if there is no creation of a common value system within an organization then there really cannot be said to be an institution in existence.

If we search for a more sensitive assessment of the quality of an institution, then we can think about the extent to which a common ethic is created within the organization and the level of internalization of that ethic among the members of that organization. As noted already the organizational culture literature (see also Morgan, 1997) argues that there can be a variety of cultures existing within a single institution. This diversity of cultures that raises the possibility of the incomplete socialization of members will characterize some, if not many, institutions. If indeed the creation of a common value system—a common "logic of appropriateness"—is the best way to understand an institution, then the extent of variations within that culture can be utilized to judge the relative success of the institution and the process of institutionalization.[18]

We might even go further to ask if the internal culture that has been created is indeed appropriate for the challenges facing an institution and the tasks that it must perform. An inconsistency in cultures is likely to develop across time as an institution

[18] Given the influence of Philip Selznick (1949; see below pp. 27–8) on this body of literature, the creation of that common value system can be seen as a measure of the success of the leadership of the institution. Similarly, Barnard placed the onus of creating the common culture on the leadership.

continues to recreate an internal value system that is incompatible with a changed environment of the institution. Some of the most egregious examples of dysfunctional organizational cultures being perpetuated come from military organizations and the tendency of generals to fight the last war. The failure to adapt is not, however, limited to military organizations as "myopic learning" (Levinthal and March, 1994) or "pathological learning" (Olsen and Peters, 1996) has been identified in a large number of organizational settings. This would add a more direct performance element to the discussion of institutions, something akin to the project of the "empirical Institutionalists."

Summary and Conclusion

The new institutionalism began with the attempts of March and Olsen to recreate, or to save, their favored version of political science. They believed that this preferred approach to the discipline was being threatened by the incursions of both economic and social-psychological explanations for political problems. Both of those alternatives emphasized the role of the individual in making political choices and tended to conceptualize the individual largely as an autonomous actor. The autonomous nature of action was more apparent in the economic models, but was also evident in behavioral approaches.

The March and Olsen perspective on institutions proposed several important theoretical components for political science as a discipline. One such element was the return to the institutionalist roots of the discipline, and to a sense of the collective, as opposed to individual, roots of political behavior. Individuals are important in the normative institutionalist model and still ultimately they must make choices within institutions, but those choices are largely conditioned by their membership in a number of political institutions (see also Clemens and Cook, 1999). In this view, the structure–agency problem is resolved through the individual accepted and interpreting the values of institutions.

A second crucial element of the March and Olsen view is that the basis of behavior in institutions is normative rather than coercive. Rather than being guided by formal, stated rules the members of institutions are more affected by the values that are advanced, and to some extent, which constitute their organizations. As we have already pointed out, although this normative element of the March and Olsen theory is appealing in many ways it also constitutes a serious weakness in theoretical terms, given that it may make the theory unfalsifiable. There is no independent means of ascertaining whether it was values that produced behavior, and no way of arguing that it was not the root of the behavior. That some sort of criticism can be made of some other forms of institutionalism, but that makes it no less an issue of concern for the normative version.

In summary, the normative institutionalism has been a major statement about the role of collective action in political life. It rejected the methodological individualism that had come to dominate political science and sought to promote a renewed interest in organizations and formal (and less formal) structures. At the same time, however, this approach to politics may have raised more questions about governing than it has been able to answer. The emphasis on norms and the logic of appropriateness is appealing, but very difficult to measure or to separate from other aspects of organizational behavior, and hence substantiating a case for this mode of explanation remains difficult.

CHAPTER 3

Rational Choice Theory and Institutional Theory

The second approach to institutions, which we will discuss, is to a very great extent the antithesis of the first. Indeed, the growing dominance of rational choice theories in political science was a principal concern motivating March and Olsen to advocate their normative version of "the new institutionalism." Given that rational choice theory depends for its analytical power upon the utility-maximizing decisions of individuals, it would appear that attempting to relate that theory to institutions and the constraining influence of institutions would be contradictory and inappropriate. Individuals are assumed to be autonomous and individualistic actors who are using any decision situations to maximize their own utility.

Despite the individualistic basis underpinning their analytic approach, rational choice institutionalists have understood clearly that most political life does occur within institutions (see Tsebelis, 1990), and that to be able to provide a comprehensive explanation of politics their theories must address the nature and role of political institutions. There, thus, has been a flowering of rational choice literature on political institutions, including legislatures (Tsebelis and Money, 1997; Kreppel, 2003), cabinets (Laver and Shepsle, 1995; Strom and Müller, 2008), bureaucracies (Miller, 2000; Huber and Shipan, 2002; Moe, 2006), the courts (Stearns, 2002; Hammond et al., 2005) and the institutions of the European Union (Pollack, 2007; see also Egeberg, 2004). These models have also been used to analyze whole political systems in comparative context (Scharpf, 2000; Tsebelis, 2002).

Rational choice theories must also be able to cope with somewhat more amorphous institutions, such as the legal system (Robinson, 1991; Hathaway, 2001) and electoral systems (Taagapera and Shugart, 1989; Norris, 2004) in order to have the analytic generality and power that their advocates argue those theories do have. We have already pointed out that the term "institution" means a variety of different things to different people, and these less formalized structures and understandings are crucial to the maintenance of society. Some economic theorists (Becker, 1986) have gone so far as to apply rational choice analysis to social institutions such as marriage. Although the predictions of the rational choice analyses are infrequently tested directly (but see Coneybeare, 1984; Huber and Shipan, 2002), their more formal modeling discussions are capable of providing interesting insights into the nature of social structures and the behavior of individuals within those structures.

Despite the possible contradictions (at least according to March and Olsen), there are several different approaches to institutions that depend upon the underlying logic of rational choice approaches. Dunleavy (1991, pp. 1–2) contrasts "institutional public choice" with "first principles public choice," and Shepsle (2006) discusses "canonical rational choice" but the logic is the same for both strands.[1] Hans Keman (1996a) has made somewhat the same distinction, arguing for the utility of "institutional rational choice" and Fritz Scharpf has written about "actor-centered institutionalism" (1997) as a means of using rational assumptions for understanding institutions while at the same time emphasizing the importance of individual actions.

In all of these theoretical approaches institutions are conceptualized as collections of rules and incentives that establish the parameters on the behavior of individuals. These rules establish the conditions for rationality (see Duquech, 2001; Jones 2001, 2003; Christensen, 2011), and therefore establish a "political space" within which many interdependent political actors can function. Thus, in these models the individual politician is expected to maneuver to maximize personal utilities, but his or her options are inherently constrained because they are operating within the rule set of one or more institutions.[2] Thus, unlike some versions of institutional theory, there are clear actors contained in the picture, rather than just a set of rules and norms.

There is also a significant and growing body of institutional theory that is based on transaction costs economic theory. Oliver Williamson (1993, 1996) and Douglas North (1990) have been central to developing this body within economics and there have also been important political applications.[3] Giandomenico Majone (2001), for example, has applied this logic to understand better the role of nonmajoritarian institutions and credible commitment (a term pioneered by North). Likewise, common governance problems such as implementation and policy coordination can be understood through the lens of transaction costs, and transaction costs can even be used to develop a more general model of governance (Nooteboom, 2007).

Unlike the other economics-based approach to institutions, these transaction-costs models focus less on rational action by individuals and more on understanding ways to design structures that reduce their difficulties in making decisions and interacting with other institutions. Transaction costs become an analytic tool that can be utilized to shape institutions and their interactions, rather than involving autonomous rational action of individuals. While individuals may attempt to use this instrument to design institutions to suit their own purposes, the concept itself

---

1 By this distinction Dunleavy is contrasting scholars who work on the "puzzles" of individual behavior as opposed to those who are concerned with the more constrained behavior of individuals within institutions.

2 This model does appear to reside very clearly in the March/Simon school of bounded rationality, as opposed to that of the more dogmatic rational choice maximizers.

3 The logic of transaction costs is usually associated with Ronald Coase in economic analysis but North and Williamson have been more central to applying the concept to organizations and institutions.

is less linked to individual rational action. In policy terms the use of transaction cost analysis can be used to design programs in ways that make changes away from the status quo more expensive in transaction terms (Wood and Bohte, 2004), thus locking in the preferences of the designers. (See also Durant, 2006.)

Whether defined specifically as institutional or not, the various rational choice approaches to institutions all presume much of the same egoistic behavioral characteristics found in rational choice approaches to other aspects of political behavior. In addition, however, the institutional variants of the approach focus attention on the importance of institutions as mechanisms for channeling and constraining individual behavior. The fundamental argument of the rational choice approaches is that utility maximization can and will remain the primary motivation of individuals, but those individuals may realize that their goals can be achieved most effectively through institutional action, and find that their behavior is shaped by the institutions. Thus, in this view, individuals rationally choose to be, to some extent, constrained by their membership in institutions, whether that membership is voluntary or not. Further, they may be particularly interested in the behavior of other people to be constrained, with one important example being the desire of former political leaders wanting the actions of new leaders to be constrained (see Colomer, 2000).

One important difference between institutional public choice and other versions of the theory is the source of preferences and definitions of personal interests. For most rational choice theorists those conceptions of preferences being pursued by individuals are exogenous to the theories and are of little or no concern to the theorists. Institutional versions of the theory, however, must be concerned with how individuals and institutions interact to create preferences (see Katznelson and Weingast, 2005). The argument is that even if individuals may become involved with an institution, including one such as the market that is assumed to be favorable to individual utility maximization, they must quickly learn more accommodative norms and accept institutional values if they are to be successful within those institutions (North, 1990; Ostrom, 2007). As institutions become more successful they become more successful in shaping individual preferences, sometimes even before they formally join the institution. In institutional rational choice some preferences, for example a general drive toward utility maximization, appear to be exogenous, while some preferences also may be endogenous to the organization.

The dominant position of exogenous preferences in rational choice institutionalism is beginning to be altered somewhat. In particular, models involving learning and adaptation are becoming more important in the field. In this view of institutions there is a continual adaptation of the rules, rather than more discrete choices that are largely unquestioned within the institution, with individual members largely accepting them (Ostrom, 2005). In addition, some scholars (see Levi, 1997, p. 24) working within the rational choice tradition have come to accept that preferences are to some extent contingent upon involvement with a particular institution, rather than general preferences that extend across all situations. The nature of preferences is increasingly considered to be at least in part contingent upon situations and interactions.

The Rationality of Institutions

The apparent contradiction in rational choice institutionalism raised by March and Olsen is resolved in practice, if for no other reason than that individuals realize that institutional rules also constrain their competitors in whatever game of maximization those competitors may believe themselves to be involved in (Weingast, 1996). A set of rules can arise, or be imposed, within organizations that structures behavior and establishes the bounds of acceptability. Further, the existence of those rules ultimately benefits all participants, and perhaps also society as a whole. Institutions are capable of producing some predictability and regularity of outcomes that benefits all participants in an institution, and also clarifies the probable range of decisions available to societal actors not directly involved in the process of any particular organization. Thus, businesses may benefit from a regulatory regime established by government, even though they may complain about some of its particular constraints.[4]

This capacity to produce collective rationality from rational individual actions that might, without the presence of the institutional rules, generate collective irrationality is a central feature of the rational choice perspective on institutions. Indeed, as much as being a mechanism for understanding the nature and behavior of institutions, as is true for most other versions of institutionalism, this body of literature appears principally interested in the manipulation and design of institutions. Unlike most of the other approaches to institutionalism the rational choice school assumes the existence of a behavioral element—individual maximization—and points out that individual maximization will produce dysfunctional behavior such as free riding and shirking. This approach then proceeds to design institutions that will constrain the behavior of those individuals to produce more socially desirable outcomes.

The recognized capacity of institutions to constrain individual behavior also provides rational choice analysts an important gateway for approaching institutional design. Unlike most other approaches to institutionalism, rational choice theorists do have an explicit theory of individual behavior in mind when they set about manipulating political structures, and that theory is assumed to apply in any institution. Thus, those theorists can advocate the development of institutions that possess incentives (both positive and negative) that should, at least within the parameters of their theory, produce the pattern of behavioral outcomes desired by the designers. Within this approach institutions are conceptualized largely as sets of positive (inducements) and negative (rules) motivations for individuals, with individual utility maximization providing the dynamic for behavior within the models.

[4] For example, some of the major opposition to trucking and airline deregulation in the United States came from the affected industries themselves (Derthick and Quirk, 1985). This pattern appears to have been repeated in a number of other national settings.

Varieties of Rational Choice Institutionalism

We have so far been discussing rational choice theory as if it were a single, integrated entity. There are, however, a variety of different rational choice perspectives on institutions, despite the tendency of some critics to lump all these perspectives together as one (Green and Shapiro, 1994; Rothstein, 1996). In particular, we will discuss principal–agent models of institutions, game-theoretic models of institutions, and rule-based models of institutions as components of the broader rational choice approach. Despite the significant internal differences among the approaches discussed below, these models also contain some fundamental and important similarities. These similarities in the rational choice approaches include:

(a) **A Common Set of Assumptions.** The different variations of the rational choice version of institutionalism all assume that individuals are the central actors in the political process, and that those individuals act rationally to maximize personal utility. Thus, in this view, institutions are aggregations of rules that shape individual behavior, but individuals react rationally to those incentives and constraints established by those rules. Also, most individuals are expected to respond in the same way to the incentives so that designing institutions is a relatively simple process.

Following from the above analysis, institutions are argued to be defined by rules and by sets of incentives. This conception is not unrelated to the notion that institutions are defined by values, but the underlying compliance mechanism assumed within the structure does appear to be different. Whereas compliance within normative institutionalism is moral and normative (see Etzioni, 1963), it is more calculative in the rational choice version of institutionalism. In the terms used by Scott (1995a), most rational choice analysis tends to be "regulative" rather than "normative" or "cognitive."[5]

(b) **A Common Set of Problems.** As noted, rational choice approaches all are concerned with ways of constraining the variability of human behavior and in solving some of the classic problems that arise in political and other forms of collective decision-making (Bates, 1988). In particular, most of rational choice approaches are attempting to solve the "Arrow Problem" (Arrow, 1951; 1974) of how groups of people can make decisions that satisfy the conditions of a social welfare function without having that decision imposed through hierarchical means.[6] Institutions create what Shepsle (1989) referred to as a "structure induced equilibrium" through their rules on voting, so that certain types of outcomes are more likely than are others.

A second major problem that rational choice institutionalism confronts is the problem of the commons (Hardin and Baden, 1977). In situations in which rational individual

---

5 It can be argued that in normative institutions individuals are assumed to acquire the same values in an institution and hence behave in certain ways, while in the rational choice version they all have *ab initio* the tendency to maximize personal utility and therefore respond similarly to incentives.

6 Kenneth Arrow argued that in most choice situations differences among individual preferences will prevent the formation of a social welfare function that can satisfy conditions such as transitivity of outcomes and nonimposition. Institutions are argued to offer a way out of that trap.

action can produce collective irrationality, the common solution is to create institutions. For example, if the rational attempts of fishermen to maximize their own income results in depletion of fish stocks, then some form of institutional arrangement can produce solutions that are viable in the longer run. While those institutions are usually conceptualized as depending on authority, they may also work through developing mechanisms for voluntary cooperation.

The other problem common to the rational choice perspective on institutions is coordination and control of the public bureaucracy. The theory posits that there is a problem of ensuring that organizations, as well as individual bureaucrats, will comply with the wishes of political leaders—the familiar problem of principals and agents. The basic task of institutional design, therefore, becomes to develop configurations of institutions that will ensure compliance by their members with the wishes of their "principals" (Horn, 1995).

(c) **A Tabula Rasa.** Unlike other models of institutions being discussed here, the rational choice perspective assumes that institutions are being formed on a tabula rasa. The outcomes of the design process are being determined by the nature of the incentives and constraints being built into the institutions. The assumption appears to be that the past history of the institution or organization is of little concern and a new set of incentives can produce changed behaviors rather easily. This view is in marked contrast to the historical institutionalists, but also appears to be incompatible with the normative institutionalists who would assume some persistence of values once they are learned and internalized by individuals. Again, however, the models based on some aspects of learning are adding more of a temporal dimension to this perspective.

Institutions as Rules

The first version of rational choice approaches to institutions, usually associated in political science with the work of Elinor Ostrom (1986; 1990; see also Ostrom et al., 1992), can be seen as utilizing rules as a means to "prescribe, proscribe and permit" behavior. This version of institutionalism is also common in institutional economics and economic history (see Aligica and Boettke, 2009). For example, Douglass North has discussed institutions as "the rules of the game for society or, more formally, . . . humanly devised constraints that shape human interactions" (1990, p. 3). For North and other institutional economists (Eggertsson, 1996) one of the most crucial set of rules defining the institution of the market is the property rights regime developed within a political system. Without the capacity of government to make and enforce those rules the market could not function. This simple fact appears lost at times on politicians on the political right who assume that the "free market" is the solution for all the problems of society, and that market is a natural occurrence.

This version of the rational choice approach conceptualizes institutions as aggregations of rules with members of the organizations—or institutions—agreeing to follow those rules in exchange for such benefits as they are able to derive from their membership within the structure. This definition is actually very little different from definitions of institutions employed in normative institutionalism, both relying upon establishing standards of behavior to establish the nature of the structures. The principal difference arises in the differential degrees of formality, and particularly enforceability, implied by the terms "norm" and "rule." Further, the standards of behavior within the rational choice version tend to be designed into the system, while those in normative institutionalism tend to be more evolutionary.

The rationality component of the behavior in this form of institutionalism becomes apparent in two ways. The first is that individuals can gain some benefits from membership in an institution and therefore are willing to sacrifice some latitude of action in order to receive those benefits. Among the more important benefits might be some greater predictability of the behavior on the part of other individuals if they all are constrained by their institutional membership. Thus, unlike Mancur Olson's (1965) famous conclusion that rational individuals would not belong to most political organizations, this approach to institutions argues that they can do so quite rationally, and will do so quite readily.

Another element of the rationality of rule-based institutions comes somewhat closer to Olson's analysis of organizations and institutions. Ostrom argues that the leadership of an institution has a pronounced interest in having their rules followed. Her research has been particularly interested in institutions devised to cope with some of the thornier problems of public policy, for example common pool resources and the "tragedy of the commons" (Hardin and Baden, 1977; Ostrom, 1990) that can result from the exploitation of those resources. In this policy, setting rules are crucial for regulating the behavior of individuals when their rational pursuit of individual gain might produce outcomes that would be collectively undesirable. In the setting of "the commons" some mechanism for making and enforcing binding decisions is crucial to the success of the institution. Without those rules the policy area would degenerate into something of the egoistic free-riding and defection conceptualized by Olson.

An interesting variation of this constraint argument is that national, or other collective, actors may have some of the same incentives for joining institutions that individual actors may experience. For example, nations may have an incentive to join institutions such as the European Union or NAFTA. First, organizations of this sort can constrain the competitive behavior of their competitors and produce a relatively level playing field for all actors. Further, a country can use the external institution as a scapegoat to impose policies on their public that might otherwise be politically unacceptable (see Mann, 1997). Membership in the European Monetary System, for example, may be a mechanism for imposing a more restrictive economic policy than might otherwise be politically feasible, and thus countries such as Belgium and Italy have been able to constrain the power of unions and other domestic actors that have at times made economic management difficult.

Decision Rules

The alternative view of the role of rational choice theory in institutional analysis also depends upon rules, but these rules are conceptualized as fulfilling a significantly different purpose. Kenneth Arrow won the Nobel Prize in 1972 largely for his contributions to welfare economics (1951), specifically the observation that it was impossible to develop a social welfare function that would be guaranteed to generate a decision satisfying the preference orderings of all participants in a society. The only route around that problem was the imposition of a decision by the authority of some dominant actor. That is to say, most voting systems do not produce decisions that perfectly match the preferred alternatives of participants in ways that would maximize their collective welfare.

Institutions are a means for eluding this fundamental problem of collective action. Institutions provide a set of agreed upon rules that map preferences into decisions. In any one decision the rules may produce outcomes that violate the criteria advanced by Arrow, or other criteria coming from welfare economics or even from democratic theory. The virtue of the institution is that the rules are agreed upon in advance so that the participants realize what they are agreeing to when they join the institution.[7] Further, given that members of an institution will participate in a number of decisions, they can make up for losses on one round in subsequent iterations of the "game." From the perspective of rationality, institutions provide a stable means of making choices in what would otherwise be an extremely contentious political environment.

This approach to institutions is also associated with a Nobel Prize, although perhaps somewhat less directly than Arrow's. One of the pioneering works in this tradition was by James Buchanan[8] and Gordon Tullock, *The Calculus of Consent* (1962). These two scholars provided a public choice interpretation of constitutions and hence of the foundations of political institutions. They conceptualize writing constitutions as a question of institutional design (see also Sartori, 1997) and as a process that could be performed best if the framers considered what the decision rules contained within their documents did to the aggregation of preferences. Among other things Buchanan and Tullock provided in their discussion of constitutional rules was a rational justification of the common practice of majority voting.

For Riker (1980) and then Shepsle (1986) the role of decision rules has been to produce an equilibrium where one might not otherwise exist. Part of the Arrow problem was that without some form of imposition there would be no equilibrium answer but rather a cycling of largely negative outcomes. Rules, once agreed by the members of the institution and then to some extent imposed on their successors,

[7] Of course, some members may be born into a set of institutions and cannot make that free choice—more on that later.

[8] Buchanan won the Nobel in 1986.

produce the constraints on free action necessary to produce stable patterns of policy choice. As noted, there may be multiple equilibria that can work, and no set of rules is a priori preferable[9] to another, but some form of rules is needed.

Another way to conceptualize the importance of rules in institutions is to identify the ways in which those rules create veto points, or veto players, in the institutions (Cameron, 2000; Tsebelis, 2002). The design of decision-making structures creates a number of points at which there must be a positive decision for the decision to go forward. Therefore, political structures that have more veto points, for example presidential as opposed to parliamentary systems or federalism (Scharpf, 1988) versus unitary regimes, will find it more difficult to make decisions, and will require more bargaining among the players. The range of possible policy outcomes in these systems is therefore more limited. This approach to making the design of institutions and patterns of decisions also provides a strong basis for pursuing comparative politics from this perspective (Kaiser, 1997). That having been said, identifying the veto players is not a simple task in all situations, and the preferences of the players involved in making policy may be more complex than some simple models would have us believe (Ganghof, 2003), making the political process less predictable.

Individuals within Organizations

The third version of rational choice institutionalism can be described as "individuals within institutions." The perspective here is one in which the rational actor is attempting to utilize institutions to fulfill his or her individual goals. For example, William Niskanen (1971) has argued that the leaders of bureaucratic organizations in government use their positions to maximize personal utility, usually through instruments such as larger budgets and larger allocations of personnel. These allocations are assumed to generate for the "bureau chief" personal benefits such as a higher salary, a thicker carpet, and greater personal prestige. Also working within the context of bureaucracies, Anthony Downs (1967) examined the strategies which the rational actor can pursue to enhance personal utility as well as to enhance organizational performance. Rather than a constraint, therefore, the institution and its resources become a locus for individual aggrandizement.

Similar modes of analysis have been developed for looking at legislative organizations. Here the question is how does the rational legislator work to enhance his or her own career (Fenno, 1978; Fiorina, 1987), to exercise legislative oversight on bureaucracy (McCubbins et al., 1987), or perhaps even to pass legislation in committees (Krehbiel, 1991). The modeling of these institutions is in many ways more difficult than for bureaucracies, given the multiple roles played by legislators and their

[9] Some rules may be preferable to others on grounds other than the capacity to invoke stability. For example, people may choose simple majority rule over other decision rules simply because it is familiar and appears democratic.

having to play the "game" against a number of equally (it is assumed) self-centered legislators.

The theories covered in this body of research, and especially Niskanen's, have been criticized any number of times (Coneybeare, 1984; Blais and Dion, 1991). Despite that criticism, they constitute a powerful analytic tool for examining public bureaucracy, legislatures, and other public organizations. They are, however, in many ways less theories of institutions than theories about how individuals use formal structures as an ecology within which to maximize personal interests. They become theories of institutions as the personal actions begin to produce actions by the institutions, with the institutions frequently becoming reified as rational actors themselves, rather than the reflections of the collective actions of the individuals within them.

The normative institutionalism follows in the intellectual tradition of bounded rationality, founded on the work of Herbert Simon (1947). However, bounded rationality may also help understand some aspects of rational choice institutionalism (see Dequech, 2001). One of the consequences of belonging to an institution is that it places bounds on the rationality of the individuals who are members. In the normative institutionalism those constraints are largely internalized by the participants, but for rational choice institutionalism the constraints are more external, but there are certainly constraints. Thus, the individual who joins an institution may not see that institution as an unlimited source of personal power and rewards, but rather as a more limited ecology for the "games" that he or she wants to play. Pagano (2007), for example, discusses how an analysis based on bounded rationality tends, like the normative institutionalism, to make preferences of individuals internal to the structures rather than exogenous. He makes the observation that in this version of rationality preferences may become endogenous but basic instincts, for example to maximize utilities, may remain exogenous.

Principal–Agent Models

Interactions among institutions, and between individuals and institutions, can be considered from the perspective of principal–agent models. This perspective can be applied within organizations as well as serving as a means of understanding interactions among groups of institutions within the public sector. For example, within a public organization the leader of that organization (whether minister or administrator) may operate as the agent for his or her fellow employees. Numerous studies of public budgeting, for example, discuss the importance of a leader being able to fight his or her corner and bring back the budgetary goods for the organization (Heclo and Wildavsky, 1974; Wildavsky, 1992). Likewise, the Niskanen model of bureaucracy could be recast and be more realistic (Hood et al., 1984; Blais and Dion, 1991), if the "bureau chief" were cast as the agent for the employees. The major effect of the expansion of a bureau is not that the chief gets more money or benefits but that there are more desirable managerial posts for subordinates.

The principal–agent model is also widely used for certain groups of public institutions or organizations. For example, this has become perhaps the standard means of analyzing regulatory policy, especially in the case of the United States which has a number of independent regulatory commissions (McCubbins et al., 1987; Cook and Wood, 1989). The problem identified here is how to design these structures so that the principal (Congress) can ensure that the agent (the agency) fulfills the principal's wishes. Strategies have included using incentive structures so that the agents have some motivation to comply—especially by overcoming information asymmetry (Banks and Weingast, 1992), and the use of oversight (McCubbins and Schwartz, 1984; Lupia and McCubbins, 1994) as a means of ensuring compliance.

This approach is rarely as self-consciously interested in institutions as institutions as are several of the other approaches, although it must address some of the same questions we are raising about institutional theory. If, for example, an institution is to act as an agent for some other political actor in society, how can we define an institution and is it sufficiently integrated as an entity to fulfill that function? For example, some regulatory agencies have a variety of functions and have some latitude to choose among them, at least in terms of the emphasis placed on one function or another (see Niskanen, 1971, on multipurpose organizations). Can these institutions really function as an agent, or are they able to choose their own principal and their own signals (see Eisner et al., 1996)?

Further, these models tend to vastly oversimplify the complex nature of regulatory policy. For example, many of the major changes in the behavior of agencies in the United States have been a result of changes in the administrative law doctrines applied by the courts rather than institutional design of the principal–agent relationship. When in the early 1970s the courts substituted the "hard look" doctrine[10] for the previous lenient interpretation of the latitude permitted to agencies to construct their own interpretations of congressional statutes (Gormley, 1989). We may be able to conceptualize the courts as another principal for the agents, but that appears to do violence to the general conceptualization of the model.

Game-Theoretic Versions of Institutions

As mentioned above, compliance is one of the principal concerns of the rational choice version of institutional theory, and to some extent of all institutional theory. The problem of compliance can also be conceptualized as a set of games played between actors (usually legislators) attempting to ensure the compliance of other actors (usually bureaucrats), while those bureaucratic actors generally seek greater latitude for action. The problem for the actors who design the "game," therefore, is to construct a pay-off matrix that makes it in the interest of those actors to comply (Calvert, 1995; Scharpf, 1997). In this game, the designers must also do something

[10] See *Greater Boston TV Corp v. FCC*, 444 F. 2d, 841.

to ensure that the legislators also uphold their end of implicit or explicit bargain between the sets of actors.

The bureaucrats in this model are not assumed to be evil but only self-interested, and they naturally desire greater latitude to pursue their own versions of the public interest in their policy area, as well as any individual interests (as in the Niskanen model) they are able to advance through the activities of their organization. Likewise, the legislators are not assumed to be pursuing inappropriate goals,[11] but rather are merely attempting to ensure that their own version of good public policy is the policy that is implemented at present and in the future, a goal very much in accord with ideas of democracy (Rose, 1974).

If this game is played only once then defection and noncompliance is usually relatively costless for any participant; he or she can win by any means available and there is no opportunity for reprisal. The literature on game theory points to the importance of repeated games as a means of establishing greater cooperation and mutual compliance among the participants in a game. Axelrod (1984), for example, points to the development of "tit-for tat" strategies in repeated plays of Prisoners' Dilemma[12] games. Players are punished when they defect and are rewarded when they cooperate, and over time settle down to an equilibrium of mutual compliance. These experimental results appear to be repeated in real-world bargaining situations. For example, Peters (1997a) points to the tendency of "games" among nations within the European Union to be played differently when they are conceptualized as only one iteration of an ongoing political process. These assumptions are, therefore, markedly different from the normative view of institutional behavior, which would assume that the actors would behave appropriately because of their acceptance of institutional values.

The game-theoretic conception of institutional theory shares a great deal with the principal–agent model. Both are centered on the compliance problem, assuming that legislators are attempting to identify ways to prevent defection by bureaucrats. The difference between the two versions of rational choice institutionalism appears to lie in how the process of compliance is conceptualized. In the principal–agent model the process is conceptualized as being performed largely through rules, with both sets of actors attempting to commit the other to complying with the terms of their tacit bargain.

Questions about Institutional Theory

With some picture now of the principal ideas behind rational choice approaches to institutions, I will proceed to ask the same series of questions that were asked

[11] This is, in fact, a more benign view of legislators than is seen in other rational choice models of legislative behavior. See, for example, Fiorina (1982).

[12] The Prisoners' Dilemma is one of the classic games. In it actors must make independent decisions about whether to cooperate or not or to defect, with cooperative behavior producing far better outcomes for the players.

about the normative approach. Despite the numerous alternative ways of thinking about rational choice within institutions, the differences among the answers to these questions are not very different. As I have already noted, there is a common set of assumptions and principles that undergirds this work and which provides a reasonably integrated conception of how political institutions function.

What Is an Institution?

We will now proceed to answer the questions we have set for ourselves. Given that we have at least four alternative views of institutions within this broad umbrella of rational choice analysis, the answers may not be simple, and some nuancing of answers will be required. Indeed, in some cases the characterizations of these sub-approaches will be quite different. This may at once speak to the power and flexibility of this approach to politics, as well as to its tendency to become all things to all people. If the same general perspective on political action appears in so many guises relative to institutions, is it falsifiable, or is it just a general viewpoint on political life that really adds little to the armamentarium of the researcher in the discipline?

The first question then is what is an institution? These various sub-approaches are not entirely clear on this point, although they do vary somewhat in their clarity. The degree of clarity is largely a function of whether they began life attempting to be theories of institutions or whether that role has been thrust upon them by my reading of them. For example, the Ostrom approach does provide a reasonably clear definition of an institution. She argues (Kiser and Ostrom, 1982, p. 179) that institutions are:

> . . . rules used by individuals for determining who and what are included in decision situations, how information is structured, what actions can be taken and in what sequence, and how individual actions will be aggregated into collective decisions . . . all of which exist in a language shared by some community of individuals rather than as physical parts of some external environment.

At the other end of the spectrum Buchanan and Tullock never produce a stipulative definition of an institution, but rather talk in terms of constitutions and constitutional rules. The manner in which those rules are seen as working are, however, very similar to Ostrom's definition of an institution.

The scholars stressing the role of institutions as decision rules sometimes assume a definition of institutions, using almost a common sense descriptive definition of specific institutions, or of structural features of politics—law or corruption. What these scholars do that is important in developing theories of institutions is to differentiate exogenous and endogenous institutional questions (Shepsle, 1986; Weingast, 1996). Exogenous institutions are taken as fixed factors for a model, with the focus of the analysis being on their consequences for political life.[13] In the case of endogenous institutions, the question becomes why institutions take on particular forms. Neither of these views provides an unambiguous definition of these questions, but they do point to significant features of institutions that require further research.

Finally, the principal–agent model of institutions provides a very clear definition of institutions as structures of relationships between principals and agents. What this body of theory does not do, however, is to differentiate clearly those relationships encountered within an institutional format from the more general case of principal–agent models. This omission may be by design, that is, the analysts may assume no significant differences, but the question does appear important. If we adopt the Ostrom view of institutions then principal–agent relationships should be conceptualized as being constrained by a set of organizational rules in addition to the more individualistic assumptions that govern their usual forms of interaction, and hence must be considered as fundamentally different.

In all of these definitions, or protodefinitions, of institutions, there is a reliance on rules in separating the institutional from the noninstitutional. The implicit argument is that individuals left to themselves would be too individualistic or behave too randomly, and therefore some means of structuring their behavior is required for the collective good. The only contrary case would be researchers who are simply interested in the way in which exogenously formed institutions affect behavior. Thus, in this view, individual utility-maximization is the source of explanation, but it is far from the normative standard it is sometimes argued to be by critics of rational choice approaches. On the contrary, utility-maximization appears in a context in which individual behavior is something to be constrained and shaped, rather than something to be loosed upon others.

Institutionalization

Once we know what an institution is, we must then ask how they come into being. Institutions do not appear automatically because they are needed, but must be created (but see Sugden, 1986). The various rational choice perspectives tend to be better at defining institutions than they are in describing and explaining the processes by which institutions are created. This is perhaps to be expected, given the general orientation of the approach. It is strong on providing explanations for behavior within existing sets of rules than it is in explaining the processes through which those rules are created. More than the other approaches the rational choice version

[13] Many scholars of institutions would argue that few if any political institutions in real life are so stable that they could be treated in quite this way. One of the important research questions is how do institutions evolve, whether by accident or design.

takes institutions as givens, or as something that can be easily created, rather than the consequence of a historical and differentiated process.[14]

The general assumption, coming in part from Hayek (1967) appears to be that if there is a logical need for the institution it will be created, given that actors are rational, or that it will emerge. As Terry Moe (1990, pp. 217–18), one of the leading rational theorists working in institutionalism argues:

> . . . economic organizations and institutions are explained in the same way: they are structures that emerge and take the specific form they do because they solve collective action problems and thereby facilitate gains from trade.

This is a highly functionalist explanation for the emergence of institutions, leaving aside almost entirely the necessity for human agency.

In a more comprehensive treatment of the emergence of institutions Jack Knight (1998) discusses three alternative models of the formation of institutions. He argues first that institutions can emerge from the evolutionary emergence of conventions and norms, an explanation more like normative or sociological institutionalism.[15] More in the rational choice stream of analysis, he argues that institutions may emerge from exchange and the need to establish equilibrium in markets through mechanisms such as contracts. Finally, institutions may emerge as bargains, and especially as bargains intended to resolve problems caused by unequal distribution of resources in society—perhaps as a justification for the power of the State in controlling some aspects of the economy. The notion of agency is discussed little in these models, nor is there any clear understanding of when one is more applicable than another.

The major exception to the somewhat negative generalization about the role of agency in forming institutions is the "endogenous" version of the "decision rules" version of rational choice. The principal question for this perspective is, in fact, the logic of forming institutions and the structure of the rules that are selected to match (and shape) particular decision situations. For example, how can regulatory systems be designed in order to maximize the effective control of legislative organizations over the bureaucracy, and how can these be made to persist beyond the duration of any particular legislative period (Horn and Shepsle, 1989). Also, how can electoral systems be designed to generate certain types of desired outcomes, for example decisive majorities for the winning party, or fair proportionality of outcomes. Similarly, institutional voting rules can be structured to produce a variety of different outcomes, or to distribute power in desired ways (Garrett and Tsebelis, 1996).

---

[14] One exception to this generalization is some game-theoretic analysis that assumes that institutions can learn across time and are "path dependent" (Arthur, 1988; David, 1994), very much like the assumptions guiding historical institutionalism in political science.

[15] That having been said, the model actually discussed is based on game theory.

Sened (1991) provides perhaps the clearest explication of this endogenous, rational choice approach to institutions. He argues that institutions arise from the desire of one or more individuals to impose their will on others.[16] Further, those individuals must have the capability to manipulate the political structure in order to create such an institution, and must anticipate that they will be better off with the institution than without it. This runs counter to the general emphasis on uncertainty in most accounts of organizational formation and their preference for general welfare and opposed to individual welfare goals for institutions (Tsebelis, 1990). This argument does make the formation of institutions a rational action for the initiators, just as opposition may be rational for individuals who would be better off without the institution, or with some other institution.

The logic of the failure to provide explanations for the formation of institutions can be seen in Mancur Olson's early work on organizations and institutions. Given that he found that membership was irrational, it seems that formation would be even less rational, if that term admits comparison. The way that was found around that problem at the time was that entrepreneurs (Frohlich et al., 1971; see also Kingdon, 2003) would be the imperfection in the system that would *drive it* forward. That is, particular individuals would have to perceive that they could gain from the creation of an institution, and be willing to invest (time and other resources) in its creation. This solution is consistent with the approach, given that it depends upon the utility calculations of individuals, but appears more applicable to the formation of small groups than to the formation of larger social and political institutions. Even there, however, the actions of individuals may be crucial, as seen in the dominant role of the "founding fathers" in writing the Constitution of the United States, or a few leaders in formulating the designs for other constitutional arrangements.

For some versions of the rational choice approach the origin of institutions is irrelevant. If the interest of an analyst is entirely in modeling the consequences of particular sets of decision rules on behavior or policy outcomes, then where those rules have come from appears of little or no concern. While that absence of concern might be so, the debates surrounding the formation of rules may say a good deal about their presumed effects, and therefore about what the rules really "mean." If we return to the example of the U.S. Constitution then the "intent of the framers" has been a powerful component of interpretation since the document was written. Thus, for an analyst coming from the normative perspective on institutions the understandings reached when forming the rules may be as significant as the actual rules themselves.

Change in Institutions

Much the same can be said for arguments about how institutions change. These ideas do not appear particularly well developed. Again, in some versions of rational choice

[16] The ability to impose their will into the future may be an important element of this activity, as with the framers of constitutions.

analysis institutional change is not particularly important, given that the analytic purpose is to assess the impacts of structure on behavior and policy. This is another statement of the fundamental analytic difference between variance theories and process (institutionalization) theories of institutions (Mohr, 1982). Institutional change is simply exogenous to a model in which the purpose is to explain outcomes that result from the particular institutional arrangement in place, and therefore change generally is ignored, except as a new modeling problem once it does occur.

To the extent that change is conceptualized in these models it is a discrete event, rather than as a continuing process of adjustment and learning. In this way, change in this model is similar to that in historical institutionalism (see Chapter 4). Change may occur when the existing institution has failed to meet the requirements for which it was formed. The definition of "failure" is not clear either, but is probably related to the definition of a "good" institution described below. What is most important is that change is a conscious process, even if it involves tinkering with existing institutions, rather than the continuous process assumed in most other theories of institutions. This reliance on the emergence of a new set of institutions appears to beg the usual functionalist question, however, of how this adaptation will take place.

It is important to contrast institutional change in this version, or these versions of, institutionalism with that arising in the March and Olsen version. These views on institutions each answer half of the basic question about change. The rational choice version of change is good at identifying why conscious change may occur in a world of stable preferences[17] and institutional failures. March and Olsen, on the other hand, think of change as occurring more through the reshaping of preferences and adaptation of preferences and possibilities within the institution. As in the "garbage can". preferences may change to correspond with what the institution has found that it can accomplish, and both the institution and the individuals change.

The capacity to design institutions and to make designed institutional change to some extent contradicts the emphasis on equilibrium in rational choice institutional theory. The ability to alter and replace equilibria has, however, been inherent in rational choice versions of institutionalism from their inception. William Riker, for example, argued (1980; see also Colomer, 2001) that one set of rules that produced equilibrium had no claim of precedence over any other, so that change was actually quite natural. This view is in marked contrast to other versions of institutionalism that assume that the status quo does indeed have some claim to survive.

Individual and Institutional Interaction

The third question we will be addressing with reference to rational choice institutionalism is how do individuals and institutions interact. As demonstrated above, this

[17] A stable preference is one of the underlying assumptions of these models, so that what is rational at one point in time is still rational at a subsequent point (see Eggertsson, 1996).

interaction is bi-directional. On the one hand, institutions are argued to shape the behavior of individuals; the central purpose of existence for this approach appears to be to demonstrate how structures outside the individual shape the behavior of individuals within them. On the other hand, individuals are also assumed to shape the behavior of institutions, and by definition individuals must be the cause of institutional activities. Unless we engage in personification and assign the properties of humans to institutions, institutions must be the product of human action.

In the rational choice perspective another way to think about the linkage of individuals and institutions is to inquire about the status of individual preferences in the theories. As we have pointed out above, the usual way to think about institutions is that they map the preferences of their members (or other individuals) into a set of outcomes. In such a model individual preferences are assumed to be exogenous to the model. It may also be that institutions create preferences, very much as was argued by the normative version of institutionalism discussed already.

Again, the answers provided by the five subspecies of rational choice institutionalism will be somewhat different, especially for the manner in which individuals shape institutions. One of the five approaches has as its central question the manner in which individuals' choices create institutions, as well as their capacity to mold institutions effectively to produce desired outcomes (see above, p. 54). The other four, however, tend to be almost silent on the question of the origins and design of institutions. Even though the rules that shape behavior must come from somewhere, there is little specification of that source, and the rules appear at times simply to be.

For example, Ostrom's analysis of rules goes into great details concerning the nature of the rules and the various types of rules that exist within an institution, but does not say how and from where those rules do emerge. There appears to be a functionalist assumption in the analysis, for example, that rules are created as and when they are needed by the institution (or by society), and that there is a rather close temporal correspondence between the social need for a rule and its appearance. Further, there appears to be an implicit assumption that the rules selected will be functional and will address the decision-making situation effectively. These are happy assumptions, but not ones necessarily borne out in fact. Other students of organizations and institutions (Crozier, 1964) have argued that often formal rules are dysfunctional responses to the problems created by the formalization of organizations, and that the more institutions are formalized through rules the greater will be the attempts to evade those rules.[18]

One more general argument about individuals and institutions in institutional theory is that the purpose of the structures is to shape individual decisions. This shaping can be done through rules, through constituting contracts, or through shaping

[18] Theories of "autopoesis" (Luhmann, 1990) argue that society is more efficient at self-organization than at the creation of effective rule-making from central institutions.

the payoffs offered in an analytic (or possible real) game. Thus, the generalized methodological individualism serving as the basis of the rational choice approach appears in institutional analysis. The decision-makers in the scheme remain individuals seeking to maximize their utilities. Individuals shape the institutions and then have their decisions shaped by the previous institutional choices. The paradoxical element (Grafstein, 1992; see also Bicchierri, 2009) of this linkage is that humans design and create institutions but then are constrained by them.

The paradox advanced by Grafstein points to an even more basic question about institutions and individuals, which is why are institutions successful in constraining behavior in some circumstances, but not in others (North, 1998). That is, in some cases individuals comply readily with rules and respond to incentives, while in others they do not. For example, even normally law-abiding citizens tend to avoid many aspects of tax law when given the opportunity. Further, the incentives offered to join labor unions were powerful at one point in economic history, but tend to be declining in relevance for many contemporary workers. Thus, the capacity to constrain behavior varies across time and across situations, so that care must be exercised when attempting to generalize about the capacity of an institution to control behavior.

Institutional Dynamics

Yet another question about institutions is what are the underlying dynamics of this approach. That is, most institutional theories are good at explaining stability but are less good at explaining how institutions function internally, how they make decisions, and how they change (see above). As I have discussed, or will discuss concerning other approaches to institutions, institutional theory tends to be weaker on agency than it does on structure when explaining social behavior. In the rational choice perspective the individuals involved provide agency as they pursue their own interests, albeit in the context created by the institution.

Institutional Design

One important dimension of the formation of institutions within rational choice is the conscious design of institutions. We said above that rational choice theory was not very good at describing where institutions come from, and why they emerge. That statement was potentially unfair, given that more than any of the other approaches to institutions the rational choice advocates admit, and even encourage, explicit thinking about the conscious design of institutions (Kliemt, 1990; Goodin, 1995; Weimer, 1995). In some ways the principal purpose of understanding institutions in this approach is to be able to manipulate outcomes in subsequent rounds of design. Although there is a concern about design there is little in the way of explanation about what choices would be made. The assumption appears to be that if people understand the consequences of institutional choices there will be little doubt about the decisions to be made.

The concern with designing, and alternative approaches to institutional design, corresponds rather neatly with the schools of rational choice institutionalism we have already discussed. For example, the rules-based analysts think about ways to design superior rules, for example property rights, and ways to make those rules more readily enforceable in order to obtain their desired outcomes (Moe, 1984). They are especially concerned with creating desired outcomes that can persist across time, and in the face of changing players. One thing that may distinguish the rules approach from other versions of rational choice institutionalism is their willingness to think about incremental adjustment of rules, rather than more fundamental redesigning. Rules may be absolute statements, but they also are almost infinitely adjustable to changed demands and to new information. This is in marked contrast to the more fundamental changes associated with other forms of rational choice institutionalism. That having been said, however, if veto points are a manifestation of rules then incremental adjustments may be more difficult, as changes in the number of location of potential vetoes can drastically alter the dynamics of institutions (Hallerberg, 2003).

Similarly, scholars more committed to the ideas of principal–agent theories pursue some of the same goals in their design, for example an outcome that will persist, but believe that goal would be achieved through the creation of contractual relationships, and information sharing (Banks and Weingast, 1992) among the relevant actors. The principal–agent school of scholarship has even had the opportunity to design institutions in the real world. For example, much of the large scale reform of the civil service system in New Zealand was guided by rational choice logic, especially the idea of creating principal–agent relationships in government. The principal argument on behalf of this approach was its capacity to serve as a means of controlling public bureaucracies (Boston, 1991; Horn, 1995). To some extent this is simply formalizing relationships that existed within the bureaucracy already, but if nothing else it has the advantage of making the existing relationships more apparent to the participants, and therefore perhaps more enforceable.

Game theorists are concerned with designing institutional games that will enable the players to reach equilibria that produce the socially desired outcomes. As with much of the other game-theoretic discussion of institutions, this design task must be conceptualized in the context of an extended series of games in which the players have the opportunity to punish any defectors on one iteration of the game. The budget "game" is a particularly good example of this characteristic (Wildavsky, 1992; Kraan, 1996). Bureaus must come back to the legislature each year for funding, so that any deception or misuse of funds in one year is likely to be punished in the following year(s). Therefore, organizations may be willing to accept short-term losses in order to maintain the confidence of the central agencies responsible for the budget. One of the more interesting uses of game theory for institutional design is the analysis of possible constitutional changes in the European Union. Steunenberg (2000) examined the various proposals for creating the co-decision process with the European Parliament and *ex ante* determined that only one was viable.

All these scholars assume that their knowledge of, or perhaps assumptions about, the manner in which institutions function can inform the actual design of institutions. For example, building on work that has been conducted in more empirical versions of comparative politics, rational choice institutionalists have begun to make suggestions about the design of institutions. Perhaps the clearest case of design is in the selection of voting systems, where a substantial body of literature and experience enables the prediction of the consequences of institutional choice. Also, as the former socialist countries of Central and Eastern Europe have democratized they have had the opportunity to choose among a range of alternative models of democracy, and may have done so with a knowledge of the logical consequences of the rules they adopted. As institutional designs are moved from setting to setting, the rational choice model tends to assume that the same incentives and the same constraints will be effective in different political settings, and hence deny what other scholars of comparative politics has come to understand about the importance of social and cultural variables.

The rational choice approach to institutions, or economic approaches more generally, also remind us that creating institutions is not a cost-free activity. The creation of an institution requires the investment of time and talent, and may require the use of other more tangible resources if a design effort is to be successful (see Hechter, 1990). Thus, one part of the rationality in this approach to institutions is determining whether the investment of resources is worth the possible benefits derived from the institution once created. In the case of the mechanisms used to cope with common-pool resources an institutional solution may be the only possible approach, while for less clear needs to constrain individual behavior more cooperative solutions may be possible.

The Good Institution

The rational choice perspective on institutions purports to be a formal, analytical statement about institutions, but that scientific pretense obscures a strong normative element at the heart of most versions of this approach. Institutions, in the rational choice perspective, are designed to overcome identifiable shortcomings in the market or the political system as means of producing collectively desirable outcomes. Therefore, a good institution is one that is capable of coping with common pool resources well and efficiently, or making good decisions, usually while maintaining commitment to other powerful norms such as democracy. Given the link between the diagnosis and the prescription of failures within other structures, it is not surprising that a good institution may have different meanings for different versions of rational choice analysis.

The problem that Ostrom and her colleagues were attempting to solve was that of the frequent disjuncture between individual and collective rationality. Their argument is that the rules that define an institution are the best mechanism for integrating those two levels of rationality. Rational individuals become willing to accept constraints on their own behavior because they know that other actors are also constrained by the same rules, and that there is an organizational means of enforcing these limitations on individual utility maximization. Given that perspective on rationality, a good institution is one which is capable of making rules that constrain individual maximization when maximization is collectively destructive, and which can enforce its rules once made. This constraint is perhaps especially significant across time, so that a political leader may be willing to accept constraints on his/her behavior if s/he can be sure that future leaders will also be constrained.

The capacity to enforce rules is also an important element of the principal–agent model of rational institutionalism. In this setting, however, the basic purpose of the rules may differ from those in Ostrom is analysis. In the principal–agent model of institutions rules are essentially "meta-rules" about how to make fair and binding deals between those two sets of actors. Once those deals are made, then there must be some means of enforcing the arrangements, just as the courts enforce private contractual agreements that have the same principal–agent nature. In the public sector the enforcement of rules may be difficult to obtain, given the difficulty in detecting all forms of shirking and defection,[19] and the difficulties in punishing either individuals or organizations. Further, the concept of commitment, or the capacity to ensure that the same rules are enforced in the future, is crucial to the assessment of these principal–agent relationships.

Finally, given the economic basis of these rational choice models of institutions, one of the primary considerations in their evaluation is efficiency. This attribute need not necessarily be strict market efficiency, although for some institutions, for example the public bureaucracy and its constituent organizations, it may well be conceptualized as such (Niskanen, 1971; but see Self, 1995). Rather, in an institutional context, efficiency refers to the capacity of a political organization to map a set of preferences expressed by the public into a policy decision in a way that produces the least unacceptable decision. At a minimum an efficient political institution will produce decisions that do not threaten the overall legitimacy of the political system.

The rational choice literature on institutions has tended to concentrate on two types of public institutions—the public bureaucracy and legislative committees—and the types of decision problems faced by those collective actors. The efficiency questions may, however, be different for the two types of institutions. For bureaucracies the basic question is finding ways to ensure that these unelected actors do not "shirk" or adopt their own views of policy. For legislative committees the question is how to take a set of disparate preferences and reach a decision that

[19] Unlike the private sector there is no clear metric (money) to measure performance so that determining adequate performance may be more difficult. This problem is exacerbated when government contracts for commodities such as policy advice (Boston, 1991).

its members can accept, that does not violate rules of democracy, and that will be acceptable to the larger legislative body from which the committee is drawn.

Summary and Conclusion

A simplistic characterization of rational choice theory would not see any place for institutions in the approach. Even perceptive critics of the approach, such as March and Olsen, however, recognize that there is a place for both formal and informal structures as a means of channeling individual rational action. Further, even the harshest critics must admit that the blending of rational choice perspectives and a general institutional outlook on political life can supply a number of important insights into politics. In particular, more than the other views of institutionalism this approach tends to provide a lucid analytic connection between individuals and their institutions through the capacity of institutions to shape the preferences of individuals and to manipulate the incentives available to members of the organization.

The approach is not, however, without its theoretical and analytic problems. The most daunting of these problems is the difficulty in falsifying the predictions coming from this body of theory. It is very difficult to find any situation in which individuals could be said to not act rationally in the context of some possible set of incentives or another. Despite the apparent formalization, the predictions of rational choice analysis are rarely sufficiently specific that they are subject to unequivocal tests. Further, most scholars working within this intellectual tradition appear more interested in the logic of the analysis than in the applications of the results of that analysis so that there is little direct confrontation of theory and evidence.

In addition to the basic problem of analysis, there are several other issues that limit the utility of the rational choice approach to institutions. One such issue is that there are sometimes little relationships between the institutions described in theory and the institutions with which the members of those structures are familiar. The need to create abstractions and simplifications in order to facilitate the construction of models removes much of the detail that defines life in an institution. Further, the models are largely incapable of generating the type of predictions of policy outcomes that would be required if these models are to be more than interesting representations of the complex realities that they are meant to describe.

CHAPTER 4

Legacy of the Past: Historical Institutionalism

Another important approach to institutions in political science has been self-described as "historical institutionalism." Although they acknowledge borrowing the term from Theda Skocpol,[1] Steinmo, Longstreth, and Thelen (1992) were central in making a coherent statement of the approach and in advocating the broader application of historical institutionalism in the discipline. The basic, and deceptively simple, idea is that the policy choices made when an institution is being formed, or when a policy is initiated, will have a continuing and largely determinate influence over the policy far into the future (Skocpol, 1992; King, 1995; Pierson and Skocpol, 2002). The standard term for describing this argument is "path dependency" (Krasner, 1984; Pierson, 2000), meaning that when a government program or organization embarks upon a path there is an inertial tendency for those initial policy choices to persist.[2] That path may be altered, but it requires a good deal of political pressure to produce that change.

Presented in such a straightforward manner the concept of historical institutionalism is indeed very simple, but there is a great deal more to the concept. Several analytic questions that we have raised about all the various forms of institutionalism appear in an extreme version in this particular version. In particular, the problems of explaining change has been a central concern in historical institutionalism (see below). Further, the linkages between individuals and institutions within historical institutionalism were not as clearly defined as in several of the other approaches in institutionalism. That deficiency has to some extent been remedied but even then remains somewhat vague, so the role of agency remains less clearly defined.

Further, it is difficult to separate this version of institutionalism from the others, and some rational choice institutionalists also have attempted to document the pervasive effects of early choices about property rights and other rules of economic interaction (Alston et al., 1996; Hall and Soskice, 2001). Indeed, in their development of the idea of historical institutionalism Steinmo, Thelen, and Longstreth appear quite comfortable with some aspects of the rational choice versions of institutionalism,

---

1 See Thelen and Steinmo (1992, p. 28).

2 As we will point out below, however, it may be difficult to differentiate the impact of institutions from simple persistence and inertia of policies (see Rose and Davies, 1994). See also Genschel (1997).

and feel compelled to find some way of differentiating their own research from that of the more economics-based researchers (see also Katznelson and Weingast, 2005). Scholars such as Avner Greif and David Laitin (2004) also have applied game theory to understand institutional change in historical context.

In addition to the explicitly rational choice versions of institutionalism in economics there are strands of economic institutionalism that also have a pronounced historical element. For example, Douglass North earned a Nobel Prize for his contributions to economic history that focused on the way in which economic institutions have enduring effects and shape economic outcomes long after the initial decision to create those institutions. Similarly, the work of Coase (1937), Posner (1993), O. E. Williamson (1985; 1996) and numerous other scholars (Milgrom and Roberts, 1988; Gibbons, 2006) on the theory of the firm has a decided institutional element. The basic argument advanced by these institutional economists is that firms have been developed as a means of reducing the transaction costs that exist in an open market, and that careful design of economic structures is as central to generating efficiency as is the market itself. These works also argue that once created institutional structures (including the structure and behavior of private sector firms) are difficult to alter.

The concept of path dependence has also been analyzed from the perspective of economics. Altman (2000; see also David, 1994) has argued that the inefficiency of real markets, as compared to the hypothetical market of theory, produces the outcome of path dependence. These inefficiencies produce numerous local optima and firms, once they find such a local optimum, seize it and that local optimum becomes the dominant solution to the problem. Phrased more in terms of the operations of government programs, a particular program addressing a policy problem may not be the best in the abstract but once it has been shown to produce some positive results it will dominate other solutions that may, in principle, be superior but which will require movement from that existing and seemingly functional program.

Historical institutionalism was virtually the first version of the new institutionalism to emerge in the discipline of political science.[3] One of the earliest research statements was Peter Hall's (1986) analysis of the development of economic policy in France and Britain. Hall did not refer to "historical institutionalism" per se, but he did point to the importance of institutions in shaping policies over time. His analysis of the impacts of institutions did contain all the basic components of the historical institutionalist approach. The basic argument being advanced by Hall was that to understand the economic policy choices being made in these two countries (or any others) it was necessary to understand their political and policy histories. The choices

[3] March and Olsen published their seminal article (1984) before the emergence of the earliest statements of historical institutionalism, but in fairness it was not yet as clear a statement of their theoretical perspective as later (1989; 1994) works.

being made during the 1970s and 1980s reflected very clearly (in Hall's analysis) the long-established patterns of economic policy-making in those two countries.

Despite the importance of Hall's analysis this was not an influential or explicit statement of the virtues of institutional theory for the discipline of political science as was the somewhat earlier March and Olsen attack on the direction of the discipline (1984). Hall made a clear statement that policies at any one time are influenced by policy choices made earlier, but was relatively less clear about the institutional nature of those choices. The same outcomes could be the result of normal incremental patterns of policy-making found in most industrialized democracies, rather than an explicit influence of institutions over those policies. One factor that did emerge very clearly, and which was to become a principal part of Hall's subsequent (1989; 1992) published work, was the crucial role that ideas play in shaping policy. This independent role for ideas was also to become a major part of the historical institutionalist approach seen more generally.

Based on Hall's research, as well as the accumulation of evidence concerning policies in a number of socioeconomic policy areas, the more explicit statement of the approach emerged. As already noted, this statement of historical institutionalism focused on the influence that a variety of institutional factors can have over policy choices and over the performance of governments. Once governments make their initial policy and institutional choices in a policy area the patterns created will persist, it is argued in this approach, unless there is some force sufficient to overcome the inertia created at the inception of the program; this is referred to "path dependency" in historical institutionalism. Given that public organizations do tend to routinize their activities and to create Standard Operating Procedures (perhaps even more than do private sector organizations), the forces of inertia are likely to be substantial in government.

One of the more interesting extensions of historical institutionalism is that path dependency does not have to occur only in the simple, straightforward, manner described above. Just as students of organizations have argued that one rule tends to beget another rule to compensate for the inadequacies of the first rule (March and Simon, 1957; Crozier, 1964), so too can institutional rules and structures generate attempts to solve the problems that they themselves have caused. Similar to the concept of "sedimentation" in the sociological institutional theory (Tolbert and Zucker, 1996), this view of organizational life provides a more dynamic way of conceptualizing path dependency in operation (see Cheung, 1996; Kreuger, 1996). It also makes the impact of institutional choices across time all the more interesting for analysis.[4]

Pierson (1997) has identified a similar pattern of response to past decisions in the institutionalization of the European Union, and in the response of the governing structures of the Union to seemingly dysfunctional choices made during the

[4] This fits closely with the idea of "policy as its own cause" (Wildavsky, 1979; Hogwood and Peters, 1983) found in the public policy literature.

formative stages (see also Krasner, 1988, p. 67). This adaptive process provides historical institutionalism a more dynamic conception of policy than might have been expected from the name or the initial formulations of the approach. In particular, if the initial choices made by the formulators of a policy or institution are inadequate institutions must find some means of adaptation or will cease to exist (see Genschel, 1997). That having been said, however, organization theorists have noted that some "permanently failing organizations" do manage to survive.

Historical institutionalism in this view implies a course of evolution, rather than a complete following of the initial pattern (see Crouch and Farrell, 2004). Indeed, one version of path dependency can be seen as related to processes of evolution in biology (see Hathaway, 2001, pp. 113–17; Garud and Karnøe, 2001). Path dependency in this view is not a mortmain on institutions and their policies. Rather it is (as the phrase implies) a path that is likely to be followed in the absence of other pressures (see Huber and Stephens, 2001). There will be change and evolution, but the range of possibilities for that development will have been constrained by the formative period of the institution. The intellectual question which arises is whether even the punctuations in the equilibrium of the institution are constrained by those choices or if there is a wide (or unlimited) set of possibilities open.

In some conceptions of historical institutionalism there is also a strong evolutionary element, some not unrelated to the logic of evolutionary biology. The literature on American Political Development (Sanders, 1999; Carpenter, 2001), for example, contains a strong logic of path dependency in its research, but also has, as the name implies, a developmental and almost evolutionary perspective. For example, John Geering's study of American political parties has demonstrated the evolution of party ideologies (2001). Also, Desmond King (1995) has demonstrated the development of racial and social policies in the United States, doing so largely from the perspective of historical institutionalism.

Finally, some versions of path dependence are closely related to game theory and other economic versions of institutionalism. In particular, the literature on the impacts of sequences of choices on final policy choices demonstrates that the initial choices made in a sequence of voting tends to influence, or determine, subsequent outcomes. These choices then can create a least a temporary equilibrium. This literature emphasizes the importance of agenda control in decision-making bodies (Hammond, 1986), with the appropriate strategies chosen at the beginning of the decision-process affecting the final decisions.

We also need to understand that path dependence is perhaps not as strong a force as some of the early literature had imagined. For example, Alexander (2001) and other critics have pointed out that many institutions are not as "sticky" as might be thought. This has been especially true in comparative politics when attempting to understand transformation of political systems, and the ability of transitional regimes to institutionalize the changed (and often democratic) regimes.

In summary, although path dependence and historical institutionalism have become very widely used in political science, there are important questions about the meaning and the validity of this concept. While the common sense conception of historical institutionalism—that institutions are often slow to change once created—is difficult to contest, the more detailed academic understanding of the concept is more difficult to sustain. As we will develop below, there are a number of questions about path dependence that need to be considered when assessing the utility of historical institutionalism in the discipline.

What Is an Institution?

The most basic question in the consideration of institutional analysis is what constitutes an institution in each of the approaches. In some ways the answer for this basic question provided by historical institutionalists is more vague than in most approaches. They (Thelen and Steinmo, 1992, pp. 2–4) define institutions by means of examples, ranging from formal government structures (legislatures) through legal institutions (electoral laws) through more amorphous social institutions (social class), and appear willing to accept all of this disparate set of structures as components of the institutional apparatus that they will use to explain political phenomena. They also stress the point that the institutions in which they are interested are "intermediate," meaning residing somewhere between the generality of states as entities (and actors at least in international politics) and individual behavior which served as the focus of behavioralism in political science. While for March and Olsen (pp. 29–32) the nemesis that motivated them was rational choice theory, for Thelen and Steinmo the arch enemy appears to be behavioralism and an excessive (in their eyes) focus on individual behavior and individualized motivations for action in politics.

Interestingly, some other scholars (as cited by Thelen and Steinmo) provide definitions somewhat closer to a stipulative definition of the term. Peter Hall (1986, p. 7), for example, argued that institutions were "the formal rules, compliance procedures, and standard operating procedures that structure the relationships between people in various units of the polity and economy." Rather than focusing on formalized structures, this definition provided a sense of institutions as rule and procedures—in line with both Ostrom's versions of rational choice institutionalism and also some aspects of March and Olsen's normative perspective. Likewise, Ikenberry (1988, pp. 222–3) argues that the range of institutional concerns extends from ". . . specific features of government institutions to the more overarching structures of state, to the nation's normative social order." Even these definitions, however, tend to define institutions by example rather than by their fundamental, denotative characteristics.

One element of the operational definition of institutions that stands out in the historical institutionalist literature is the role of ideas in defining institutions. Although there is some discussion of formal structures, and of the procedures within those structures, in much of the literature using the approach the concept of the influence of ideas comes through strongly. Take, for example, Ellen Immergut's (1990; 1992a; 1992b) analyses of health care policies in a number of European countries. She is very clear in the influence that ideas concerning the practice of medicine have on the public programs that are adopted. There is certainly some discussion of the formalized structures of government involvement in health care, and the difficulties that multiple "veto points" present. The dominant factor in her analysis of what determines health policy, however, is what medical practitioners in the different countries believe is best practice.[5]

Similarly Peter Hall's more recent work (1989; 1992) turns from more structural explanations of economic policy to examine the influence that ideas have on those policies. He is especially concerned with the impact of Keynesianism and monetarism on policy. These ideas are the functional equivalents of the logic of appropriateness in normative institutionalism; they constrain the limits of acceptable action of government. More particularly, the ideas tend to provide a set of ready solutions for policy problems that arise within their domain. As Hall points out (1989), for much of the post-war period Keynesian ideas provided solutions for policy problems, while a revolution in policy ideas in the 1970s meant that later monetarism became the conventional source of those economic policy solutions, with supply-side concepts also vying for recognition and dominance.

Although the historical institutionalist approach emphasizes ideas, scholars have argued that there is also a "discursive institutionalism" that is even more associated with ideas and, rather obviously, discourse (Chapter 8 in this book; Bourdieu, 1998; Kjaer and Pedersen, 2001). The scholars working in this tradition also focus on ideas, but tend to do so almost to the exclusion of structural considerations. This approach is also discussed in terms of "constructivist institutionalism," meaning that institutions are essentially ideational constructions. Further, Hay (2006) argues that constructivist institutionalism is concerned with using ideas to understand change *after* the initial formation of the institution, while historical institutionalism is more concerned with the role of ideas at the formative moment.

Arguing that ideas are central components in defining institutions can go only so far in solving the problems raised by historical institutionalism. On the one hand, historical institutionalists focus on common sense concepts of formal institutions, for example legislatures or bureaucracies, similar to the focus of the empirical institutionalists (see pp. 92ff.). On the other hand, however, they rely on relatively an amorphous concept such as ideas to define the institutions. In some cases, for example the U.S. Forest Service or the Canadian Mounted Police, bureaucratic agencies are seen as embodying particular ideas and invest heavily in training their personnel to accept those ideas.[6] Jorgen Gronnegaard Christensen (1997) further demonstrates that organizations have powerful weapons to maintain their existing patterns of behavior, even in the face of determined efforts at reform.

---

[5] Some of the rational choice literature on institutionalism talks about "veto players" rather than "veto points." This emphasizes their focus on the behavior of individuals within the institutional context of rules and incentives (see Tsebelis, 1995).

[6] For example, environmental organizations tend to embody those ideas, just as military organizations are said to embody ideas such as "Duty, Honor, Country."

How Are Institutions Formed?

The emphasis of historical institutionalism is much more on the persistence of organizations after they are formed than it is on the facts of their initial creation. To some extent, the emphasis on embodying ideas in the structures that support institutions may be taken as a definition of the formation of institutions. It can be argued that when an idea becomes accepted and is embodied into a structural form then the institution has been created. As with the case of the normative institutionalism, however, this may be almost a tautology; the institution exists when an idea is accepted, but that acceptance is indicated by the presence of a structured institution.

What may be more important for the question of formation in historical institutionalism is the definition of when that creation occurs. The choice of when the relevant date from which to count future developments will be crucial for making the case that those initial patterns will persist and shape subsequent policies in the policy area. For example, when King (1995) was considering the development of welfare politics in the United States and the United Kingdom he began the analysis from the passage of major pieces of legislation in 1909 (United Kingdom) and 1932 and 1935 (United States). In at least the case of the United Kingdom the story could have begun with the Poor Laws (Himmelfarb, 1984) with the laws adopted in the early twentieth century being in some ways extensions of those laws. Or, if the analysis began with the creation of the "welfare state" during the post-war Labour government then the path that we would expect policy to follow would be substantially further left of center than that being discussed by King.

The question of what is a defining event, or what changes are incremental and what changes are fundamental, is a familiar one in political science (Hayes, 1992). Dempster and Wildavsky (1980), for example, ask the simple question of how much change constitutes an increment, as opposed to a more fundamental shift in a policy or a budget—a punctuation in the terms of the historical institutionalists. The familiarity of this question, however, does not make it any easier to resolve in practice. For purposes of understanding historical institutionalism, the question becomes whether the movement away from a presumed equilibrium position occurs by evolution or by revolution. The answer may be that both types of change occur, but accepting the revolutionary concept of change does require somewhat greater justification in a body of theory premised upon stability and continuity.

There is an important question of agency involved in the formation of institutions in the historical institutionalist perspective. The formative moment is crucial in this approach, and the logic of path dependency follows from that formative moment. It is clear that ideas are important elements in the formation of the institution, but ideas do not act on their own but require policy entrepreneurs (Kingdon, 2003) or some analogous actor to use the idea to create policy and to create institutions. Other approaches to institutions have a strong element of design (Alexander, 2005) but historical institutionalism appears to lack any significant emphasis on actors.

Katznelson and Weingast (2005) have attempted to integrate rational choice versions of institutionalism with historical institutionalism. They attempt to link one version of institutionalism that is very strong on agency with another that is much stronger in its use of structure, and therefore can provide the mechanism for driving action within an approach that appears to lack agency. In particular, preferences held by individual actors help to explain the choices made by individuals, whether individually or involved in interactions with others. To some extent these preferences can be derived from the organizations and institutions within which the individuals function and these help to maintain the path along which the institution is moving. This argument is also closely related to the logic of normative institutionalism in that preferences are considered to be more endogenous than would be true in conventional versions of rational choice institutionalism.

Institutional Change

The one area that historical institutionalism might be expected to have a particularly difficult time providing convincing explanations is the question of institutional change. The entire analytical framework of historical institutionalism appears premised upon the enduring effects of institutional and policy choices made at the initiation of a structure. Thus, the approach appears much better suited to explain the persistence of patterns than to explain how those patterns might change. That having been said, there are within the approach some promising avenues for exploring change. Further, other scholars have begun to link institutions to other aspects of political change in ways that may help historical institutionalism out of the trap of apparent immobility.

To understand change, or the relative lack of change, in historical institutionalism it is important first to conceptualize more completely how path dependence operates. Initially, path dependence was largely an inductive finding about technical choices and policy choice, and the behavior of formal structures in the public sector. As the thinking in historical institutionalism has evolved more complex understandings of path dependence have emerged. As noted above, in economics the understanding is one of numerous local optima and the associated difficulties for organizations (firms) moving in order to (perhaps) find a better solution. The same logic can be seen in the attempts of public programs to protect themselves against threats of terminations or modification, even if objectively those changes might be socially beneficial.

Paul Pierson (2000) has argued that path dependence can be explained through positive feedback from the initial policy choices and the manner in which that feedback reinforces those initial policy choices. Pierson does not, however, note the extent to which organizations that have somewhat vague measures of success and failure can code the observed outcomes as positive and use them to support their own policy views, and maintain some form of equilibrium in the face of significant challenge. Finally, Padgett and Ansell (1993; see also Clemens and Cook, 1999) have argued that institutionalization creates roles (see above, pp. 30–2) and those roles in turn create interests that help to maintain the institution.

Major Change

Historical institutionalism has treated change through the concept of "punctuated equilibria" (Krasner, 1984). As this phrase implies, there is an expectation in the approach that for most of its existence an institution will exist in an equilibrium state, functioning in accordance with the decisions made at its initiation, or perhaps those made at the previous point of "punctuation." These policy equilibria are not, however, necessarily permanent and institutions are considered capable of change within the context of the approach. Just as economic theory points out the existence of multiple equilibria in markets, so too for political institutions there may be a number of points of stability that are equally viable. The same concept of punctuated equilibria has been used in more general studies of public policy, and agenda change as a contribution to policy change (Baumgartner and Jones, 1993).

Although institutions are permitted to change within this conception of institutionalism, there are several problems with the conceptualization of change within the historical institutionalist model. One problem is that there appears to be little or no capacity to predict change. The concept, or "metaphor" of "punctuated equilibrium," was borrowed from neo-Darwinian evolutionary theory in biology, and implies some environmental dependency for institutional change. The punctuations in the equilibrium are assumed to occur when there are "rapid bursts of institutional change followed by long periods of stasis . . ." (Krasner, 1984, p. 242). That punctuation can be a sufficiently clear explanation *after* the fact, but it also comes very close to being tautological. That is, when a major institutional (evolutionary) change does occur then, after the fact, it can be argued that there was a sufficient force available to produce a movement away from the equilibrium and inertia affecting an institution. How do we know? The change did occur, did it not (?), so there must have been sufficient pressure to generate the observed shift. There appear to be no a priori criteria for determining when there is sufficient political or environmental "pressure" to generate a change.

Let us take one specific institutional change as an example. As almost the first act of the new Labour government in 1997, Chancellor of the Exchequer Gordon Brown granted considerable autonomy to the Bank of England, long directly controlled by the government of the day (Busch, 1994). This was an institutional equilibrium that clearly had been punctuated, but it is not at all clear that this could be explained by the logic of institutional analysis. If we take Peter Hall's discussion of the roots of British economic policy then this shift appears to go against established patterns. It also contradicts other versions of historical institutionalism, given that the older institutional arrangement presented fewer veto points to a political leader than does the new structure. In short, here is a major institutional change that does not appear explained well at all by historical factors, but yet after the fact can be made to appear almost inevitable given what we learn about the values of the new government by their haven taken the action.

Another, although very similar, way to look at the process of change in historical institutionalism is the idea of "critical junctures" (Collier and Collier, 1991) that has been used to describe and explain change in Latin American governments during the twentieth century. The argument is very much like that those governments did indeed have a great deal of inertia and that change would not occur unless there were a conjuncture of a variety of internal political forces that individually were not capable of generating significant change but which together could produce such movements. The agenda-setting literature (Baumgartner and Jones, 1993; Bohte, 1997) has discussed some of the same phenomena in the guise of "critical institutional events."[7]

Institutions also appear capable of change through learning and can move among equilibria by responding to new information. That information may come from experiences as they move along their own "path," or the information may come from the experience of other institutions. Hugh Heclo (1974), for example, has argued that social policy in Britain and Sweden during the 1950s and 1960s could be explained by the differential capacity of bureaucracies in those two countries to learn from their own and other experiences. More recently, Olsen and Peters and their collaborators (1996) have examined the manner in which public bureaucracies learn from their attempts, and the attempts of other countries, to implement reforms. Here again there are a variety of degrees of success in adaptation. Countries with well-institutionalized systems which might have been thought capable of resisting pressures for change (the United Kingdom) actually changed substantially while less institutionalized systems (the United States) actually resisted change rather completely. If we return to our example of the Bank of England, it may be that the Labour government had learned from the relatively greater success of the *Bundesbank* in Germany in controlling inflation and decided that this institutional structure also could work in the United Kingdom.[8]

If we remember that the power of public ideas (Reich, 1990) is a central part of historical institutionalism, then institutional change to some extent becomes a question of how to change ideas. Policy learning, more so than institutional learning, examines the reframing of policy issues and with them the possible reframing of the associated institutions. Paul Sabatier (1988; see also Sabatier and Jenkins-Smith, 1993) addresses the policy learning question as one of conflict between alternative visions of policy and a political process for resolving those differences in views.

---

[7] The purpose of this literature is to explain policy choices, not changes in institutions, but the two types of change may be closely bound together in the operation of actual policy processes.

[8] As noted, the British government also could have been said to be learning from its own past, as the Bank had enjoyed considerable independence prior to World War II.

Further, Peters, Pierre, and King (2005) demonstrate the importance of political conflict, and especially conflict over policy ideas, as a source of change in policy and in institutions with the development of alternative conceptions of policy being the source of "punctuations."

Finally, Paul Pierson (1996; see also Pierson and Skocpol, 2002, pp. 708–9) has pointed out that evolution should be an important process of change in the historical institutionalist analysis.[9] The approaches to change discussed above all depend upon creating a distinct separation from past policies, while Pierson argues for that more gradual change is also possible. In his view most institutional designs contain at least some unanswered or some dysfunctional elements that generate a subsequent need for change. Thus, incremental adjustment—one of the oldest identified processes in political science (Lindblom, 1965)—can be seen as a means of institutional adjustment to changing demands and to inadequacies in the initial design.[10] Using this method, however, assumes that the status quo is not too far from some desired position; if it is, then simple incrementalism may not be sufficient to general adequate change.

Gradual Change

As already noted, historical institutionalism began with a model of change that depended upon large-scale change that would occur infrequently. This notion of change is in marked contrast to the prevailing model, in American political science at least, of incremental change (Hayes, 1992). Many, if not most, policies appear to change rather gradually over time, through gradual accretion of new program elements, or perhaps the removal of other elements. There are, of course, also examples of policies that have changed dramatically in the manner proposed by the original historical institutionalist literature. For the theory to represent a major alternative in political theory it should be able to cope with both gradual and radical change.

In response to the numerous critiques of reliance on "punctuated equilibrium" Streeck and Thelen (2005) and others have developed several more gradual approaches to change within the context of historical institutionalism. These approaches to change all assume that the basic structure of policy will remain intact but that there will also be some changes. Further, not all of these changes will be functional for the actual delivery of the policy—some may be simply means of appearing to change in order to maintain the status quo, while attempting to satisfy political demands for change.

---

[9] For a more rational choice perspective on institutional evolution see Knight (1992).

[10] Pierson and Skocpol (2002) argue that institutions may be layered because of their processes of development, a concept similar to "sedimentation" in the sociological studies of institutions (see below, pp. 140–1; see also Schickler, 2002).

As well as focusing on large-scale change, the original work in historical institutionalism tended to assume exogenous sources of change (see Mahoney and Thelen, 2010). The assumption was that if stable institutions and their policy were to change they would have to do so in response to exogenous shocks that were sufficient to overcome the existing equilibrium. The more recent developments in this approach also accept that change may result from exogenous forces, with the institution adapting to its own internal dynamics in order to preserve itself and to establish a new (and perhaps moving) equilibrium.

Thelen and Streeck propose four alternative strategies for change within this framework. The simplest of these forms of change is *displacement*, in which existing patterns of rules within an institution are transformed. This is in many ways simply a restatement of conventional ideas about organizational and policy change. This form of transformation is occurring in most institutions on a continuous basis, and they may cumulate into more significant transformations. As with incremental theory there is a significant question of how much change is an increment and when more significant change occurs (Dempster and Wildavsky, 1980).

Layering implies change resulting from imposing new rules on top of, or alongside, existing rules. This style of reform often results from changes in partisan control of government, so that the new government imposes its own preferences without bothering to alter the existing structures. One clear example is the layering in of new civil servants in Mexico and other Latin American countries when there is a new government. That new government does not go through the arduous process of firing sitting public servants but merely adds its own adherents on top of the government they inherited.[11]

Third, rules may *drift*. Mahoney and Thelen (2010, p. 16) argue that drift occurs when rules change in response to changes in the environment. Although not included in the discussion of change within historical institutionalism, there is also a substantial literature on drift in government regulations (McCubbins et al., 1987). These changes occur more from internal changes in the regulatory organizations and their preferences. There may be some reaction to changes in the regulated industries (the environment) but most appear to arise from changes in the regulatory organizations themselves.

Finally, *conversion* refers to the process of using existing rules and structures in different ways. This can be seen somewhat more easily with the behavior of organizations rather than rules per se. There are the classic examples of private sector organizations such as the March of Dimes and the YMCA that transformed their operations in order to survive (Zald and Denton, 1967). In the public sector after the end of the Cold War, the U.S. military went through a period of emphasizing its

[11] This is true even after there is real change of parties after elections, when the PRI lost its long-term hold on the Mexican government.

capacities for coping with domestic crises or fighting the drug wars, for fear of losing their budgets and autonomy.

These four models of gradual institutional change do enable the historical institutionalist model to contend with change more effectively than if the only option for change is more radical change. Taken together these four ideas about change contain a number of relatively ordinary processes of organizational and institutional change. The theoretical question that remains, however, is whether these models actually fit with the basic assumptions of historical institutionalism. If that model is indeed constructed on the persistence of patterns, and the economic logic of maintaining local equilibria, then these rather simple processes appear to be just added on to the model with little theoretical coherence.

Summary

In summary, historical institutionalism was not originally a fertile source of explanations for change in organizations and institutions. We have been able to point out that change is not totally antithetical to the approach, but it certainly has not been a central element in this approach to institutions. To uncover the explanations for the changes that do occur we are forced to move outside the approach itself to identify other dynamics (learning or environmental change) that can generate sufficient political pressure to produce a change. There appears to be no such dynamic element within the theory itself to motivate these incremental changes, unless one accepts the dysfunctions of initial design as sufficient cause.

Even if we accept the dynamic of adaptation to remedy dysfunctions, however, there must be some mechanism to recognize the dysfunction as well as a political mechanism to furnish the remedy. The sociological version of institutionalism would almost certainly argue that the cognitive constraints imposed by institutional membership would tend to make recognition of dysfunctions less likely.[12] Likewise, the assumptions of problem-solving through gradual evolution may underestimate the degree to which attempts to remedy organizational faults may actually reinforce some of those problems rather than actually help. The stable mindset of any institution will support only a limited range of possibilities, and most members of the institution will have a difficult time "thinking outside the box" associated with the dominant ideas of the institution.

These analytic problems with change emphasize the weakness of agency in historical institutionalism (see Peters et al., 2005). The more extensive changes involved in "punctuated equilibria" are more dependent upon external forces, but the more

[12] Desmond King's (1995) study of the evolution of labor market policies in the United States and the United Kingdom demonstrates the forces of persistence rather than functional adaptations when dysfunctions are encountered. This is an institutional version of the familiar problem of cognitive dissonance in social psychology.

gradual changes do appear to require agency. The transformation of rules, or their replacement, within the more gradual models might be related to external forces but still require those external changes to be interpreted and framed (Hacker, 2005) to be capable of motivating change. Thus, as noted in several places already, organization theory can become useful as a complement to historical institutionalism to provide the necessary dynamic (Egeberg, 2003).

In summary, theorists of historical institutionalism have been making a number of important efforts to integrate ideas of institutional change into their models. That effort has, however, to some extent emphasized some of the weaknesses in the approach. That is, historical institutionalism per se does not provide any dynamic for change, other than large scale changes seen as punctuations in the equilibrium. Even those, however, depend upon some exogenous shocks rather than any internal dynamic. And those changes may further depend on the manner in which the external shocks are perceived and framed within the institution.

Linking Individuals and Institutions

Unlike several of the other approaches to institutionalism the historical institutionalists are not particularly concerned with how individuals relate to the institutions within which they function. There appears to be an implicit assumption of the approach that when individuals choose to participate in an institution they will accept the constraints imposed by that institution, but that linkage is not explored directly by the scholars working in the tradition. Indeed, there is a certain sense of *deus ex machina* in the historical institutionalist approach, with decisions taken at one time appearing to endure on auto-pilot, with individual behavior being shaped by the decisions made by members of an institution some years earlier.

That assumption is essential to being able to tell causal stories using a historical institutionalist approach. The structure-agency problem familiar in the social sciences arises very clearly in this approach in that although the structural elements of an institution may establish conditions that make certain outcomes much more likely, there is still a need for the individual decision-makers involved to translate those constraints into action. If there is not that linkage of individuals and institutions it is difficult to determine how those earlier decisions are translated into contemporary policy choices.

There is also the question about the other linkage between institutions and individuals, that is, how are institutions shaped by individuals. This is one of the enduring questions for institutionalism, and the answer provided by this model is not at all clear. The most facile answer is that individuals make the institutional decisions that then persist throughout the future life of the institution. Still, it is not clear in all or even most cases exactly how those decisions are translated from the individual to the institutional level and how they become more than individual understandings.

In some case the formative policy choices are translated into law, and then that law functions as the basis for subsequent institutional actions. If that is, however, the definition of the linkage then this can perhaps be better understood as a legal, rather than an institutional, model for explaining behavior. We can easily discuss law as being an institution (see Lindahl, 2001), but that seems to drive the explanation back one more step. That is, how does law (as an institution with its stable rules and values) explain change observed in other institutions? Phrased somewhat differently, there are questions of individual compliance with rules and law after they are initially formed within the institution (Scott, 2008).

Finally, there is the question of the role that ideas play in shaping individual behavior within institutions. Ideas are a central aspect of the historical institutionalist perspective, and the capacity of the structures to "sell" those ideas to current or prospective members of the institution is crucial for making the linkage of structure and actor. Some of this linkage may result from self-selection as individuals attracted to a particular set of ideas will come into the institution ready to accept those ideas. That self-selection behavior is very similar to the attraction of individuals for institutions argued to exist in the normative institutionalism. One version of institutionalism talks more in terms of ideas and one in terms of norms and values, but the logic is very similar.[13] Likewise, the importance of ideas has some similarity with the discursive institutionalism, although the dominance of one idea over some time in historical institutionalism is markedly different from the somewhat indeterminate nature of discursive institutionalism (see Chapter 6).

Institutional Design

Given that we have argued that historical institutionalism is not at all clear on the origins of institutions, or on the linkage between individual decisions and institutional choices, it is not surprising that this approach is almost silent on the design of institutions. It is almost silent, but not totally so. Indeed, it could be argued that design is perhaps the central question for the historical institutionalist, given that the initial choices of policies and structures are argued to be so determinate of subsequent decisions within the institution. Thus, design may be the selection of ideas that will motivate the institution during the remainder of its existence.

These formative choices for institutions do not appear to be, within this version of the theory, the product of a conscious design choice or any explicit model of designing government structures (see Alexander, 2005). Rather, these formative choices appear to reflect the particular confluence of political or technological forces at play at the time of the time of formation of the institution. The historical institutionalists

[13] There may be an important difference between ideas and norms. The former concept appears concerned primarily with how external events are structured, while norms are more internal to the institution. See also Immergut (1997).

often do a good job of describing those political forces and the manner in which they produced the initial policy decisions, but that is more the product of politics than the conscious design of policy or the design of government institutions. This approach appears to eschew any ideas of rationalistic design in favor of a more political conception of policy choice. That having been said, some scholars have attempted to build on the lessons of the past and use those lessons to design institutions in different settings (Luong, 2002).

Interestingly, consciously *redesigning* existing institutional frames appears to be a more significant component of the historical institutionalist model than does the initial design. This place for purposeful change is simply because redesign involves a conscious reaction against the existing institutional and policy frame. It may become obvious that the framework in place is no longer functional (if it ever was; Sykes, 1998), and that there is a need for a redefinition of the nature of the institution. If there is a dominant institutional frame in place then the best way in which to generate change is to produce a superior alternative frame to replace it.

Although there is a place of redesign in the historical institutionalist framework, there is still a need for agency in this process. The logic of historical institutionalism is that institutions should persist unless there is some force that diverts them from their established paths. While major technological or economic changes might be expected to generate change, but even then the need for change may not be self-evident but will have to be conceptualized and the members of the existing institutional structure will have to be convinced.

The Good Institution

The final question to be asked concerning historical institutionalism is what constitutes a good institution in this model of political life. Unlike the first two models of institutionalism I have discussed there is little explicit normative content in this approach. This approach to institutions is very much a statement of what is (at least in the conceptualizations of its advocates), as opposed to what should be. The fundamental purpose of the approach appears to be to explain the persistence of institutions and their policies, rather than to evaluate the nature of those policies and institutions. Ideas are important, but more as a means of defining the institution rather than as a means of assessing the virtues of the institution.

The above having been said, one way to think about the quality of an institution in the historical institutionalist model is their adaptability. This criterion appears to be a direct contradiction of the basic premises of persistence within the model, but yet it does make some sense. In particular, the work of scholars such as Pierson (1996) points out that many initial choices are dysfunctional and hence the successful institution will have to change. Even if the initial choices were appropriate, the policy environment in almost all areas has been changing rapidly, so that adaptation becomes essential.

The other normative statement that could be teased out of the historical institutionalist version of the approach is that good institutions are those that can translate their ideational basis into action. If, as scholars such as Peter Hall argue, institutions are based on ideas then those institutions should be judged on how well they are able to make effective policies that implement those ideas. On the one hand, this definition of the good institution may become almost tautological, like several other versions of institutional theory. That is, if institutions are defined as being defined on the basis of on putting ideas into action, they perhaps should not be judged on how well they put those ideas into effect. Even then, however, the historical approach to institutions did not purport to contain a strong normative element as do several of the others, so that it may be unfair to make this assessment of its capacity in this regard.

The models of change that have been developed tend to undermine this conceptualization of the "good institution." Concepts such as "drift" and "conversion" that are utilized to describe institutional change imply that the ideas used to define the institution, at least at its inception, are not being put into effect later in the life of the institution. If the ideas do not provide a stable platform for assessing the performance of an institution, then there is little means of arguing whether an institution is in fact persisting.

The Limits of Explanation

One of the more interesting aspects of the historical institutionalists' approach is that their explicit purpose is to deal with the demands of comparative political analysis. These scholars have envisaged their approach being able to explain differences across political systems. Hall (1986), for example, is quite clear in his arguments about the effects of different histories and different institutions on the economic policies, and subsequent economic performance, of France and the United Kingdom. This comparative purpose is rather different from the normative approach, and even the rational choice models of institutionalism, that appear to offer explanations that are less anchored in specific times and places. Steinmo's later work on tax policy (1993) also points to the persistence of certain approaches in Britain, Sweden, and the United Kingdom.

The most obvious question to be asked concerning the explanatory capacity of this body of theory is can objective researchers differentiate the historical institutionalist explanations from other forms of historical and inertial explanations? The answer to that fundamental question appears to differ depending upon which version of historical institutionalism one chooses to focus attention upon, and in particular what version of explanation for path dependence one chooses to accept. The answer further depends upon what role policy ideas are assigned as a defining characteristic of institutions, as opposed to just having an independent influence of their own over policy. Finally, the answer depends upon how well one can differentiate the arguments of the historical institutionalist from those of the empirical institutionalist discussed below.

Let me deal with those three points in turn. First, as already noted, there are several versions of historical institutionalism in use in the discipline. If we focus our primary attention on the Thelen, Longstreth, and Steinmo version that has functioned as the manifesto for this movement then there may be some questions about how clearly one can separate historical institutionalism from the influences of history on policy, taken more generally (see Mahoney, 2000). In other words, what does adding the term "institutionalism" in the title of the approach add to the explanatory capacity of history as an approach? The term does make the approach more respectable in a discipline that has rediscovered institutions, but it is not clear what else is being added. The principal object here is that of being able to postdict decisions with 100 percent accuracy, and the difficulty in imagining history having operated any differently. Calling this persistence of policy encountered in almost all policy situations "institutionalism" appears to convey little concerning the dynamics of the institutions themselves.

The second part of the answer to the underlying question depends upon whether ideas are seen as having an independent status and influence of their own, or are they considered simply as components of the institutions that convey and implement them? For some scholars ideas are argued to possess a significant explanatory power even without their institutional trappings. Robert Reich (1990), for example, has argued for the "Power of Public Ideas" as a factor in explaining the development of the public sector. Martin Rein (1998) also discusses ideas as one of the three principal factors explaining policy choices in contemporary political systems. Giandomenico Majone (2001) also has emphasized the importance of ideas in policy discourse although his discussion appears closer to the discursive model discussed below. In short, the advocates of the approach of historical institutionalism must be capable of explaining why ideas are institutional and are not, at least in principal, independent of the institutions. Institutions may adopt and embody ideas, but it is not clear that they actually determine the nature of the institutions.

Finally, it is not always clear how some self-proclaimed versions of historical institutionalism differ from the empirical institutionalist approach. Take, for example, Ellen Immergut's (1992a; 1992b) analysis of health policy using the concept of "veto points" to define the crucial junctures that arise from institutional structures. The existence of these veto points within institutions represents an historical legacy of their founding, but they also represent enduring structural features of those institutions. As pointed out already the concept of a veto point is very little different from the earlier Pressman and Wildavsky (1974) concept of a "clearance point" for implementation analysis. For both concepts it is assumed that a decision must pass through a number of formal points in a chain of linked decisions before it can go into effect, and that actors at those points are capable of making or breaking the policy.

The concept of "veto point" is used more generally than is that of "clearance points," referring as it does to decisions made at any point of the policy process (see

Tsebelis, 2002). On the one hand, the "veto point" idea is focused very much on structural barriers within the institution itself. The Pressman and Wildavsky concept, on the other hand, places a great deal of emphasis on the blockages that exist throughout the complex chain of events required to put a program into effect. Given the increasing use of nongovernmental actors in implementation, these problems include problems arising from social actors that are involved in the policy process. If the above analysis is true then there may be little to separate empirical institutionalism and historical institutionalism.

The most difficult question to ask about historical institutionalism is whether the explanations be falsified, the standard Popperian (Popper, 1963) test for an adequate scientific theory. Just as rational choice theory can almost always develop an explanation that demonstrates that the actors were acting rationally, so too the historical institutionalist can always generate an explanation that demonstrates the impact of previous decisions and inertial tendencies. There appear to be few *ex ante* criteria of proof available here; how large a deviation from an inertial path is needed to argue that the historical explanation was not effective in a particular case? Further, there are no basic premises, for example, to maximize self-interest or act according to a set of institutional norms that can be used to make predictions about behavior.

Historical institutionalism comes close to being just a version of normative institutionalism, given its tacit acceptance of "logics of appropriateness" in shaping behavior. The concentration on ideas, and the routes through which ideas shape behavior, may be little more than saying that there are such logics of appropriateness within policy areas and within specific government institutions. If, however, all that these scholars are arguing is that there are such logics that have some durability over time it is not clear that there is really a distinct approach to institutions. Historical institutionalism then might as well be subsumed as a component of the March and Olsen normative approach, albeit with a well-developed interest in history and the impact of institutions across time. Given the emphasis that March and Olsen place on history, again it may make more sense just to consider this variant a part of normative institutionalism.

Further, and as noted above concerning several of the other manifestations of institutional analysis in contemporary political science, this version of the approach appears extremely effective at "explaining" what happened and in weaving a narrative that does capture a good deal of the reality of historical influences. At times, however, these characterizations of history come close to being functionalist accounts; things happened the way they did because they had to, given the historical and institutional forces at work at the time. The problem is that there are cases in which institutions do change in unexpected ways and this approach appears at something of a loss to explain those changes. Further, the functionalist explanations often are not convincing, given that often there is no clear explanation for why things had to happen the way they actually did.

Summary

In many ways the historical institutionalists are, when considered carefully, the most surprising of the schools of institutional theory in political science. The initial impression created is that of a static and conservative explanation of policy, and with that a prevailing assumption of hyperstable institutional structures. After a more thorough reading of this literature, however, a clear dynamic of adjustment can be distinguished, and the approach appears to offer a greater scope for explanation than might have been expected. In addition, the historical institutionalists do provide an avenue of looking at policy across time, while many of the approaches are more bound in time and even in space. The initial formulations of the approach had rather extreme conceptualizations of change, but these are now augmented by more gradual, if somewhat troublesome, versions of institutional change.

There are, however, also several severe problems with the historical institutionalist explanations of policy and political life. The most basic difficulty is that this rendition of institutional theory provides little or no capacity to predict change. As pointed out above, the assumptions of this model are almost certainly not as static as its critics would have us believe. The approach still appears, however, incapable of doing other than postdicting changes in the equilibria that otherwise characterize the predictions of this approach. This deficiency is not fatal, given that the model can be considered as more descriptive than explanatory or predictive, but this certainly does limit the overall scientific utility of the account of institutional theory. This deficiency does, however, highlight the importance of the absence of a clear model of agency within the approach.

Further, this version of institutionalism has some difficulties in distinguishing itself from other approaches. Historical institutionalism argues for the dominance of decisions made early in the existence of a program or organization. By attempting to overcome the critique of being excessively static, however, the advocates of the historical approach have had to rely upon explanations such as "ideas" that make them appear like the normative institutionalists, or like cognitive theories in sociological institutionalism, or perhaps most closely like discursive institutionalists for whom change is dependent upon the clash of ideas.

That lack of sharp distinctions, in some ways, is a strength of historical institutionalism. If it is similar to the other approaches then the historical approach can be integrated with most if not all the other versions of new institutionalism, and perhaps create something of an integrated institutionalist theory for political science. As we will point out at the end of the volume there does appear to be something that can be considered the "new institutionalism." Historical institutionalism is a central part of that body of thinking about political life. Despite that centrality, the approach does have particular problems that limit its own capacity to explain and to predict the behaviors, and the fates, of institutions.

CHAPTER 5

Empirical Institutionalism

Much of the research on institutions we have been discussing is explicitly and purposefully theoretical. There has been some attempt to test the predictions of rational choice theory and economic institutionalism (Alston et al. 1996) and the historical institutionalists utilize a base of historical experience to develop their generalizations about institutional behavior (King, 1995; Thelen, 2004). Other institutionalist scholars, however, have attempted to test several of the prevailing conceptualizations concerning the impact of differences in institutions more empirically. This type of comparative analysis is, however, difficult to implement methodologically. On the one hand, there are relatively few countries in which institutions have varied significantly across time, so that attempting to demonstrate the effects of structure with a quasi-experimental design (Cook and Campbell, 1979) is difficult, if not impossible. There have been some interesting examples, for example Israel adopting a semi-presidentialist system similar to that of France with a directly elected Prime Minister (Diskin and Diskin, 1995; Shugart, 2005), but these opportunities for testing theory directly are very infrequent.

On the other hand, the differences among countries that do appear in any cross-sectional analysis tend to be associated with a wide variety of social and cultural values that could confound any statistical findings (see Peters, 1998) presuming to document the impact of structural variables. Are differences observed between social or economic policies in the United States and the United Kingdom a result of institutional differences, or of any number of other political or socioeconomic factors, or both? The probable answer is "both," but assigning relative weights to them is difficult with such a small sample to apportion explained variance among various causal factor countries. Attempting institutional factors and the other relevant factors is almost certainly impossible, especially when the United States is the only true example of presidentialism among the industrialized democracies.

Despite the inherent research problems, attempts at empirical research on the impacts of structure are extremely valuable for advancing the institutionalist arguments. If institutions do have any significant effects these effects should be demonstrable through the methods usually associated with empirical social science. If the expected results do not manifest themselves then we must question whether these variables, despite their face validity, are as crucial for understanding political life as their advocates would have us believe. The alternative possibility would be that institutions are important for establishing a framework of action but that other proximate variables, such as political interests and the decisions of individual political actors, are more directly related to policy choices.[1]

Building an Empirical Theory of Institutions?

The above discussion is, of course, just another way of stating the familiar "structure-agency" problem of explanation in the social sciences (Dessler, 1989; Hay, 1995). It may also be the case that, as Przeworski and Teune (1970) argued, systemic level variables—whether appearing as the proper names of countries or as institutional structures—do not have any substantial effect on political behavior. If we then utilize a variant of the "most similar systems design," and change only one system level variable then we should expect little difference in behavior. The remaining political relationships would be sufficiently strong, and also sufficiently persistent across time, that this one simple structural manipulation will have no real effect on patterns of decision-making.

The above argument can be illustrated by thinking about the Federal Reserve Bank in the United States. If it were transformed into a less politically independent status would its deeply ingrained anti-inflation values in economic policy persist despite that structural change?[2] Interestingly William Riker, generally an advocate of the institutional form of federalism, has argued that the institution itself had little or no influence over public policy decisions (1962; 1980). His argument was that individual preferences would still dominate in making public policy, regardless of institutional structure and that institutions were really little more than "congealed preferences" from earlier policy choices. That meant that the institutions could themselves be highly mutable, and that although structures produced an equilibrium in political forces, there were many possible equilibria.[3]

Ove Pedersen's (1991, p. 132) critique of several versions of the new institutionalism is particularly important here. Pedersen raises the question of the status of system level variables in an interesting way. His point is that if we argue that institutions are in essence collections of values, or of rules, or of cognitive frames, then what actually explains any observed differences in the outputs of government? Why not say that rules are the operative element rather than some superordinate entity—the

[1] Such a formulation is not incompatible with the rational choice version of institutionalism, given that it assumes that rational individuals will make choices in accordance with the rules and incentives structured by their institutions.

[2] This is in many ways a historical institutionalist argument assuming the persistence of those values (see Chapter 4).

[3] This is in part a function of Riker's commitment to rational choice analysis, and the dominant of individual preferences over institutional formats. This distinguishes his work from that of rational choice institutionalists such as Shepsle discussed in Chapter 3 For both strands of thinking about institutions, however, institutions are highly mutable, in marked contrast to the historical institutionalist.

institution—composed from those rules? It could be argued that the longevity and predictability of those rules (or preferences) may constitute the institutional aspect of the relationship to outputs, but then there is the question of how to distinguish the long-term from the short-term impacts of the rules. In short, what is the utility of using the label institution, or "new institutionalism" for empirical analysis rather than simply looking at rule-based behavior, or the impact of particular rules or norms? Some scholars argue that social theory will advance primarily through identifying the underlying factors in social processes, such as rules or values in the case of institutions.

Thus, when we begin to examine the impact of structural characteristics of institutional arrangements in the public sector on the behavior of individuals, and on the policy outputs of government, we want to be able to specify the dynamics by which the formal structure creates any observed differences in behavior. There is no shortage of descriptions of institutional arrangements and their presumed effects, but as valuable as these descriptions are they often do not add up to a comprehensive explanation for the behavior of governments. Nor do these descriptive accounts necessarily explain much about the policy choices made by governments. As we noted above, one of the powerful aspects of rational choice versions of institutionalism is they could specify clearly the behavioral and causal assumptions that drove their theories. Unfortunately, few if any of the empirical institutional theories can make such a claim, so that there are often a number of credible findings without a strong theoretical basis for explanation.

Varieties of Empirical Questions

There are several renditions of empirical institutionalism, just as rational choice institutionalism had a variety of different perspectives within the same approach. Rather than offering alternative theoretical perspectives, however, most versions of empirical institutionalism are asking the same question—do institutions matter?—about a number of different institutional arrangements and options (see Weaver and Rockman, 1993). The answers are to some extent predetermined, given the institutionalist concerns of the researchers, but the variety of different questions (and similar answers) does point to the richness, and research potential, of this body of literature.

Presidential and Parliamentary Government

The most developed body of empirical literature on institutions examines the impact of differences between presidential and parliamentary regimes on the performance of political systems. This is one of the standard "chestnuts" of political science, going back at least to Woodrow Wilson's more normative (1884; 1956) writings about American government, but the question remains important, especially during an age in which a number of countries have only recently designed their own versions of democracy. Although based to an increasing degree on empirical observations, this literature also retains some substantial theoretical and almost ideological elements. In particular, some scholars (Riggs, 1988; Linz, 1990; 1994) are particularly concerned about the impact of the choice of presidential regimes on governments of the Third World and the newly democratized regimes in Central and Eastern Europe. These scholars appear to have concerns about the consequences of this institutional choice, including perceived problems in presidentialism (Riggs, 1988) that extend well beyond the limited evidence of differential levels of stability.[4]

The dependent variable in these analyses, "performance," is being conceptualized in several ways. In the first place, performance may simply mean survival. One segment of the literature on presidential government, alluded to above, is concerned with the impact of regime type on the stability of governments. The argument is that presidential regimes, because of their concentration on the single executive and the absence of a means of changing incumbent governments without extraordinary actions, tend to be more fragile than parliamentary regimes. Thus, presidential institutions are argued to perform less well than parliamentary regimes, despite the long-term survival of the United States and the success of semi-presidential regimes such as France and Finland (see Pasquino, 1997).

It has been argued, however, that even if presidential regimes are successful in more developed countries the institutional format may be inappropriate for the strains of Third World governments. The temptation for elected presidents to convert the office into a less democratic system appears very strong under the pressures of economic stagnation and ethnic divisions. Further, presidents often become closely allied with the military and may become tempted to use that institution to maintain their power, which in the long-run becomes associated with extralegal forms of transition. There is, however, an increasing amount of empirical evidence demonstrating that presidentialism is not as much a predictor of instability as often thought, but rather other conditions such as the nature of the party system may be better predictors (Cheibub and Limongi, 2002).

At a second level the performance of presidential and parliamentary regimes can be measured by the types of policies that they enact. The articles contained in the Weaver and Rockman (1993) volume on the impact of institutions focus on the choices made by these types of regimes, as well as the impact of variations among parliamentary regimes. Coalition governments in parliamentary governments, for example, may be forced to make more "side-payments" to member parties than would be true for governments with a single party (Britain) or with a limited number of parties in the coalition, for example Germany. Thus, the limited coalitions should be able to

[4] To some extent the findings are biased because of the large number of Latin American regimes with presidential forms of government and their independence for longer periods of time than other Third World countries.

make more creative and radical interventions than would be true for larger and more diverse coalitions. Further, the capacity to manage government may depend upon other institutional variables, for example the strength of party discipline, rather than simply the formal nature of the regime.

Finally, the performance of parliamentary and presidential regimes can be measured by their capacity to legislate at all (see Cox and McCubbins, 2001). The division of powers inherent in presidential government is argued to make legislation more difficult.[5] The two branches will have their own concerns and policy styles, whether or not there are partisan differences (see below). Those institutional values may make generating the coalition necessary to pass legislation through the legislature, whether one house or two, substantially more difficult than when the executive is drawn directly from the legislature in a parliamentary regime. Having a parliamentary form of government does not guarantee effective government, but it may make achieving that easier. That having been said, however, the checks and balances built into the system may make monitoring and accountability easier than in a more unified political system.

Arend Lijphart (1984; 1994) also has examined the impact of choices of political institutions on the relative effectiveness of governments. He has, however, been at least as much concerned with the differences among parliamentary governments as with the differences between presidential and parliamentary regimes (see also Steinmo and Tolbert, 1998). In particular, Lijphart has attempted to assess whether majoritarian parliamentary systems (such as the United Kingdom) are more able to govern effectively as is usually argued. The contrast is with consensual systems, for example the Netherlands, that depend upon coalitions that might have to trade some effectiveness in order to gain greater representativeness.

Lijphart's quantitative analysis leads him to argue that consensual, coalition governments are both more effective and more representative.[6] He finds that the instability associated with majoritarian governments tends to reduce the effectiveness of governments, perhaps because of the same logic as credible commitment for nonmajoritarian institutions (see below; see also Vibert, 2007). Consensual governments, on the other hand, provide predictability and stability in public policies. Likewise, Kenneth Janda (2011) finds that configurations of political parties are crucial for explaining success and failure in governance.

Lijphart's analysis in some ways begs the question that is raised by other students of parliamentary institutions. The advantage of majoritarian government may not be so much that it will make the proper policy choices but rather that the policy choices that are made are more likely to be the product of a single conception of good policy,

[5] For an analysis of these issues from a rational choice perspective see Weingast (2002).

[6] Steven Kelman (1988) makes a similar argument about the difference between adversarial and cooperative styles of decision making. Kelman's analysis is within the context of the United States, but his logic is very similar to that of Lijphart.

and perhaps even more directly linked to the votes of the public (but see Rose, 1974; Castles and Wildenmann, 1986). The concern is whether an executive elected to office is able to make government perform in the way that he or she wants. Although that rarely happens in an ideal manner, the institutional structure of majoritarian systems appears more likely to enable a prime minister to shape policy than do those of consensual systems. Thus, differences in outputs such as economic performance may be as much a function of poor policy choices as the structural features of the system.[7]

The parliamentary versus presidential dimension of policymaking also is associated with the capacity of governments to deliver "credible commitments" (North, 1990; Thatcher, 2002; Coen and Thatcher, 2005). Certain policy areas, such as monetary policy or financial regulation, may be more effective if there is some certainty that the policy will persist for some time. Clearly credible commitments may be more likely in consensual, parliamentary governments than in presidential systems. That said, however, for most of the post-war period the U.S. government had a broad consensus on foreign policy and many aspects of domestic policy that persisted through a number of changes of party control for the presidency.

Divided Government

A special case of the discussion concerning presidential and parliamentary systems is the "divided government" (Sundquist, 1988; Fiorina, 1996) or "separated institutions" (Jones, 1995) discussion in the United States. In this debate the impacts of the institutional configuration—separate but equal institutions—is compounded by the frequent control of these institutions by different political parties. Indeed, "divided government" has been the norm for most of the post-war period, with both houses of Congress and the Presidency being controlled by the same party in only 10 out of 66 years during the post-war period.[8]

The conventional wisdom is that divided government makes it difficult for government to function effectively, with "gridlock" the probable outcome of the arrangement. David Mayhew (1991), on the other hand, argued that the U.S. federal government has performed little differently when it was divided and when it was not. Using a set of measures of the significance of legislation Mayhew found evidence that the bills passed during periods of division were little different than those

[7] If economic performance in the United Kingdom is no better than that of the consensual systems, the cause may be as much a number of socioeconomic factors as the policy choices made by government. Assuming otherwise appears to attach much too much importance to the decisions of the public sector.

[8] Americans appear to prefer this pattern of government. Not only do they vote for this at the federal level but for state governments as well. In 2010, atleast 20 of the 50 state governments had at least one house of the party other than that of the governor.

passed during the relatively scarce times of unified government. There have been a number of critiques (Kelly, 1993; Herzberg, 1996) of the methodology that Mayhew used in supporting his contentions. In particular, Mayhew's argument depends upon a coding of policy decisions as "major" and that judgment is open to a number of interpretations.

In addition, Krehbiel (1996) has argued that gridlock can occur in a presidential regime even without partisan division between the institutions, when there are institutional conflicts as well as partisan conflicts. Unlike Mayhew's work, however, this analysis is based entirely on rational choice analysis of the possibilities of forming coalitions. These coalitions could bridge political party lines and either facilitate or hinder policy-making. One source of this deadlock might be ideological, as when conservative Southern Democrats teamed with Republicans to block, or at least delay, social legislation during the 1950s and 1960s (Rohde, 1991).[9] There could also be coalitions based upon regional interests (farming in the Midwest or industry in the"Rustbelt") or perhaps on minority status (both gender and ethnicity) within the Congress.

Divided government is usually discussed as a peculiarly American phenomenon, but there are other interesting and important examples (see Elgie, 2001). The most interesting is France, where the constitution of the Fifth Republic makes a divided government possible (Pierce, 1991; Elgie, 2001), and indeed this has occurred twice, referred to as periods of "cohabitation" in French (Duverger, 1987). First in 1986–8, Socialist President Francois Mitterrand had a Premier from the political right.[10] Later, for the period 1993–5 he again had to rule in conjunction with a rightist prime minister. More clearly in the first instance, but even in the second, government proceeded with little apparent interruption. Again, however, it can be argued that divided government can occur even with the same parties in the Elysee and the Matignon, given personal and institutional priorities of the two offices.

Australians also argue that their government has begun to behave as if it were virtually divided, given the tendency of the Senate to have no clear majority and to function as a check on the usual powers available to a prime minister in a parliamentary regime, especially in a majoritarian Westminster system (Winterton, 1983; Joyal, 2005). Canada might have the same sort of division but a different basis of selection and the senior statesman status of most of the members of the *Senate* tend to reduce the effective extent of division within Canadian government.[11] Although

---

[9] Even during the "Boll Weevils," conservative Democrats (generally Southern) coalesced with Republicans to impede proposals coming from the Clinton administration.

[10] These were first Jacques Chirac (himself elected president in 1995) and then Edouard Balladur.

[11] Canadian senators are not elected but rather appointed for life (actually until age 70) by the governor general. There is a tradition of keeping the senate in partisan balance, but the divided government characterization does not appear as applicable (see Tuohy, 1992, pp. 28–30).

not a Westminster parliamentary system the case of Germany may also be instructive for thinking about the consequences of divided institutions (Thaysen, 1994; Sturm, 2001). For the life of the *Bundesrepublik* there often has been a partisan majority in the upper house (Bundesrat) different from that in the lower house (Bundestag), so that German chancellors often have functioned in something like a divided government, despite the strong position accorded them in governing by the German constitution.[12] The power of the Bundesrat was especially evident in blocking attempts by the Schroeder government to reform the German social policy system to make the economic system more competitive (Schmitthenner and Urban, 1999).

One interesting question about presidential and parliamentary regimes is the extent to which parliamentary regimes may be becoming increasingly "presidential" (Von Mettenheim, 1996). There are a number of political and governance transformations that appear to be changing within parliamentary regimes. Electoral campaigns are increasingly centered on the candidates for prime minister, rather than on political parties and their platforms (Peters, 1997a).[13] Once in government prime ministers now tend to have greater control over policy than might be expected in a regime exercising collective responsibility. This pattern of prime ministerial power over the remainder of the cabinet was especially evident in the United Kingdom under the Blair government and his desire to centralize policy-making and media coverage and since that first week he solidified his personal control over public policy and the institutions of government. Further, conceptions of ministerial responsibility to parliament have also been diluted (Marshall, 1989; Sutherland, 1991a, 1991b; Bogdanor, 1994) so that executives function as much like their counterparts in the private sector, or like cabinet secretaries in Washington, as they do like ministers operating within the traditional model of the ministerial role.[14]

Variations within Parliamentary Institutions

Parliamentary democracies occur far more often among the developed democracies. Although broadly parliamentary in form, there are also important differences among these governments, and we can investigate the impacts of differences empirically as well. For example, as mentioned above, Arend Lijphart (1984, 1994) has

[12] The system is sometimes referred to as "Kanzlerdemokratie," or "Chancellor democracy" (Helms, 2000). The chancellor is able to exercise a great deal of control over the lower house but is more at the mercy of the constituent states in the Bundesrat.

[13] For example, on the day that the 1997 general election campaign was announced all quality daily newspapers in the United Kingdom discussed the campaign in presidential terms.

[14] This is with respect to formal responsibility for action. Having to be a member of parliament in most systems does make the role different. In systems such as Austria, Norway, and France where ministers either must or can be outside parliament the differences with an American cabinet member may be minimal.

argued that there are two groups of parliamentary governments—majoritarian and consensual. Majoritarian regimes are characterized by the capacity of one or another party (or perhaps a small coalition) to win sufficient numbers of seats to form a Government. Consensual parliamentary regimes, on the other hand, can only form a government through forming coalitions. The process of coalition building, in turn, requires making "side-payments" to a potential coalition party, and with that there is some lessening of the consistency of government programs.

Political science has developed an extensive literature explaining the formation and persistence of cabinets in parliamentary democracies. There are a variety of models explaining this crucial activity in governing, but the dominant approaches tend to be that of the minimum winning coalition and the alternative of the ideological proximity of prospective coalition members (Back, 2003). Obviously these differences in coalitions should be expected to influence patterns of decision-making by governments. Further, the increasing prevalence of both minority and oversized coalitions also affect the capacity of government to govern, and to take difficult policy choices (Volden and Carrubba, 2004).

Finally, rules for decision-making within cabinets (and governments more generally) are components of the institutional apparatus and also influence policy choices. For example, the Swedish government is required to make collective decisions, so that there must be some degree of accord among the ministers. The German government, on the other hand, has the *Ressortsprinzip* giving each minister substantial control over his or her own policy area. Again, these rules affect the governance capacities of these governments, as well as their capacity to make more specialized decisions about policy problems.

Federal and Unitary Governments: The Varieties of Multilevel Governance

Another of the classical institutional questions addressed in political science is the allocations of powers among levels of government. The general distinction made in this regard is between federal and unitary regimes, but as is very often true for simple dichotomies, this distinction conceals a great deal of internal variance in both the federal and the unitary states. Federalism in particular tends to represent formal constitutional arrangements but even those arrangements tend to evolve after the basic constitutional settlement and represent the political evolution of their political systems.

Within federal systems there are markedly different levels of central coordination in political systems that are to some extent designed to offer substantial autonomy to the subnational governments (see Hueglin and Fenna, 2005). Perhaps, most fundamentally, federalism implies some form of shared sovereignty, with both the central government and the subnational governments able of claiming sovereign status. Although the two levels can claim some sovereignty, in some systems (e.g., Germany) the central government is able to coordinate most of the policy action, while in others (Canada, the United States) the constituent units have much greater autonomy.

Just as federal states have a good deal of variation, so too do unitary regimes. In general authoritarian regimes tend to be especially concerned with creating uniformity and in exercising control. That said, however, many democratic regimes such as the United Kingdom also exert a good deal of control over their local governments. On the other hand, local governments in Sweden are able to make a number of decisions on their own so that in many ways they can act more as if they were in a federal than a unitary state, even if the formal institutional rules are clearly unitary.

The increasing importance of the European Union in governance has produced interest in the concept of "multi-level governance" (Bache and Flinders, 2004) as a means of conceptualizing the relationship among levels of government in contemporary political systems. While many analysts in federal states tend to consider this concept as just another way of thinking of intergovernmental relations, the term has become extremely popular for examining the complex interactions within the European Union. Further, the creation of multilevel governance has increased the influence of subnational governments, even in states that are nominally unitary.

While these differences are significant for formal descriptions of political systems, they may also be important institutional explanations for the actions of political systems. The most obvious consequence of choosing one form or another of these patterns is the likelihood of differences in public policy. The federal systems are designed to provide greater flexibility and autonomy in policy, and therefore there should be more variation and more opportunities for innovation. There may, however, also be political consequences of choosing a federal format, with more opportunities for public participation, more capacity to solve problems closer to the local community, and perhaps therefore greater political efficacy and trust. Again, the logic of designing institutions in this empirical form is the capacity to shape both policies and politics.

Legislative Institutionalization

Most of the research on institutions and institutionalization has focused on the executive branch of government, especially the public bureaucracy. There has, however, been a significant amount of empirical research on the institutionalization of legislatures. This literature is based on the seminal article by Nelson Polsby (1968) on the institutionalization of the U.S. House of Representatives. Polsby (1968, p. 145; see also 1975) argued that the House of Representatives had changed over time in the direction of becoming more "institutionalized," meaning that it had well-established boundaries for roles, internal complexity and universalistic criteria. Polsby's research has been followed by a variety of other attempts to document and to measure institutionalization in a number of other legislative bodies. For example, Squire (1992) examined a series of indicators of institutionalization in the California state legislature. Hibbing (1988) applied the concept to the House of Commons in the United Kingdom, Opello (1986) did so for the Portuguese parliament, and Loewenberg (1973) and Gerlich (1973) did so for a number of European parliaments.

Not all the discussions of legislative institutionalization have praised the concept (Cooper and Brady, 1981; Judge, 2003). Judge, for example, has argued that like many aspects of institutions measuring legislative institutionalization is difficult, if not impossible. Further, he and other critics wonder whether the presumed institutionalization of legislatures actually is related to the performance of legislatures or to the behavior of governments more generally. Despite that, the concept has been influential in the development of legislative studies. Indeed, it has become conventional to discuss institutionalization as one of the fundamental characteristics of a legislature.

This version of institutional theory concerning legislatures is labeled as "empirical" because, unlike some other approaches, it does provide very clear ideas about the empirical indicators than can be used to measure its concepts. Further, this corpus of theory involves a dynamic conception, with institutionalization being a process rather than just an end state. If anything, the approach may be excessively empirical, with the concepts seeming to be determined as much from the operations used to measure them as vice versa. This possible defect of operationism was demonstrated rather clearly by Squire (1992, pp. 1027–8) who had some difficulty distinguishing the commonly used characteristics of professionalization in legislative bodies from those used to measure institutionalization. Squire consequently questioned the independent meaning of the latter concept. Despite that significant weakness, the research on legislatures does contribute another arrow to the quiver of institutional analysis, and does provide some useful ideas about measurement of the attributes of other institutions.

The institutionalization literature on legislatures also has the capacity to predict the behavior of individual legislators. One of the criteria for understanding institutions is their capacity to shape individual behaviors, and to some extent their political fortunes. For example, Berry, Berkman, and Schneiderman (2000) found that more institutionalized legislatures insulate their members from external political shocks and enable those legislatures to survive threats to their incumbency. The institutionalization and the associated professionalism of the legislatures, thus tend to create a stronger boundary between these institutions and the political environment.

In short, legislatures can be conceptualized as institutions that vary in their degree of institutionalization. That is, they differ in the extent to which they are successful in imposing a set of common values on their members. Most of these values are those of professionalization, and the acceptance of the idea that a legislative office is a full-time career. The assumption of institutionalization is that there are some common conceptions about how that office is best managed, regardless of the political values the member may have. In this same manner of thinking, institutionalization implies the development of larger legislative offices and more centralized services to the legislature as a means of ensuring that the legislature can compete effectively with the information available to the political executive through the permanent bureaucracy. This conception appears based in part on the role of American legislatures as "transformative legislatures" (Polsby, 1975) as opposed to the "arena legislatures" found in most parliamentary regimes, but it does also indicate something about the structure and functioning of legislatures in general.

Institutions and Implementation

As well as being a question for legislatures and the formation of public policy, there are also important structural questions about how policies are implemented. This body of theory is based largely on the Pressman and Wildavsky study of implementation first published in 1974 (for a review, see Winter, 2003). The argument is that the (frequent) failures of implementation can be seen in structural terms. Their analysis of the failure of an economic development program to be implemented in Oakland, California pointed to the presence of some 70 separate "clearance points" that had to be passed successfully if the program was to go into effect as intended. Even if the probability of passage of each point is 0.99 the a priori chances of the program being implemented are less than fifty-fifty; at 0.95 percent the probability drops to 0.004.

While scholars had been aware for some time (Hood, 1976) of the difficulties associated with making programs function as they were designed, the Pressman-Wildavsky analysis provided a way of analyzing the structural causes of that problem. This problem was becoming more common as this initial study was being written, but has become endemic as the implementation of policies increasingly is brought about through partnerships, alliances, contracts, and a variety of other schemes mingling public and private organizations, and requiring complex agreements among the actors (Pierre, 1998). Those schemes are almost obligatory for political and budgetary reasons, but they do present a huge potential for implementation failures (for ways around these and other problems in implementation see Bowen, 1982).

Ellen Immergut's (1992a) analysis of policy-making more generally has some of the same features as the "clearance point" concept. She talks more generally of the "veto points" that exist in a policy-making system, and the need for decisions to clear each of these successfully if a program is to be adopted and then implemented (see also Weaver, 1992; Kaiser, 1997). The argument in comparative terms is, rather obviously, that countries with more of these points are more difficult locales in which to make effective decisions than are less complex systems. In her empirical research she contrasts the extreme complexity of the Swiss political system (Linder, 1997) with the more linear politics of Sweden in making health policy.

A final institutional, structural analysis of implementation structures is provided by Benny Hjern and David Porter (1981). They argue that the best way to understand implementation is not through a top–down conception of a piece of legislation being pursued by a "formator" with a particular set of policy desires, with any deviation from those desires representing failure (Lane, 1981). Hjern and Porter rather conceptualize implementation as taking place through a complex structural arrangement of interests and organizations that almost by definition will adjust the meaning of any piece of legislation to fit their own conceptions and their own political interests. Policies should, it is argued, be designed to be sufficiently robust to sustain this degree of modification and still accomplish its desired goals (see also Ingram and Schneider, 1990). Their conception of the "implementation structure" is essentially that of a group of organizations with continuing linkages, something very similar to the network idea discussed in Chapter 7.

Another interesting institutional question is the nature of central banking and the impact of alternative institutional arrangements on economic performance (Goodman, 1992). The fundamental variable here is the degree of independence of central banks from direct political control. The contrast often made is the independence of a bank such as the Bundesbank in Germany or the Federal Reserve in the United States. These banks can employ monetary policy instruments (open-market operations, interest rates, reserve requirements) regardless of the wishes of the government of the day, and often do so in direct opposition to the wishes of that government (Woolley, 1984; Alesina and Summers, 1993). The assumption is that this independence enables central banks to make decisions on strictly economic, rather than political, grounds.

Central Banks

There have been several interesting institutional experiments about the independence of banks. Almost immediately after gaining office in May 1997 (for the first time in 18 years) the Labour Party in Britain removed the Bank of England from direct political control and gave it a much greater degree of independence in setting monetary policy (see Busch, 1994). The institutional arrangements still are not so independent as those of the Bundesbank, but do approach that degree of independence. Although the British economy had been performing well under the previous conservative government the Labour government wanted to ensure an independent source on monetary policy, as well as prepare itself for possible entry into the European Monetary Union (but see Rees-Mogg, 1997).

A similar change in control of the central bank occurred in Italy, if somewhat earlier. After years of massive government deficits and questionable financial support for state-owned industries the Italian government decided in 1981 to separate the Banca d'Italia from the Treasury. The deficits continued to mount, until the Maastricht requirements for entering the European Monetary Union forced the government to reduce spending drastically, but the Italian financial system may have been placed on a firmer footing by this change. In this case the structural change may have been a necessary but not sufficient change to produce the policy results desired.

The question for empirical institutionalists is, of course, whether the differences in monetary policy institutions make any real difference for economic performance.

The "quasi-experiment"[15] with the Bank of England will provide one test within a single economy. We can also look at the recent performance of the economies of countries with independent banks and those with more politically dominated central banks (see Grilli et al., 1991; Davies, 1997). There is some tendency for countries with autonomous central banks to control inflation better than those countries with more politicized banks. On the other hand, however, there is almost no relationship with economic growth, or if there is one it is that more independent banks are related to somewhat slower growth.

Rational choice institutionalists have also been concerned with the impact of independence of central banks, but have addressed that question from the perspective of the role of veto points in the decision structures as well as the formal structures (see Tsebelis, 2002, pp. 240–6; Hallerberg, 2003).

Institutions and Development

Finally, institutions have been argued to play a major role in the process of political development, and more recently in the transition from authoritarian to democratic forms of government. This debate was actually begun some decades ago by Samuel P. Huntington (1968; see Remmer, 1997), but his views on the role of institutions and institutionalization in development have tended to be less influential than those of scholars who emphasized more cultural variables in promoting change.

This tradition of cultural studies of development has tended to persist into the present time in major works such as Robert Putnam's studies of social capital in Italy (1993), and his and followers' extensions (Perez-Diaz, 1994; Gyimah-Boadi, 1996) of the same basic logic to other geographical areas (including to the United States by Putnam, 1995). The logic of this approach to democratization is that to be effective there must be a cultural underpinning of trust, among individuals and between individuals and institutions. The concepts of "social capital" and "civil society" are really ways of saying that without the right set of social values structural manipulations and constitution writing will produce little positive result.

The domination of the cultural approach is being challenged, however, by more structuralist perspectives that argue that if the appropriate institutions are put into place then the appropriate values will then follow.[16] For example, the work of Stepan, Linz and others has pointed to the need to build institutions that can promote simultaneously democracy and stability in regimes undergoing change—especially those

---

[15] It is a quasi-experiment because of the inability to control other factors in the environment. A good or a poor economic performance after this change may not really be due to this one institutional innovation, but there is no way to be absolutely sure of that.

[16] In terms of the other theories of institutions this argues that the March and Olsen creation of appropriate values will stem from the creation of structures that will inculcate those values.

going through the joint challenges of democratization and movement to a market economy. This approach argues, although perhaps not so boldly, that if effective institutions can be constructed and then managed in time (and perhaps not very much time) the appropriate values will also be created.

The Questions of Theory

We now have a better idea of the nature of the literature on empirical institutionalism. We should, therefore, turn to the questions that we have been applying to all bodies of institutional theory. Given that this body of literature is more empirically based than the others, the answers might be expected to be somewhat more definitive than for the other approaches. In some ways that is true, but in others the researchers often take the definitions of institutional forms as givens without clear conceptual definitions.

What Is an Institution?

As noted, the research concerned with presidential and parliamentary government often takes those institutions as a fact of political life, rather than an entity in need of conceptual elaboration. For example, there has been relatively little work on the differences that exist within the category of parliamentary regimes. Those differences may, however, be quite important as when one contrasts the Westminster traditions of majority governance and adversarial politics (Lijphart, 1994) with the traditions of minority government and party cooperation found in Norway (Strom, 1990a), or with several other countries with long experiences with multiparty cabinets. Even seemingly simple internal rules concerning whether ministers make many decisions independently or whether decisions are made collectively will influence governance within these systems.

Within the presidential category there are also obvious differences between the United States as the archetype of presidentialism and the "semi-presidential" system of France and Finland (Duverger, 1980; 1988; Pasquino, 1997), as well as the way in which presidential politics is played out in Mexico (Camp, 1996) and other non-European countries (Mainwaring, 1991). Presidencies vary in terms of their legislative powers, their appointment powers, veto powers and a host of other constitutional rules that define their roles in governing and define many aspects of the governance process (see Perez-Linan, 2007).

For a great deal of the research discussed here the absence of conceptual and even empirical elaboration is somewhat justifiable. In most cases it is clear that a regime is either presidential or parliamentary, so the researcher can simply proceed to discuss the apparent effects of those differences. There are some cases in which the differences are not so clear, for example the semi-presidential regime in France, or perhaps that of Finland (Nousiainen, 1988). Further, in some countries there are sufficiently marked changes in the ethos of politics to question whether or not there are formal institutional changes as well (Foley, 1993; Peters, 1997b). For example, as the 1997 British election was being announced, all the major papers in Britain pointed out that the election would be "presidential," that is, it would focus on the ideas and leadership potential of the potential prime ministers. In short, the assumptions about the obvious nature of the differences among political types are not always justified.[17] Given the normative definitions of institutions by March and Olsen, a change in the style of governing may be considered as important as a change in the formal structures.

For the implementation structure version of empirical institutionalism the definition of an institution is substantially less clear. The basic orientation of this approach is similar to that of network theory, as discussed in the following chapter. In such a view the institution is formed more from interactions of the actors than from any particular conscious choice or decision, as may be expected when selecting presidential or parliamentary government forms. To some extent these institutions are discovered, as administrators attempt to implement a program and find that they are incapable of doing so alone but need the other members of this "institution."

How Are Institutions Formed?

This question is in most ways not relevant to this version of institutional theory. Empirical institutionalism primarily takes as given the political and social institutions of a society and then attempts to determine whether those institutions have any impact on the behavior of their members. The process of institutionalization does, however, provide some element of a dynamic within this body of theory. As noted above, concerning legislative institutionalism there has been a process of change and professionalization in many legislatures, with the addition of bill-drafting organizations and more personal staff, the adoption of longer sessions, and the creation of a more differentiated and powerful committee system. Legislatures before those changes may have been institutions but they are certainly more institutionalized after those developments.

The concept of implementation structures also involves the creation of structural relationships among organizations. The passage of a new piece of legislation will require creation of a network of actors concerned with the implementation of that legislation. In some instances that legislation may mean simply reviving, or further burdening, another "implementation structure." New legislation frequently, however, involves the formation of a new structure to put it into effect. These patterns of relationship may have been relatively unstructured initially and may have involved the constituent organizations only tangentially, but they will require some sharing

[17] The scholars doing this work clearly understand that they are simplifying, and for good reasons. The question is what does this simplification say about the meaning of the institutions in a more theoretical sense.

of values and some formalized patterns of interaction if they are to be effective in making a policy work.

For implementation structures the one question about formation that does arise is the now familiar debate between "top down" and "bottom up" conceptualizations of the implementation process (Sabatier, 1986; Linder and Peters, 1989). The former view argues that implementation is ultimately a question of the application of law, and therefore should be seen as a hierarchical process. This hierarchy is considered necessary to ensure the just and adequate enforcement of the law in question (Hogwood and Gunn, 1984). The alternative view is that even though implementation is about law, it is also about the relationships between public employees and their clients and is also dependent upon the knowledge of the lower echelons of the bureaucracy. In this view, if an implementation structure is not designed with those relationships and skills in mind it will not be effective.

Given that basic distinction in the way in which implementation is conceptualized, are there also differences in the way in which implementation structures are formed? For the "top down" conception the template for an implementation structure is readily available—the organization would simply reproduce the pattern found in any one of hundreds of other hierarchies in government. The creation of an implementation structure in the bottom-up view is more problematic and more variable. It would require the negotiation of a relationship among a number of organizations and their agreement to cooperate among themselves, and with the organization charged with primary responsibility for the policy, over the implementation of the policy. The structure that might emerge from such a negotiation is likely to be more of a network or partnership rather than the hierarchical structuring that still characterizes most government organizations.

All the above having been said, one of the apparent failings of the empirical institutionalists is in not having a clear conception of the origins of institutions. Karen Remmer (1997) mentions this as one of the four "paradoxes" of contemporary institutionalism. She refers to all branches of new institutionalism in a very undifferentiated manner, but this critique appears particularly applicable to the empirical institutionalists, given their explicit concerns with contemporary institutional structures. They argue that certain structures are more effective than are others, but fail to ask why the seemingly ineffective structures are selected as often as they are.

How Do Institutions Change?

Some of the same problems encountered when asking how institutions are initially formed arise when asking how do they change. The empirical institutionalists have been more concerned with the effects of existing structures than they have been with these dynamic questions about their origins or their transformation. For much of the work in this tradition institutions are a given, rather than an entity that requires any great degree of explanation. The above having been said, there are some ideas about change in some versions. As already noted, the legislative institutionalists such as Polsby are concerned with the process of institutionalization within legislatures, a process not dissimilar to those discussed by Eisenstadt and other sociological theorists in reference to bureaucratic institutions. Legislatures in most countries have become more professional and more institutionalized, often as a means of counteracting the increasing powers of political executives. This implies that in this perspective institutions change in response more to external stimuli than to their own internal values, although statements of that sort are rarely discussed.

Similarly, in the research discussing differences between presidential and parliamentary systems, one of the capabilities in question is the capacity of the political systems to respond to innovation (Feigenbaum et al., 1993). This does not mean that the institutions themselves will necessarily change, although most organizational theorists would tend to argue that they would have to adjust their structures somewhat to satisfy changed environmental demands. There is also some sense in several of the discussions of these institutional arrangements that some adaptation does take place, so that effective institutions will learn how better to cope with environmental challenges. So, although change is not a central question for the empirical institutionalists, there are some dynamic elements built into their conceptions of institutions that at least begin to address the question of change.

Institutional Design

The design of institutions appears more central to this version of institutionalism than to others, with the possible exception of rational choice institutionalism. Although there is little interest in any theorizing about the natural evolution of institutions, the scholars contributing to this body of literature have very real intellectual and academic interests in the subject. Further, for many of them there is also a clear concern about being able to offer effective advice to government. This is especially true for advice to governments of those countries in which democracy is a relatively new phenomenon. The Linz (1990; 1994) and Riggs (1988) discussions of presidential and parliamentary government, for example, are clearly attempts to utilize empirical evidence from the recent past to convince governments in the process of democratic transformation what the probable consequences of certain institutional choices would be, and therefore what their institutional choices should be. More recent analysis has indicated that some of the conclusions drawn in the literature on presidentialism may be incorrect, or at least exaggerated (Cheibub and Limongi, 2002), but these studies do at least raise some considerations for design.

One factor that distinguishes this version of institutional theory from most of the others (again the rational choice version may be the main exception) is the sense that there is a virtually free choice of institutional forms available to institutional designers. Historical institutionalists might argue that in most instances there are important constraints on the capacity to make such a choice, at least after an initial choice. Further, for the "empirical institutionalists" the design choice appears to be up to political elites. This view that assumes rather unconstrained choice appears to run contrary to some of the important argument of both historical institutionalists and normative institutionalists who identify constraints rather than opportunities when confronted with the design question.[18]

The arguments of the historical institutionalists may be muted somewhat in the case of a newly formed, or reformed, political system, but those of the normative institutionalists may still have substantial weight. For example, even if the evidence on the effects of presidentialism were stronger than it is, questions of legitimacy may prevent other constitutional choices. In Latin America for example, the history of presidentialism—whether an unfortunate export from the United States or not—may make other forms of government appear inappropriate to the population. Further, if not familiar and legitimate in a system, parliamentary institutions may generate at least as much instability as would presidential ones. Similarly, as the countries of Central and Eastern Europe have institutionalized their democratic systems they have adopted a range of solutions that balance the desire for democracy with the need for maintaining some stability, again in pursuit of legitimacy with their populations. To argue otherwise would be to go against much of the inherent logic of institutionalism as it has been developing in political science.

Related to the choice between parliamentary and presidential government is the place of institutions in the development of democracy. The collapse of authoritarian governments in many parts of the world has produced a need for functioning models for developing and sustaining democracy. While some of these models concentrate on the development of appropriate social and cultural patterns, notably a functioning social infrastructure (Putnam, 1993; Armony, 1998) many other models focus on the design of appropriate institutions (Stepan and Skach, 1993; Power and Gasiorowski, 1997; Sartori, 1997; Melo, 2007). In some instances the design element required is a governing system that can bridge among previously hostile social groups (Burton and Higley, 1987; Higley and Gunther, 1992; Adams, 1999), with questions of decision-making appearing, at least in the short-run, subordinate to stability. In others it is for organizations that can make decisions effectively while still being open to demands from a divided and often fractious public opinion.

The question of design also raises a question of how well the evidence can predict specific outcomes of institutional choices. As noted above, the evidence for the effects of presidential and parliamentary regimes is not as clear as some of the analysts have argued. Further, as some of the differences among institutions have tended to diminish, then design becomes less capable of predicting outcomes. Likewise, the predictive capacity of federalism as a formal constitutional arrangement is not as great as might be expected given the differences among federal

---

18 The more common assumption of constrained choice is a version of bounded rationality in which either existing institutional arrangements or emerging institutions constrain behavior.

systems (Hueglin and Fenna, 2005) and the autonomy of some local governments within unitary regimes. For example, the commune governments in Sweden have substantially greater autonomy than do subnational governments in some federal systems.

Individuals and Institutions

Another of the basic questions we are asking about institutions is how do individuals and institutions interact? The general pattern encountered in institutions is one of mutual influence. Individuals may have their behavior and their values changed by membership in an institution, but institutions also must adjust as they recruit different types of people. For the empirical institutionalists the direction of influence appears to be more unidirectional; the behavior of individuals is assumed to be largely determined by their participation in the institution. A president is expected to play the role of president, and not to act like a prime minister (although prime ministers are said increasingly to act like presidents).[19] Given its close relationships with the presidential/parliamentary debate, the divided government literature posits much of the same unidirectionality.

This unidirectionality of influences can be observed in almost all the versions of empirical institutionalism we have been discussing, although in varying degrees. As the illustration above indicates the influence of institutions over individuals can be seen very strongly in the discussion of presidential and parliamentary government, although even here strong leaders may be able to shape the office more to their own liking. The different forms of parliamentary government may constrain a leader even more than the differences between presidential and parliamentary systems. The leaders in a Danish or Norwegian system with minority governments and strong norms of collegiality would have little opportunity to act as a president, while several British and Canadian prime ministers have been able to act in a very presidential manner.

The empirical institutionalists are, therefore, very close to the normative institutionalists in the importance they attach to the common values existing within an institution, and in their assumptions that those values dominate individual preferences for the members of an institution. If anything the empirical institutionalists ascribe an even less significant role to the individual, whether prime minister or legislator, than do the normative institutionalists. In particular, the empirical institutionalists appear to lack any clear ideas about how institutions might be transformed in response to different values of their members. Certainly individuals, such as particularly active prime ministers (Margaret Thatcher, for example) may alter institutions but there is no particular theoretical argument to capture of the logic of that change.

---

[19] Also, after his reelection in 1996, President Clinton announced that he wanted to act more like a prime minister running a collegial cabinet system.

Empirical institutionalists also are not clear about the mechanisms that link individuals and their institutions. As noted above, the principal mechanism appears to be the roles that individuals play within an institution, so that individuals attempt to conform to the expectations of the position. The other mechanism that appears to be important is leadership and/or personality of individuals who occupy those positions. That being said, however, there is no explicit theoretical explanation for these linkages between individuals and their institutions.

The Good Institution

The fundamental questions for empirical institutionalism, despite the name I have attached to it, are ultimately normative. More than perhaps any other institutional approach discussed in this book the empirical approach attempts to identify "what works," and to some extent why it works. To a great extent the empirical approach identifies the good institutional arrangement as one which meets these more operational criteria of virtue. For the empirical institutionalist the question is what impact does an institutional arrangement have on the performance of government, with different scholars being concerned with different types of performance. For some institutional analysts the most important measure of the success of an institution is its survival, or perhaps the survival of the regime as a whole. For other scholars, the question is one of economic, rather than political, performance, so that the good government is one that produces economic success.

As well as being concerned with fundamental questions of the survival of governments or overall economic performance, other questions about the good institution, or set of institutional arrangements, have to do with the capacity of the system to make decisions. The question is not so much whether those decisions are good or bad, but rather whether the institutions are capable of making decisions. In these views of institutions, the better ones are those that can make decisions, and particularly those institutions that can make major decisions rather than just the continual series of incremental decisions. Part of the argument on behalf of parliamentary regimes, for example, is that the integration of the legislative and executive powers permits more effective decisions than in the "separated powers" of the presidential systems.

Summary and Conclusion

Just as there were a number of different approaches to rational choice institutionalism, there are also a variety of different empirical approaches, to institutions and institutionalism. The most common approach is to *differentiate* presidential and parliamentary institutions and determine their impacts. Rather than attempt to develop an alternative perspective on institutions and their nature and origins, however, these various empirical approaches classify types of institutions and then attempt to determine whether those arrangements have any real impact on the performance of government. Only rarely do they begin to offer a theory of institutions per se, but rather are concerned with the apparent impacts of institutional arrangements.

We should not, however, be too quick to dismiss the empirical institutionalists as atheoretical, and therefore not as significant a contribution to the discipline as other approaches to institutionalism. First, there is indwelling in the descriptions of institutional arrangements an argument that formal structuring of interaction do determine, or at least influence, behavior. While some theorists (Campbell and Petersen, 2001) might argue that this structuring operates through norms, others that it comes through rules, and still others that it comes through manipulation of incentives, the empirical institutionalists argue that the important fact is simply the arrangement of the operative elements, not what those elements are. Even if the theoretical development within this approach is not as great as in some other approaches, the literature developed does fulfill some of the goals of March and Olsen in launching the "new" institutionalism. It has pointed out that structures and institutions do matter; if not always a one-for-one correspondence of structure and performance there does appear to be some influence. Further, the methodological and theoretical assumptions are most definitely not individualistic ones against which March and Olsen were reacting in their original call for a new institutionalism in political science.

CHAPTER 6

Ideas as the Foundation of Institutions: Discursive and Constructivist Institutionalism

The last of the several "new Institutionalisms" to emerge has been labeled variously as "constructivist institutionalism" or more recently as "discursive institutionalism." Both of these versions of institutional theory focus on the role of ideas in shaping institutions and the behavior of individuals within those institutions. In some ways positing that institutions are shaped by ideas is not a new idea, and Peter Hall's (1993) work on the importance of ideas also laid the foundations for this approach.[1] Indeed, in many ways historical institutionalism also emphasizes the importance of ideas in defining the policy trajectories that institutions will follow. In the course of the chapter I will, however, identify points at which the various versions of institutionalism based upon ideas diverge.

In this chapter, I will focus on discursive institutionalism, given that it appears to be gaining greater intellectual traction than does the constructivist versions of this general approach. The discursive version of institutionalism has been advanced primarily by Vivien Schmidt (2008; 2010). Previously scholars such as Colin Hay (2001; 2006) and Nicholas Jabko (2006) had discussed some of the same concepts in terms of constructivism. Schmidt, however, created a stronger conception of this ideational logic in her discursive model. The basic logic of this approach is that institutions are defined by ideas, as well as by the manner in which these ideas are communicated within the structure. Unlike some, or indeed most, conceptions of institutionalism, this version is not based on hierarchy or formal structures but is based more on shared communication.[2]

The constructivist version of institutionalism has been more apparent in the study of international relations than it has been in the study of domestic politics and policy (see Chapter 9). While this approach has been concerned with understanding institutions, it to some extent has also been concerned with theoretical issues in that subdiscipline rather than with institutionalism per se. The constructivist version of institutionalism became embroiled in the debate between more realist and

[1] Hall's work has also been closely associated with the development of historical institutionalism (see Chapter 3).

[2] There is an obvious connection with the Habermasian ideas of communications and discourse within this approach (Habermas, 1989; 1996).

constructivist theories in international relations (see Abdelal et al., 2006). An institutionalist perspective is almost contradictory to the more anarchist assumptions found in much of conventional international relations theory (see Wendt, 1992), so that it becomes more than just a statement about structures existing at the international level.

By including discursive institutionalism, and constructivist institutionalism, as one of the variants of institutional theory, we include an approach that depends much more heavily on ideas than do the other versions discussed in this book. Normative institutionalism also places norms and values in a central position in their explanations, but that version of institutionalism does not focus so clearly on the role of substantive policy ideas. Much of the logic of normative institutionalism is defining appropriate behaviors within an institution, rather than emphasizing the goals and ideas that are pursued by the institution.

While explanations based on interest have been dominant in political science there is also a significant strand of thought emphasizing ideas (Goldstein and Keohane, 1993; Braun and Busch, 1999; Gofas and Hay, 2010) as independent sources of explanation. Discursive institutionalism therefore represents a particular variant of a more general approach emphasizing the significance of political ideas. While explanations based on ideas and those based on interests may be artificially distinct, they do represent alternative avenues for understanding the complexities of public action and of the institutions involved in that action.

Discursive institutionalism represents by far the least structural approach to institutions of all the various approaches I am discussing in this book. While the term "institution" appears to imply structure, in this case the structure is more virtual, implying common understandings and perhaps beliefs rather than hierarchies or formal structures. The contrast with empirical institutionalism (see Chapter 5) is therefore quite marked. Whereas the empirical conception of institutions relies almost completely on formal structures and "brass plaque institutionalism," the discursive approach does not eschew such formal structures, but instead considers them to be somewhat secondary to the ideas that are held by the members and the communications that occur within the structures.

The nature of discourse and its ally constructivism (see Hay, 2006) in the study of institutions reflects the very indeterminate nature of information and knowledge in constructivist versions of the social sciences (see Kratochwil, 2009). If social facts are the products of social understandings that may be fleeting and frequently renegotiated, then institutions represent not stable patterns of action and stable rules but more transient understandings that we should not expect to be able to produce anything permanent. Yet, to some extent they do, and institutions viewed from the perspective of discourse may represent relatively stable *fora* in which continuing discussion and redefinition is occurring.

Although elaborated in somewhat different ways, the fundamental logic of discursive institutionalism is importantly similar (see Chapter 2) to that of normative institutionalism. In both cases institutions are defined largely through their ideas and their norms. Further, creating the institution in both approaches depends heavily on inculcating a set of values among the prospective members. In both cases, the actors involved in an institution are primarily involved because of the values and ideas that the institution represents, rather than from any formalistic use of rules and structures. And in both, institutional change comes through changing ideas and changing the associated norms, although the normative version tends to somewhat more strongly dependent upon top–down processes for producing the change.

Although there is the basic similarity of these two versions of institutionalism, there are also several crucial differences. The most fundamental of these differences is that the normative version of institutionalism has strong roots in organizational theory and tends to take organizations as the fundamental locus for institutional activity.[3] In contrast the discursive approach to institutions does not assume established organizational structures but rather that the institutions, and the associated organizations, emerge from the interaction of the members. Following from the interactive nature of institutions in its approach, organizational norms within the discursive form of institutionalism are more flexible and tend to be constructed through interactions, while those in the normative approach are more defined by the existing patterns of norms, symbols, routines, myths, and the like.

Following from the above difference, there does not appear to be anything equivalent to a "logic of appropriateness" operating within the discursive form of institutionalism. Appropriateness functions as a means of defining the institution and as a standard of action for the participants (March and Olsen, 1989; Christensen and Rovik, 1999) in normative institutionalism. As norms are created primarily through interactions in the discursive approach then an external standard of behavior does not appear feasible, or even desirable. Thus, as already noted, the discursive form of institutionalism is the least structured among the various versions, and provides the greatest ambiguity (and the greatest range of action) for the members of institutions conceptualized in this manner.

As well as having similarities with the normative version of institutionalism, discursive institutionalism has some strong affinities with international institutionalism and with some versions of international relations taken more generally. In particular, discursive institutionalism is similar to the constructivist strand of thinking in international relations (Finnemore and Sikkink, 1998; Howorth, 2004). In contrast to more realist approaches to international politics, in which the patterns of interactions are assumed to be structured by the exercise of power by nation states, the constructivist approach assumes that the interactions are structured more by ideas and the discourses and communications of the actors. In the constructivist approach nation states are by no means the only actors involved in

[3] The original state of the normative approach by March and Olsen (1984) discussed institutionalism as the "organizational basis of political life."

international politics, so that nongovernmental organizations (NGOs) and international regulatory organizations such as the World Bank and the World Trade Organization are also involved in shaping the ideas used to govern the international system.

The seeming affinity of discursive institutionalism with the international version goes beyond simply the constructivist use of ideas in defining interactions. To the extent that international institutionalism becomes manifest through the creation of regimes, then ideas are crucial in defining those regimes (see Rittberger, 1993). While many aspects of international politics are defined by national interests, most regimes are defined more by ideas and commitment to certain policy outcomes by a variety of actors. The actors involved in these regimes tend to be committed to the ideas prior to joining or creating the regime so that the discursive activity may not be as crucial to shaping decisions within the regimes as they are in the general model of discursive institutionalism described below.[4]

Discursive institutionalism also has fundamental points of convergence with the extensive literature on framing and reframing in policy studies, sociology, and political science. The basic logic of framing is that policy problems do not come neatly defined but instead have to be defined in a certain manner in order to be resolved. Further, if there are alternatives then the manner in which an issue is framed will determine the manner in which it is resolved. The emphasis on discourse has become a common approach to policy studies, functioning as an alternative to the more common positivist approaches (see Hajer and Wagenaar, 2003; Gottweiss, 2006). This emphasis on ideas and discourse in policy analysis may occur within existing organizational structures or it may, in turn, require the creation of alternative structures when the existing ones do not correspond to the contemporary understandings of the issue area.[5]

I will now proceed to discuss discursive institutionalism using the same categories used when discussing the other forms of institutionalism. Given the somewhat indeterminate nature of institutions within this approach several of the answers for the questions will be somewhat less precise than those for the other approaches. That said, the somewhat indeterminate nature of some parts of this approach makes change much easier than with other versions of institutionalism. Also, despite the somewhat indeterminate nature of institutions in this approach it is clear that this approach does indeed describe important aspects of institutions and does contribute to our collective understanding of institutions and institutionalism.

---

4 That said, however, continuing involved with a regime will involve continuing debates and redefinition of the purposes of that regime through a process such as those identified with discursive institutionalism.

5 The literature on organizational change, however, argues that structures may be able to adapt rather well to changing ideas and changing policy demands (see Zald and Denton, 1967 for one classic example).

What Is an Institution?

The most fundamental question about any theoretical approach to institutions is what constitutes an institution within the approach, and how is this central element of institutionalism defined conceptually. For the discursive version of institutionalism, institutions represent as much a process as a settled structure or an identifiable pattern. For the other versions of institutionalism that central concept exists ontologically distinct form the individuals who are functioning within it. In this version the institution represents more of the individuals themselves—or at least their ideas and discourses—and their patterns of interactions.

The discursive approach is based fundamentally on ideas, but ideas are employed differently in the discursive model than in other approaches (normative institutionalism and historical institutionalism in particular) in which the ideas are defined largely externally to the participants in the institution.[6] In discursive institutionalism the ideas are largely the ideas that are generated discursively by the participants in the institution. That is, ideas are important in themselves, but are more important as they are communicated and debated among the members of the institution. The ideas, therefore, are not hierarchical ordering principles for the members, but rather are the products of interaction among the members.

Discursive institutionalism discusses the communication of the ideas associated with the institution in two ways. First, *coordinative discourse* occurs within the institution as the members create, elaborate and justify the ideas that will be central to the functioning of their policy making. Again, the ideas may be widely shared among the members of the institution but they are not received wisdom but rather are more open and interactive. That said, not all members of the institution will be equal in the process of initiating and diffusing the ideas. Policy entrepreneurs (Kingdon, 2003) or "mediators" (Jobert, 1989) are responsible for generating and propagating ideas among the other members of the institution. Even if a member is not playing those roles, he or she may be more influential based upon persuasive abilities or knowledge of the issues being considered.[7]

Communicative discourse is the other form of communication associated with discursive institutionalism. To be effective in policymaking, and in actually generating changes in the economy and society, ideas have to be communicated to the society and to other policy actors in other institutions. That communication may be more difficult than is communication within the institution because those on the outside of an institution do not have the same commitment to the goals and success of the

---

[6] This is to some extent less true of the historical institutionalism because at the formative moment of an institution ideas tend to be imported and used by the actors forming the institution.

[7] This inequality is analogous to that which plagues advocates of discursive democracy. Although the system is designed to be equal among the members, in reality it rarely can be and the more capable tend to dominate.

institution and its programs. This communicative discourse may involve reframing the issues and policies, as Schon and Rein (2000; see also Bardach, 1998) argue, as a means of resolving incompatible policy frames (or discourses). That is, when there are fundamental differences over the definition of problems or possible solutions then a fundamental debate over these differences is required, often resulting in new frames that are agreeable to the full range of participants.

Paul Sabatier and Hank Jenkins-Smith's concept of advocacy coalition theory also points to the importance of ideas and finding common ideas for solving policy problems. Various groups involved in policy-making activity have their own ideas, including core beliefs that they attempt to protect.[8] They are, however, willing to negotiate more peripheral values with other groups or organizations and create winning coalitions to have legislation adopted. This reframing is a crucial component of the political process and represents a means of shaping and reshaping the ideas that in turn shape public policy.

The concept of discourse involved in creating the ideas within the institution is closely related to the general models of discourse within the social sciences. Discourse theory (Torfing, 1999; Howarth et al., 2000) focuses on the importance of ideas and the expression of those ideas as a means of understanding political action. As with the utilization of discourse within discursive institutionalism, discourse in general involves multiple discourses and interactions in defining that action. Further, all that discussion and debate involved in discourse effectively create some common patterns of thinking and understanding around the issues of policy and action.

The concept of epistemic communities (Haas, 1992) that has been used within international relations and other areas of political science is to some extent analogous to discursive institutionalism (Miller and Fox, 2001). Epistemic communities are networks or associations defined by a body of knowledge. For example, there may be an epistemic community defined by professional knowledge, such as the medical community. Or the community may not be professional but defined by particular understandings of a policy issue such as the environment (see Zito, 2001). These epistemic communities are also to a great extent defined by the interactions of the participants although they may begin with a greater common background and understanding of the policy area than would be true in most discursive institutions.

The above relationships of discursive institutionalism with epistemic communities and with the advocacy-coalition model also points that this version of institutionalism is more closely linked with policy than are the others. Certainly all versions of institutionalism have relevance for public policy, but the discursive model is very much defined by shaping public policy through discussion and disseminating policy

[8] Anthony Downs (1967) discusses that these core values are the "heartlands" of a bureaucratic organization and argues that organizations are willing to moderate their commitments to more peripheral policy ideas so long as they are capable of maintaining those heartlands.

ideas. Historical institutionalism also has a strong link to policy and much of this strand of institutionalism utilizes policies as the means of understanding the existence of the institution. That said, however, the historical approach to institutionalism contains a stronger concern with organizations and structures per se than does the discursive approach to institutions.

Finally, in discursive institutionalism the boundary between the institution and its environment is less distinct than it might be in other approaches to institutions or organizations. Because the discursive model depends upon importing ideas into the institution, and continuing to do so during the course of its existence it appears incapable of differentiating itself clearly from the sources of those ideas and must remain open to individuals who are the promoters of new ideas. The openness of institutional boundaries in the discursive model of institutionalism thus means again that structure becomes less significant than in other versions of institutionalism.

In summary, in this discursive version of institutionalism the institution is defined by the ideas of the members, and by their communication among the members. The actual content, the policy ideas of the institution, therefore, tends to be highly malleable. The institution, therefore, reflects a short-term equilibrium in the discussion of policy ideas. Further, the institution itself becomes largely a virtual entity, with rather indefinite boundaries and limited necessity for formal structures. This form of institutionalism can be used to analyze more formal structures but unlike other approaches to institutions and institutionalism there is little need for that formality of structures and memberships.

The Formation of Institutions

As can be understood from the above discussion of the nature of institutions in discursive institutionalism, the process basis of this version of an institution means that to a certain extent institutions are always being created and recreated.[9] Institutions are created, in this perspective, from the interaction of the participants and the creation of relatively common sets of internal ideas. This coordinative discourse remains largely within the institution and the individuals associated with the institution. In this perspective, institutions are, to a great extent, contingent entities that depend upon the involvement of actors.

This logic for creating institutions is to some extent similar to Anthony Giddens's (1984) concept of the mutual constitution of agency and structure. The individuals as agents are involved in the process of creating the institutional structures but at the same time the structure defines the role of the agents. The actors utilize not only the ideas that they bring with them into the institution but also use the understandings

[9] This conforms to the understanding when studying institutionalization that structures are never fully institutionalized but are always in process becoming more or less institutionalized.

created by their involvement with the institution in order to form policy relevant understandings. Schmidt (2008, p. 314) refers to those interactions of ideas as the actors using their background ideational abilities to involve themselves. In this case then the preferences of the actors involved are neither so clearly exogenous as in rational choice nor so clearly endogenous as in the normative version.

The analytic and potentially practical difficulty in this version of institutionalism is that there does not appear to be a clear boundary between the institution and the surrounding society. Even if one conceptualizes organizations or institutions as open systems (see Katz and Kahn, 1968) there is still some boundary that the structure attempts to maintain for purposes of its own integrity. In the discursive model, however, there does not appear to be any such boundary or if there is a boundary it is rather easily breached by anyone wishing to participate in the discourse. In the discussion of communicative discourse there is a concept of a general public which is involved in, or influenced by, the discourses.

Considering the formation of institutions raises the question of institutionalization as a means of understanding when a structure has been created with sufficient identity and sufficient control over members to be able to say that it is distinct from the surrounding society or polity. The discursive version of institutionalism does not appear to have any particular or distinctive conception of institutionalization, although the general discussion of formation of institutions does provide some understanding of when that process may have been completed, albeit as in all versions of institutionalism, institutionalization has to be considered an ongoing and reversible process (see Chapters 1 and 10).

Given the analogy that can be drawn between discursive institutionalism and normative institutionalism, Philip Selznick's conception of institutionalization (1957) may be of some utility. As noted (Chapter 2), he conceptualized institutionalization as infusing a structure with meaning. This definition encounters some difficulties in discursive institutionalism because the structural element—most particularly organizations—are not so central to the understandings in this version as in the normative version of institutionalism. Thus, there need not be any prior organization that becomes institutionalized within this approach, but rather the structure and the meaning appear to be created simultaneously. In the discursive model of institutions meaning may search for structure, rather than vice versa.

Institutional Change

The standard critique against other forms of institutionalism, especially the historical form of institutionalism, is that they are not good at explaining change, or even in including change within their conceptualizations of institutions. The basic logic of institutions in most conceptualizations is that they provide permanence and predictability for society, even in the midst of turbulent political activity. This predictability and stability enable institutions to regulate many aspects of political and social life and to enhance governance capacities, even if they may at times risk becoming excessively rigid.

Discursive institutionalism is more open to change than are the alternative forms of institutionalism, and indeed one might argue that the approach is perhaps *too* amenable to change for an institutionalist approach to political life. If institutions are intended to provide predictability and stability then any conception that undermines that predictability may undervalue the very nature of an institution. Thus, in this approach to institutions the usual criticism against institutionalism is reversed, and the analyst must consider the capacity to create sufficient stability.

In discursive institutionalism institutional change is defined through changes in the ideas and values that are the core of the discourse. Given that these ideas and values are created through discussion, that is discourse, among the members then institutional change much also reflect that change in that discourse. This change may occur through a variety of means. Perhaps most obviously, the change occurs in much the same way that the initial formation of the institution occurs. Therefore, policy entrepreneurship and advocacy have been identified in a number of settings as important components for policy change and, in the discursive approach, are also crucial for institutional change.

If we assume that some stability among the actors within a discursive institution has been achieved, that is some level of institutionalization has occurred, then what will upset that equilibrium? One obvious answer is that one or more of the actors involved recognizes that his or her ideas are not being advanced though the institution, or that even their self-interest is not being enhanced through continued participation (Hay, 2006). They are then left with the familiar choices of exit, voice, or loyalty (Hirschman, 1970).

The concept of the "bricoleur" is another approach to institutional change within discursive institutionalism (Carstensen, 2011). The logic here is that attempting to master all the complex ideational elements involved in most institutions is perhaps excessively taxing and perhaps unnecessary. For an agent who wants to generate change within this context rather than attempting to create an entirely new approach to the issues at hand will almost certainly encounter opposition. Therefore, the superior approach to creating change is to tinker with the existing collection of ideas and discourses within the institution and create new combinations. This role is not dissimilar to that of the policy entrepreneur, although rather than bringing an entire new policy perspective the *bricoleur* tends to fashion new approaches from elements of existing ideas. The bricolage approach, therefore, will produce more incremental change within the institution, as might be expected anyway from an approach that involves substantial negotiation and bargaining.

The *bricoleur* version of change is also obviously closely related to the advocacy coalition approach to policy mentioned above. The *bricoleur* can be conceptualized as an agent who creates the new coalition, finding ways to involve elements from the alternative perspectives that are contending for control over the policy area. This appears to imply that the *bricoleur* can act as an honest broker among the various contending conceptions of good policy in the area. While that may be true, the assumption generally is that the *bricoleur* will be pursuing his or her own policy goals and attempting to build coalitions to pursue those goals.

Individuals and Institutions

One of the fundamental questions about institutions is how they interact with the individuals who comprise them. This question is in part the familiar structure–agency division in the social sciences, but it is particularly acute in institutions because of assumptions that are usually made about the institutional role in society. In particular, there is the seeming paradox that although institutions are human creations, once they are created they constrain the activity of the individuals within them, perhaps even the individuals who created them (Grafstein, 1992). Indeed, institutions are created in order to constrain individual variability in behavior, and to provide greater stability in behavior and decisions than if the individuals were not involved with these structures.

Discursive institutionalism provides a very different solution to this basic paradox than do the other approaches to institutions. As noted, the interactive nature of discursive institutionalism implies that institutions and individuals are intimately connected in this version of the broader institutional approach. Schmidt (2008) argues that in this approach institutions are at once given and contingent. On the one hand, once an institution has been created (see above) there are, by definition, some common understandings among the participants, although that understanding may come from the argumentation and bargaining among the participants.

The contingent nature of institutions reflects the role of individual participants in defining the discursive content of the institution. In this perspective, individual interactions develop the basic ideas and discourses that define the institution and therefore the nature of that institution cannot be readily defined or constrained *ex ante*. There may be some periods of stability when the definitions of policy and ideas reach some equilibrium but that stability may become destabilized in part because the institution itself generally remains open to the recruitment of new members. Unlike the logic of normative institutionalism in which individuals coming into the institution are thoroughly socialized, the logic of discursive institutionalism is that the new participants may import new ideas that will upset the balance.

Given the nature of discursive institutionalism there is a stronger interaction between the institution and the individual than in other versions of the general approach. The institution is defined by the involvement and interaction of the individuals within it. Their discussion and bargaining over the nature of the ideas used to define policies for the institution means that the individuals shape very much the institution. That said, it is unclear the extent to which individual ideas and involvement are sufficient to constitute a discourse, or whether more extensive collections of actors are needed to press through a particular vision within the structure.

What is less clear, however, is the impact of institutions on individuals. Individual values and policy commitments will inevitably be influenced to some extent by their involvement with the institutions, and more particularly by their involvement with the other members of the institution. That said, however, the less structured nature of institutions in this version of institutionalism may reduce the capacity of the institution to shape the individual. Unlike the normative model of institutions the ideas and values in this approach are less fixed and fewer efforts appear to be expended in shaping the values of the participants.

The interactions of individuals within the institution are a central component of understanding how the institutions function within this approach, and how they can reciprocally shape their own views and those of other participants. In any significant policy area these individuals will be a rather diverse group—politicians, civil servants, interest groups of various stripes, clients, and also representatives of other associated or competitive policy areas. This diversity can be managed more readily if there is a strong epistemic foundation for the institution, when there is likely to be more internal homogeneity and also there will be a greater opportunity for some participants to exclude other actors.[10]

Another way in which to understand the interaction of individuals and institutions is through the preferences of the participants and how they shape their behavior within the institution. The origins of preferences are clear in this model, in that they tend to be exogenous to the institution, unlike normative institutionalism in which the preferences tend to be shaped by the institution. That said, the process of coordinative discourse will involve some modification of the preferences of the individuals as they confront ideas from other participants. Again, the greater the diversity of the participants in the process the more likely there will be changes in those preferences. However, unlike the normative version of institutionalism all the participants may be expected to alter their views, rather than conforming to the "logic of appropriateness" within the institution.

Finally, the familiar structure–agency distinction in the study of the social sciences must be considered when thinking about how individuals and institutions interact. This relationship is especially complicated because of the role that ideas play. In particular the nature of individual actions must be considered in light of the individual role that ideas may play in shaping the behaviors of the institution (see Blyth, 1997; Gofas and Hay, 2008).

The Operation of the Institution

Institutions are structures but they also are mechanisms through which individuals and the institution itself achieve goals. This pursuit of goals is certainly apparent in social institutions such as churches or educational systems. The institutionalist logic

---

[10] This argument is analogous to the capacity of "iron triangles" in pluralist politics to define their own boundaries rather exclusively and thus prevent representatives of their policy communities from influencing policies within the single "triangle."

in general tends toward anthropomorphizing institutions so that there are assumptions that goals exist for the structure that are independent of the individuals who comprise the institution. Individuals may adopt those goals for their own as they enter the institution, or they may attempt to alter those goals, but in most versions of institutionalism there is some collective pursuit of goals.

The discursive approach to institutionalism has somewhat less clear assumptions about the existence of collective goals within an institution. Rather, those goals are conceptualized to be interactive, variable, and less stable than in other versions of institutionalism. Managing an institution in this setting, therefore, requires not just the conventional management skills but also the skill of managing multiple and perhaps conflicting goals. Management in this context also involves creating some degree of consensus among the participants, even though that consensus may be fleeting. Given the general understanding of an institution, there should be some stability among the participants and among the goals involved in the institution there is the need to build that consensus, even if the belief pattern it is not as enduring as that expected for the normative or historical versions.

Although in some cases discourses and ideas can be used as a source of agency for transformation within structures that might otherwise become ossified, it may also be that there is a need for agency to make the discursive version of institutionalism function in a more stable and predictable manner. While it appears open and democratic to have a wide range of ideas contending and being discussed within the institution, that process may not of itself produce anything other than debate, or perhaps reach policy solutions constituting the lowest common denominator (Scharpf, 1988). Thus, perhaps the central analytic problem in discursive institutionalism is to transform discourse and multiple ideas into a decision, or perhaps at a minimum a truce in the continuing debates.

If there are such difficulties in making decisions within an institution then reverting to the rules central to rational choice institutionalism, or to common norms and symbols central to normative institutionalism may be the ways available within the institutionalist paradigm. If one moves outside that framework then leadership and entrepreneurship become the most obvious means of generating internal consistency among the participants. This is but one example of how most social science theories as yet are incapable of explaining a full process or outcome. Rather, there appears to be a need to bring together a range of variables and theories together in some form of "causal reconstruction" (Mayntz, 2002).

The Good Institution

In discursive institutionalism the criteria for a good institution are somewhat less clearly defined than they are in other versions of institutionalism. The somewhat indeterminate nature of institutions in this version of the general approach, with institutions being at once fixed and contingent, means that it is difficult to ascertain when the structure is adequately institutionalized and when it is successful in involving the members in the institution. The interaction of members within the institution defines the institution but these interactions also make the boundaries and the limits of the institution less readily defined.

The above discussion may, however, utilize too much of the conventional understanding of institutions to attempt to conceptualize an approach that is intended to be, at least in part, an alternative to those more structured versions of institutionalism. Any standard of success and failure for discursive institutions will therefore be based more on process considerations than on outputs of the institutions or internal homogeneity of the participants' values. Almost paradoxically, institutional success in a discursive model implies maintaining some openness to policy ideas and discourses that are not central to the status quo within the institution. That is, if discourse is good then more discourse must be better, and therefore if the institution is more open then it is a more successful institution.

This version of institutionalism is even more policy-oriented than most of the other versions, so that a second criterion of success would be to be able to produce successful policies. That, in turn, may beg the question of what a successful policy may be, and for whom? Given that this version of institutionalism is more open and more interactive than are others, then different actors may be expected to have different policy commitments, and hence different actors will assess the quality of the policy outcomes substantially differently. The task for successful operation of the institution is to create some form of consensus, even if it may be transient, about the particular policies being adopted.

In summary, the good institution in the discursive model appears based much more on processes of building and changing institutions than do other versions of institutionalism. The process of interaction among the participants is crucial for defining the content of the institution and its policy outcomes. While the process orientation is a useful addition to the alternative approaches toward institutions, it also is more indeterminate than are the other versions. Therefore assessing the institution and comparing institutional performance becomes substantially more difficult.

Problems in Discursive Institutionalism

The development of yet another version of institutionalism might be seen to add one more weapon to the armory of institutionalist explanations for politics and public policy. While that is certainly true, this approach also raises some important questions not only about how it functions itself as an approach, but also how it functions with other versions of the more general institutionalist approach. The discursive approach, as already been argued, is closely associated with the sociological institutionalism and its emphasis on ideas but also has ties with the historical approach. But how does the approach stand up on its own? Does it add insights about institutions that would not be available from the other existing approaches?

The first question which must be raised is whether this version of institutionalism takes the emphasis on ideas too far. It is difficult to deny that ideas are important in political life, and that many policies are shaped by ideas. Examples such as economic policy and the welfare state demonstrate clearly that ideas can be extremely important and indeed almost determinate. But these examples may well be the exception rather than the rule in public policy and governance. Many policy areas may not have as clear dominance by ideas, or have as clear sets of ideas that can shape a policy.

The factor most obviously not included in the discursive model of institutions is interest. Even if one does not accept rational choice as the fundamental organizing principle for contemporary political science, actors in politics do have interests that they attempt to fulfill, if not maximize, through the political process (see Baumgartner and Leech, 1998). While the causal linkages between ideas and policy choices may at times be difficult to identify (see Braun and Busch, 1999) the linkages between interests and policy choices often are more readily demonstrable. It is not difficult in most circumstances to identify what interests an actor (individual or collective) may have in the policy process and then to relate that set of interests to their advocacy of particular policies.

The above having been said, to what extent are ideas and interests related and reinforcing? Ideas can be used to justify interests when the exercise of raw interests might be considered inappropriate. While business interests may have strong interests in having tax cuts and business preferences they can rationalize those benefits in terms of economic growth and maintaining the free market. On the other side, unions and other groups on the political left may simply want higher wages and job security but they justify those in terms of economic growth (the Keynesian logic) and in terms of equity.

In addition to functioning simply as a potential source of policy ideas, discourses can also function as a source of preferences for participants in the policy process. One of the enduring questions about rational choice institutionalism, and indeed about rational choice theory in general, is what is the source of preferences (see Hechter and Kanazawa, 1997). There may be a general preference for maximizing individual utilities that is pervasive in the model of rational politics. But those preferences may, however, be so vague that they are of little use in explaining the policy choices of actors. The various discourses involved in institutions may be capable of providing participants with sets of specific policy preferences that can be related to their more generic preferences for utility maximization.

The use of the term equity above also points to the variety of types of ideas that may be involved in shaping public policies. In particular, the distinction between normative and more empirical ideas and theories adds a more complex dimension to the analysis of discourse and its role in institutions. Not only do institutions carry ideas about policy, they may be associated with normative statements about the good society and the good policy. Therefore, the discourses that occur within an institution can define the values of the participants as well as the policy choices that it ultimately makes.

Summary and Conclusion

The discursive approach to institutionalism has been a relatively late addition to the various approaches to the study of institutions. Although it has been a recent addition it does add several important dimensions to the study of institutions. The most obvious, and most significant, is the central role that this approach to institutions assigns to ideas. As noted the normative approach does the same, to some extent, but for the normative version the ideas of relevance are primarily internal to the organization or institution rather than policy ideas that will shape the outcomes of the policy process.

The deliberative approach also provides a more flexible perspective on institutions to those found in other approaches, especially historical institutionalism. While the stability of institutions is a central feature of most approaches, this perspective points out the possibilities of change and to some extent also the virtues of having a less structural perspective. As with the other approaches to institutions, this perspective on institutions may be best understood in conjunction with others (see Katznelson and Weingast, 2005). The emphasis on ideas here, combined to some extent with the emphasis on structure in other approaches to institutions, can provide a more complete interpretation of the complexities of institutional life than can any one approach alone.

Thus, like all approaches to institutions the discursive model answers some questions well but also leaves some questions unanswered. Perhaps the most significant unanswered questions concerns the process through which all the ideas that comprise the discourses within an institution are converted into some more or less common agreement on common policy and/or management approaches for the institution. There are always multiple ideas available to be adopted within the institution and some are selected and others are not. This selection may be temporary and contending ideas are vying to replace the dominant approach, and these processes do not appear to be understood adequately.

CHAPTER 7

Sociological Institutionalism

This book is concerned primarily with the development of new institutionalism in political science. Despite that focus, we would be overlooking a potentially important means of understanding political institutions if we did not discuss the significant body of relevant institutionalist literature existing in sociology. This literature is important to political science, just as is the increasing role of the economic analysis of institutions in our discipline (Chapter 3). If anything, the sociological literature on institutions and institutionalism is more fully developed than is that of economics, given that organizations and institutions have been a significant focus of attention in that discipline for some time.

Further, sociology has had some of the same distinctions between old and new institutionalism that has been found in political science (Selznick, 1996; Stinchcombe, 1997). The old institutionalism was characterized by the emphasis on values seen in normative institutionalism (see Greenwood and Hinnings, 1996). The new institutionalism, on the other hand, is concerned more with the relationships of institutions to their organizational fields, with elements of discourse, and institutional entrepreneurship (Hardy and Maguire, 2008).

The sociological literature on institutions is very rich but it is also somewhat perplexing. This puzzlement stems from several characteristics of the literature. First, there is not always a clear distinction between institutions as entities and the process of institutionalization by which they are created. As pointed out above (p. 23), Lawrence Mohr (1982; see also Zucker, 1977) has made the distinction between "variance" and "process" theories of institutions, or those theories that focus on the effects of different institutional formats[1] and those that focus attention on processes of creation and change of the structures themselves. There is a good deal of both categories of theory in the sociological literature on organizations and/or institutions, and the two strands of theory are not always clearly distinguished. As we will point out below, however, the sociological literature appears much stronger in explaining the process of creating institutions than it is in describing the characteristics of the institutions resulting from those processes.

[1] The obvious example would be the "empirical institutionalists" discussed in Chapter 5. In general, political science has been more concerned with this style of institutional theory than with the process of institutionalization.

In contrast, political scientists (and especially those working within the empirical and economic approaches to institutions) are better at explaining the effects of institutions than they are at describing their creation or dissolution. For most political scientists the principal reason for investigating institutions is that these structures shape public policies or influence other fundamental political processes. The sociological institutionalists, on the other hand, are interested in the existence of the institutions, their internal processes, and their relationships with other institutions in the field.

A second reason for some apparent confusion in the sociological literature on institutions is the failure to distinguish clearly between organizations and institutions. There is a rich literature on organizations and organizational theory in sociology (Katz and Kahn, 1978; Scott, 1992; Clegg et al., 2006), and that literature has an obvious bearing on the issues of institutional behavior. Some theorizing in sociology has been very explicit in making that distinction, but the majority of the literature has tended to slide all too easily from one noun to the other (Scott, 1994; see also Hirsch, 1997). In fairness the failure to distinguish clearly between institutions and organizations has not been confined to sociological analysis of institutions, with much of institutional analysis failing to make clearly that differentiation. This weakness does, however, appear more evident in the sociological literature. This is perhaps because of the strength of organization theory in that discipline, and therefore the conceptual differences tends to create more confusion here than in other approaches.

Despite those perplexities, we should attempt to integrate the insights from this literature when we attempt to understand institutionalism in political science. On the one hand, the emphasis on the creation of meaning (Meyer and Rowan, 1977; Chia, 2000) and the relevance of values in sociological theory is an extremely useful counterbalance to the individual maximization and utilitarian values inherent in the rational choice version of institutionalism. Further, the March and Olsen version of the "new institutionalism" that began the current discussion of institutionalism within political science clearly had its roots in the more sociological conception of institutions (see pp. 27ff.). Hall and Taylor (1996; see also Rockman, 1993; Peters, 1996), in fact, refer somewhat incorrectly to the March and Olsen version of institutionalism as "sociological institutionalism" (but see Friedberg, 1998).[2] Certainly many of the criticisms that have been leveled at the March and Olsen version of institutionalism also can be argued to be applicable to a good deal of the sociological literature on this subject. Not least among those critiques is that the emphasis on rather amorphous normative and cultural statements assumed to function as guides

[2] The most important point distinguishing between the normative and sociological approaches is that the emphasis on political behavior in the March and Olsen approach, as well as its greater concern with the active molding of institutions by active political entrepreneurs. As we will point out below institutionalization in the sociological approach appears to be a less purposive process.

for action in institutions in much of this (and the March and Olsen) rendering of institutionalism are not adequately defined and researchable. This makes these theories almost unfalsifiable and hence suspect on theoretical grounds.

The role of meaning in political science versions of institutionalism can be seen most clearly in discursive models of institutions (Chapter 6, this volume; Schmidt, 2010). Discursive models also emphasize the extent to which meanings within institutions, and indeed the very purpose of the institutions, are not given but are constructed through interactions. The discursive model and the other versions based on ideas all demonstrate a close affinity with the sociological approach to institutions, with the principal difference being that political scientists tend to be more concerned with the consequences of the attributes of the institutions (Bourdeaux, 2008).

The Roots of Institutionalism in Sociology

The concern for institutions within sociology can easily be traced to the leading theorists of that discipline. For example, Max Weber's theoretical work (1976) is clearly concerned with institutions and the development of "rational" institutions to meet the demands of modernizing societies. One commentator on Weber's theory of bureaucracy and other institutions (Lachmann, 1971, p. 68) argued that institutions were as central to his concepts as the idea of competition was to economics. For Weber his "ideal type" of the rational-legal bureaucracy is the highest possible form of rationality manifested in an institutional format, even if that level of rationality is almost certainly not achievable within the real world. Even more fundamentally, Weber's analysis is concerned with the manners in which cultural values infuse and shape formal organizations, no matter the level of socioeconomic and cultural development at which this process occurs. Similar to the value-based institutionalists discussed above, Weber posited a direct link between cultural values and formal structures in society including formal institutions.

Similarly, the eminent French sociologist Emile Durkheim also developed a clear conceptualization of the role of institutions in social and political life, and referred to sociology as the "science of institutions." Durkheim (1922) was also concerned with the development of rational organizations, although instead of being concerned initially with the role of values Durkheim was more interested in the role of objective societal characteristics, especially the division of labor, in organizations and institutions. These "societal facts" were, in turn, converted into symbolic systems that represented collective values for those institutions. For Durkheim, like Weber, there was a link between social forces and the nature of institutions, but the causal connection appeared much closer for Durkheim than for Weber. The linkage of symbols and institutions was more evident in part because of a greater empirical content in Durkheim's work (1986).

The American sociologist Talcott Parsons (1951; 1960) represents another branch on the tree of evolution in the sociological analysis of institutions. Parsons was one of the major proponents of functionalism in the social sciences, the basic argument of which being that societies had certain requisite functions that must be performed if they were to survive. For example, societies (it was argued) must fulfill the "adaptive" function of extracting sufficient resources from the environment to survive.[3] The performance of these functions was then related to the existence of institutions (structures), with the comparative analysis of societies being possible through different manners of relating structure and function.

More recently, Philip Selznick had a profound influence on thinking about institutions in sociology. He focused attention on the importance of understanding organizations in institutional terms, and of understanding the processes of institutionalization and institutional change. Selznick's classic study (1949) of the Tennessee Valley Authority pointed to the process through which an organization based largely on a technical process is transformed into an institution, and begins to embody values as well as merely a structural form. Thus, Selznick is interested in the process of institutionalization as much as in the institutions that result from that process. The role of organizational leadership (one of Selznick's primary foci) was to create and defend the value systems created within the institution.

Selznick's own research was supplemented by that of his students, many of whom have carried on and extended his research program on organizations and institutions. Several of these students (Zald and Denton, 1967; Zucker, 1988) focused on the processes of organizational change, and the capacity of organizations (and institutions) to persist even after their ostensible purposes have been achieved. This research reinforced the point that institutions have a capacity to defend their core values (and especially their fundamental existence) even when confronted with objective conditions that might seem to negate their utility. Further, this sociological work has emphasized the importance of maintaining routines and processes in the face of the challenges that confront any organization or institution.

Finally, S. N. Eisenstadt (1963; 1965) has been concerned explicitly with the processes of institutionalization and deinstitutionalization in society and organizations within society. Eisenstadt accepted much of the functionalism of Parsons, and attempted to demonstrate how change could be explained using a theory that was widely regarded as static and conservative. Unlike many contemporary sociologists Eisenstadt was interested in the historical dimension of change, beginning with these processes within major empires and continuing up to the establishment of the Israeli state (1958). Eisenstadt argued that institutions and individuals adapted to changes in their environments through a functionalist logic so that the behavioral patterns that evolved would be compatible with the survival of the organization.

[3] For a useful analysis of these Parsonian functions in a political context see Lipset and Rokkan (1967). For structural functional analysis of politics more generally, see Almond and Coleman (1960) and Almond and Powell (1967).

Eisenstadt further utilized role theory, and the concept of "role crystallization" as a measuring rod for gauging the development of institutions. The argument was that institutions were, in essence, bundles of roles that individuals occupy more or less adequately. To the extent that the expectations of those roles are sufficiently clear and individuals play the roles with minimal ambiguity then institutionalization can be said to have taken place (see also Zucker, 1987). The clarity of roles and the acceptance of the roles by individuals within organizations vary over time, so that institutions can vary in their degrees of institutionalization. If we refer back to the March and Olsen ideas about "appropriateness" this can be seen as analogous to the logic of appropriateness being more or less infused into the members of the institution.

Eisenstadt develops some of his conceptions of changing institutions within the context of bureaucratization (1959; 1963). As bureaucracies develop they acquire a richer and more complete set of values, as well as a more complete pattern of interactions. Eisenstadt's work is especially interesting in that he does not consider the process of institutionalization (or bureaucratization) irreversible. He was interested in the ways in which nominally bureaucratic organizations can become less institutionalized, especially in the context of changing "raw materials" with which the organizations must contend. In the most extreme case he found Israeli organizations (Katz and Eisenstadt, 1960; Eisenstadt et al., 1970) becoming less bureaucratized in response to having to cope with immigrant populations from North Africa that did not share the Western, bureaucratic values of most Israeli organizations.

Contemporary Sociological Institutionalism

Just as our discussion of rational choice versions of institutionalism pointed out for the case of economic approaches, there is a variety of different approaches to institutions within sociology. We do not have time or space to devote to a complete treatment to each of those approaches, so we will focus attention on several of the more important ones.[4] I should also reemphasize here, however, that a good deal of the institutional analysis in the discipline of political science per se draws heavily from its sociological heritage. For example, March and Olsen's (1989; 1994) analysis of government institutions is closely allied with the strands of sociological literature that stress the central role of values and symbols in defining an institution and in guiding the behavior of its members.

Population Ecology Models of Organizations

Perhaps the most interesting sociological perspective for the study of public sector institutions is the study of organizational ecology, and the associated population

[4] For a brief and extremely insightful discussion of the variety of "sociological institutionalisms," see the work of Richard Scott (1994; 1995a).

ecology models of organizations (Carroll, 1984; Hannan and Freeman, 1989; Singh, 1990). This school of analysis has been applied relatively little in political science (but see Casstevens, 1984; Peters and Hogwood, 1988; 1991; Gray and Lowery, 1996a; 1996b), but it appears to hold a good deal of promise for understanding the dynamics of the public sector as a collection of institutions, as well as for understanding the behavior of the individual organizational components of the public sector.

The fundamental premise of the population ecology approach is that organizations (or institutions) and their behavior can be understood in part through an analogy with populations of biological organisms. Just as the biological ecology model provides opportunities for only so many organisms to survive, so too the environment of organizations is capable of supporting only so many structures. For example, the market provides only so many customers and employees, and only so much capital for restaurants, gas stations, newspapers, or other types of businesses.[5] Similarly there is a limited supply of public money and political support for organizations in the public sector, so the public sector can support only so many of those institutions.

Another of the concepts developed in the population ecology approach is the organizational niche. A niche is a particular mixture of resources that enables a specific type of organization to survive. For the public sector a niche might be defined by budgetary resources, legal mandates, institutional political support, and mass political support. These combinations will permit certain types, and certain numbers, of organizations to thrive while others will not be so fortunate. Some niches are "wider" than others, permitting a wider variety of institutions to function within them successfully. For example, a policy area such as providing basic public services may be dealt with through direct public ownership and distribution.

One of the most important questions in the population ecology models of organizations is the survival of organizations in this presumably hostile environment. Without getting into the details of the various mathematical models that could be used to explain the survival of organizations (Tuma and Hannan, 1984; Aldrich, 2007), there are a number of factors that are used to describe the process of survival and the rate of "death" of organizations. One of the more important models depends upon the age of the organizations, with both very young and very old organizations being particularly in jeopardy of being terminated. Also, given the limited "carrying capacity" of any environment, the density of the population will affect the survival of organizations.

How does this approach to organizations illuminate the study of institutions in political science? In some ways it might be thought that the environmental dependency of organizations assumed in the population ecology approach might have little to add to the understanding of institutions that are largely considered volitional. The

[5] The examples of firms used here are those that have served as the basis of a number of population ecology studies.

principal contribution that this set of ideas makes is to emphasize the dependence of institutions on their environment, and their "embeddedness" in society and economy. It also points to the extent to which institutions may be in explicit or implicit competition with one another for resources and even survival, whether they be in the market or in the budgetary competition of government.

Institutionalization and Isomorphism

A second version of the sociological approaches to institutions which we will mention is concerned with the symbolic and valuative dimensions of organizations. This can be seen as a reaction of a nascent strand of rational choice reasoning in sociology that argued that organizations and their structures could be explained by the tasks being performed and by the resource base available to the organization. In such a view, organizations were almost purely utilitarian and action oriented. There was an emerging body of literature (Simon, 1947; Cyert and March, 1963) that demonstrated the difficulty of rational action in most organizational settings, but the functionalist conception of organizational behavior tended to persist.

A more symbolic conception of the character and behavior of organizations emerged from the apparent incapacity of resource-based models, for example contingent approaches, to explain adequately the nature of organizations. This research to some extent built on the prior work of Selznick, but emphasized more the manipulation of symbols within a successful organization as the best means of comprehending how and why the institution behaved as it did (Meyer and Rowan, 1977). Organizations certainly do have a task-oriented character, but they also have a very clear element which is not rational in the usual sense of that term.

From this concern with the extra-rational and symbolic aspects of organizations came an explicit sociological theory of organizations as institutions (see Strang, 1994). The fundamental perspective being employed here is that institutions are systems of meaning and that their behavior and the behavior of individuals within them depend upon the meanings incorporated and the symbols manipulated. In the public sector, Herbert Kaufman's analysis of the U.S. Forest Service (1960) is a classic example of an organization using symbol manipulation to define itself and to create a desired pattern of behavior by its members. Kaufman points to the role of training, and the use of symbols in that training, as the way of getting members of the organization to behave "in the public interest" even when they might be under strong pressures to conform to local wishes and give in to local economic interests.

Although the March and Olsen version of institutionalism does have its roots in sociological analysis, there are some important differences between their work and much of that in sociology (Campbell, 1997). Perhaps the most basic distinction is that March and Olsen tend to emphasize the normative basis of institutions while much of the sociological literature emphasizes the cognitive elements of organization theory. That is, the sociological literature has become more concerned with how the members of an institution perceive situation within their structure and the "frames" that they bring to bear on those situations in order to make decisions about them (Berger and Luckmann, 1967).

This cognitive emphasis then has more to do with perception than with evaluation. Just as professional memberships may create a trained incapacity to perceive problems and evidence in other than the professional manner, so the membership in an institution is argued to create the same sort of perceptual frame. The difference from the normative view of institutions is subtle but yet important. The cognitive view may be more basic than the normative view, given that it determines how the member of the institutions interprets data from the environment, while "all" that the normative perspective tells him or her is what the appropriate behavior would be in any situation. Both approaches may be needed for a complete explanation of organizational/institutional behavior (Scott, 1995a). The logic of the one approach will affect the members of the organization as they receive inputs on which they make decisions. The other part of the sociological process may be more significant in explaining how decisions are made.

One question that emerges from this literature is why relatively similar forms of institutions emerge in very different social and political settings. This question of "isomorphism" (DiMaggio and Powell, 1991) to some extent goes back to Weber (and perhaps some of the other founding fathers of the discipline), given that he argued that there would be a tendency toward convergence around a rational legal format for bureaucracy as societies developed (but, see Franzen, 2011). The famous concept of the "iron cage" as developed by Weber has been extended by Dimaggio and Powell to relate to a number of sociological processes by which the common institutional and organizational formats emerge, even in seemingly different objective circumstances. Their version of convergence tends, however, to be more differentiated; the argument is for convergence in particular fields but not necessarily across all fields, and further that the convergence occurs for a variety of different reasons (see Frumkin and Galaskiewicz, 2004).

The isomorphism literature is based on the logic of organizational and institutional fields, meaning that institutions within a field tend to converge on relatively similar forms. This convergence is not dissimilar to the literature on organizational learning (Levitt and March, 1988; Boxenbaum and Jonsson, 2008) as well as that on diffusion. That convergence has become one of the dominant approaches in the sociology of organizations and institutions, and provides an important means for understanding institutional change.

Sedimentation

One of the more interesting concepts to emerge from this body of sociological literature on institutions is that of "sedimentation" (see Tolbert and Zucker, 1996). This term reflects the characteristic of human life that current practices are built on the past and that beneath current practice in an organization there may be layers of values and understandings left from earlier times. Thus, if organizations or institutions were to be presented visually, they might look like rocks drawn from the sea bed in which layer after layer of deposits have accumulated and been solidified.

The idea of sedimentation reflects very clearly the historical and cumulative nature of institutions. These structures may be transformed over time, but they also retain much of their past history. However, unlike being the captive of that history entirely (as they might be to the historical institutionalists) the organizations are seen as redefining themselves as well as reflecting their past. This view of institutions has interesting consequences for the conceptualization of change in institutional theory. Rather than being a question of design and change that occurs for once and for all, change involves developing new understandings and symbols that are not incompatible with those that were in place before. This makes change slower but on the other hand more possible than a more absolutist position about replacing values might be.

The idea of sedimentation is analogous to the logic of layering in the historical institutionalism (Streeck and Thelen, 2005). In its initial formulations the historical institutionalism contained relatively little about change other than the extreme version of "punctuated equilibrium." Layering, as the name implies, adding new layers of values or structures to existing institutions in order to produce change without producing radical alteration of the existing patterns.

Organizational Archetypes: A Return to Weber?

An interesting variation on the theme of isomorphism in the sociological approach to institutions is the development of archetypes of institutional forms for comparative purposes. The logic here is similar to that employed by Weber (1949; see also Page, 1992; Peters, 1998) in his development of "ideal type" methodology for the analysis of formal organizations, as well as other aspects of social life. The variation in forms of organizations and institutions is sufficiently great that any attempt to examine them all would have the researcher bogged down in almost endless detail. Therefore, it appears more efficient to create ideal types of institutions against which to compare the institutions observed in the real world.

As well as being useful for comparative purposes, the archetype analysis is useful for speaking to questions of change in institutions (Laughlin, 1991; Greenwood and Hinnings, 1993). As we have pointed out at several places, one of the dangers of focusing on institutions for analysis is that they tend to be relatively permanent, and even inflexible, so that change is difficult to detect. The argument accompanying the use of archetypes is that institutions can only change from one archetype to another; the pressures of isomorphism may make only so many alternative forms possible or thinkable at any one time.

The movement from one archetype to the other involves then a process of deinstitutionalization and a subsequent reinstitutionalization, as one set of structures is replaced by the new alternative. As pointed out much earlier by Eisenstadt (1959), change in an institutionalized structure involves both eliminating old structures (or systems of values and symbols) and then replacing those with new ones. This view of institutional change is almost exactly the opposite of that found in the sedimentation perspective in organizational sociology. In that view an institution will represent a succession of values, with some remnant of each persisting.

Discursive Institutionalism

As sociological theory has been developing, as is true for the other social sciences, the positivism that had characterized much of the development of the discipline has been supplemented by alternative methodologies and theories. One of these has been the use of discourse analysis, and other approaches that depend more on an understanding of the rhetorical and ideational basis of social action (Fairclough, 1992). This type of analysis has been applied to a wide range of social and political phenomena, and depends upon the construction and interpretation of the ideational and narrative basis of issues. The argument is that in order to understand the role that ideas play in shaping policy one must understand the entire discourse within which it is embedded.

From that basic approach to social phenomena the discursive approach to institutions has emerged, albeit perhaps not so clearly as it has for other types of social phenomena. Institutions have tended to be discussed more in structural terms than in terms of more diffuse influences on the behavior of individuals through ideas. That said, however, when we discussed historical institutionalism (Chapter 4) we noted the importance of ideas in defining institutions in that approach. Discursive institutionalism shares the importance of ideas with historical institutionalism, but differs in that it is less concerned with the equilibrium conditions that may result from the initial selection of ideas to guide policy.

Questions about Institutions

We can now embark on asking the same questions about the sociological perspective on institutions that we have asked about all the other versions. As might be expected from what we have already said, some of the answers here will not be terribly different from those given with respect to the March and Olsen version. When that is the case we will say so and move on as quickly and parsimoniously as possible. At the same time, however, it is important not to be too facile in equating the two versions of institutionalism, given the different range of phenomena that the two are discussing and their somewhat different purposes.[6]

[6] Although different, both versions have been reactions to a perceived overemphasis on the rational and the utilitarian within their disciplines.

What Is an Institution?

The first and most basic question is what is an institution in this approach. Again, we point to the difficulties in differentiating an institution and an organization in this version of institutional theory. It could be argued, although it is probably an overstatement, that what we are discussing in sociological institutionalism is an institutional *perspective* on organizations, without a clear definition of what constitutes an institution per se. If this statement is true, institutions and organizations are virtually identical structures and there is little need to provide a second definition. The above statement points to the centrality of the process of institutionalization in the sociological literature. The sociological approach to institutions appears to be somewhat more concerned with the process of creating values and cognitive frames within an organization than it is with the end state—the differences among organizations that can predict the behavior of those institutions and individuals within them. The latter characterization is something of an overstatement perhaps, given work such as that by Goffman (1961) on "total institutions," and Etzioni (1975) and others (see Orru et al., 1991) on comparative organizational analysis. There is, however, a clear difference between these scholars and the empirical institutionalists (largely in political science) who tend to focus attention almost entirely on end conditions and institutional performance and very little on process of formation and change. Certainly there is some concern in political science with the development of institutions, for example the institutionalization of the Congress (Polsby, 1975).

Despite those apparent problems, Scott (1995a, p. 33) does provide a definition of institutions. For him:

> Institutions consist of cognitive, normative and regulative structures and activities that provide stability and meaning to social behavior.

This is a clear stipulation of what constitutes an institution, but also is a very broad statement and captures some of the theoretical controversy about the term within itself; almost nothing is left out. For example, the question of whether institutions are best understood as structural features of society or as cognitive features is defined away in Scott's definition. Such a broad definition is probably desirable, given the many ways in which the term institution is used in both scientific and everyday language, but it does not differentiate institutions from other forms of organization or social structure.

In addition to the definition coming from Scott, Jepperson (1991, p. 149) defines institutions as:

> socially constructed, routine reproduced . . . program or rule systems . . . operating as relative fixtures of constraining environments and . . . accompanied by taken-for-granted accounts.

This definition is more detailed than that provided by Scott, and appears very much like that used by the normative institutionalists. We should, however, attempt to make some differentiation between institutions and organizations, despite the similarity of the literatures dealing with each. One useful definition coming out of the economics literature (North, 1990, p. 4; Khalil, 1995) differentiates between teams playing a game and the rules of that game. That is, organizations are formed to participate within the "institutional environment" (see Davis and North, 1971) created by entities such as markets and political systems. For example, firms are created to play within the framework created by a market, and if the rules (formal or informal) of the market change then the firms must also change.

Alternative Definitions of Institutions

Scott does identify three different ways to think about the roots or organizations: cognitive, normative, and regulative. His analysis is built on the differences among these three versions of institutions in sociology and their differing implications for how institutions function and can be understood. Scott describes cognitive institutional theories as ones in which institutions are defined by their use of symbols and systems of meaning to intermediate between the environment and behavior within the institution. In this view, institutions are socially constructed by the perceptions and cognitions of their members rather than being objective entities (Scott, 1987).

The normative "pillar" of institutionalism is very close to the normative version of new institutionalism in political science; we have already pointed out the close linkage between the March and Olsen rendering of institutional theory and some aspects of the sociological theory on organizations and institutions. Indeed Scott's description of these pillars used March and Olsen's work as a principal example of the normative version of institutionalism, and pointed to its close connections to the sociological literature.

Finally, the regulative rendition of institutionalism relies on rules and control for defining institutions. This theoretical strand within sociology is not dissimilar to the rational choice versions of institutionalism already discussed (pp. 52ff.), or to the institutionalism encountered in the economics literature, for example principal-agent models and the utilization of rules. As discussed in reference to that approach, the role of institutions is to regulate behavior within its confines, and perhaps also to control social behavior more generally in society. Rules define institutions and they are also the means through which those institutions have their influence on individuals.

Individuals and Institutions

In some ways the crucial question for the sociological conception of institutions is how are individuals and institutions linked. This has been the source of some controversy in the discipline, and is fundamental to some differences among scholars over the nature of organizations and institutions. On the one hand, some scholars, most importantly Meyer and Rowan (1977), argue that institutions are primarily a symbolic manifestation of the needs of a society or a group in society for legitimation and can be decoupled from action. In the public arena Edelman (1992, pp. 1540–2) has argued that institutions that fulfill more symbolic functions are likely to be as effective as or even more effective than institutions that more closely affect behaviors.[7] Similarly, other scholars (see Preuss, 1991) have argued that in the public sector the less determinate an institution is, the more legitimacy it is likely to have. In this view, individuals and (successful) institutions tend to exist apart from one another, especially within the public sector.

On the other hand there are scholars such as Giddens (1979), who argue that institutions are manifestly not institutions if they do not shape the behavior of individuals within them. Institutions as systems of meaning do convey a sense of how their members should behave, whether that is the profit maximization of economic organizations or the altruism of religious and charitable organizations. The view that institutions must shape behavior is the dominant perspective within the sociological study of institutions, with emphasis on the manner in which individuals within organizations become habituated to accepting the norms and values of their organization.

One perspective on this controversial issue argues that the process of institutionalization progresses through three distinct stages (Tolbert and Zucker, 1996): habitualization, objectivication, and sedimentation. Beneath all those dreadful bits of jargon there is an implied movement from institutions existing merely as a fact of organizational life to a greater and enduring acceptance of the values of an institution by individuals living within it. Those theorists did not provide any unambiguous objective indicators of the passage of an organization through these stages, but the analysis is a useful way to think about the development of institutional structures. Further, this process is quite similar to the idea of institutionalization advanced by Eisenstadt as a way of understanding transformations of structures, especially in the public sector.

Change in Institutions

We have already noted that a good deal of the concern in at least one branch of the sociological study of institutions is in the process of institutionalization. This process orientation in the discipline tends to make the study of change a natural component of the field. In this particular account change occurs through institutionalization or deinstitutionalization; that is, institutionalization increases by adding more roles

---

[7] Yet another Edelman (1964; 1988) has also argued persuasively for the symbolic aspects of politics and political institutions.

and features to the institution, for example firmer commitments to the prevailing cognitive "frames" of the institution or weakening those commitments.

Sociologists can also look at institutional change in a more functionalist way, and argue that institutions must, and will, find means of adapting to changes in their environment. This form of change involves recognizing challenges in the environment and then finding ways to make the institution conform to those external forces. From the cognitive perspective in sociological institutionalism there may be dominant elements in the political culture that will limit the capacity of any institution to deviate too far from the status quo. For political science the work of Karl Deutsch (1963) on social cybernetics is one approach for understanding how institutions receive and process signals from the environment and attempt to match policies with the changing nature of that environment.

The above having been said, however, there is a strong strand in organization theory that argues that organizations will attempt to mold its environment (Pfeffer and Salanick, 1978; Oliver, 1991) to meet its own needs, rather than passively responding to that environment. That view may be especially valid for institutions in the public sector that may have the capacity to manipulate the political economy in ways that suit them. Private sector organizations may also attempt to manipulate or create markets for themselves (North, 1990). The ability of public sector organizations to build political support, however, and even to create their own clientele groups (Walker, 1983), may give those organizations even greater capacity to manipulate their environments that may not be available for private sector organizations.

Finally, the population ecology version of institutionalism would place the locus of change in the environment of the organization or institution. Organizations have greater adaptive capacity than do the biological organisms on which the original ecological theories were based, but the impetus for change still comes from outside and if the organization is not able to adapt to that changing environment then like the biological organism it must die. In this view, change is not as important within individual organizations as it will be for the population of organizations that will attempt to occupy a domain. Presumably one of the drives for change in the individual institutions will be the overall "carrying capacity" of the environment, and the types and intensity of interactions with other institutions.

The Good Institution

The final question to be addressed in this chapter is what constitutes a good institution within the sociological framework of institutional analysis. The answer here is more ambiguous than for most other approaches to institutionalism. Indeed, the sociological approach appears less concerned about the normative questions presented by institutions than do the other approaches. Organizations and institutions have been so central to the development of sociological theory that many of the normative questions have been subsumed in the empirical analysis. Further, there are several alternative sociological conceptualizations of institutions, each of which may provide a somewhat different conception about what equals a good institution.

The population ecology approach to organizations and institutions stresses the adaptive capacity of institutions and their ability to adapt to their environment. In this view, the longevity of an organization is perhaps the best measure of its success. In the ecology model, however, the institution (organization) appears to have little control over its own capacity to survive—the environment tends to determine whether its particular endowment of resources and goals will be successful. What may be needed, therefore, is some connection of this approach with strategic, managerial thinking about how institutions can adapt in order to survive (Singh, 1990).

The good organization in the logic of isomorphism is not dissimilar to that encountered in the population ecology models. Again, a good organization or institution is one that adapts effectively to the external pressures for isomorphism, whether the process for change is mimesis, coercion, or normative. What is perhaps different about the two components of the sociological approach to institutions is that the population ecology models tend to identify the possibility for a number of different types of organizations within the same population field, while the isomorphism approach tends to argue for a more limited range of possibilities.

Finally, the cognitive, normative, and regulative definitions of institutions proposed by Scott all present different conceptions of the good institution. The normative approach considers many of the same criteria advanced by March and Olsen, especially the capacity of an institution to inculcate its values into its members. Also, the regulative approach corresponds closely to a good deal of the thinking in the rational choice analysis, with the successful institution being one that is able to control the behavior of its participants (by rules or incentives). Finally, the cognitive approach concentrates on the capacity of institutions to process information and to reach the appropriate conclusions from that information. All these are important elements of the behavior of institutions and taken together they can define the behavior of members of institutions as well as their aggregate behavior *qua* institution.

Summary and Conclusion

This chapter has looked at sociological theories of institutions within the context of the history of that body of theory, as well as some basic questions concerning sociological theory. We have not, however, addressed the question of how this corpus of theory corresponds to the goals and concerns of political science, and its own conceptions of institutionalism. As we have pointed out above, one obvious connection is that the sociological literature is one major intellectual root of the March and Olsen version of institutionalism (and to a much less extent several of the others). Another obvious connection is that Weber and his conceptions of bureaucracy are at least as important to political science as it is to sociology, given that the public bureaucracy is often taken to be the closest thing to his ideal type found in the real world.

There is also an increasing interest in political science in the concepts of population ecology as mechanisms for explaining patterns of organizational formation and persistence. Just as the newspapers and restaurants used as evidence in much of the sociological analysis may come and go, so too do the government bureaus and interest groups. The difficulty for the public sector is specifying the environmental conditions under which institutions may be created and dissolved. Still, this body of theory provides a means of understanding and explaining the coming and going of public organizations.

The sociological approaches do provide an alternative to the rationalistic and individualistic ideas that dominate much of contemporary political science. March and Olsen began their campaign against those approaches in political science arguing that while the individualistic bias in the theories was misdirecting the discipline, the sociological approaches have maintained their connections with these more organizational and institutionalist traditions. In particular, the cognitive and normative accounts of institutions within sociology are in direct opposition to the rationalistic roots of rational choice theory. These institutionalist traditions continue within sociology and continue to have some impact on the study of organizations and institutions in political science.

CHAPTER 8

Institutions of Interest Representation

The majority of the political institutions we have discussed thus far are formal structures in government, for example bureaucracies and legislatures. These structures—our empirical institutionalism—are what we usually think of when the word "institution" is used in political science, but it is also important to consider the manner in which other aspects of the political world are structured. Many of the aspects of politics usually conceptualized as being less formal institutions are themselves highly structured and well-institutionalized. This structuring is true of the individual actors themselves, for example a single political party or an interest group. It is also true of the collection of organizations and other actors, for example party systems or networks of interest groups, as they participate in political life.

We could spend several entire books on the issues of political parties, interest groups, and networks (see, for example, Mair, 1997; Mair et al., 2004; Sorensen and Torfing, 2007), but in this one brief chapter we will attempt to capture some of the more relevant features of these organizational actors and systems of actors. We will discuss political parties in these terms relatively briefly, but spend more time on the changing conceptions of interest groups, and especially their interrelationships, and their relationship to formal political actors through networks and communities.

Although the literature on political parties, as well as that on interest groups, contains a number of institutional and structural features there does appear to be no distinctive theoretical contributions to the institutionalist literature. For the most part political parties and interest groups can be understood through the more general institutional theories such as rational choice, normative institutionalism, and even the sociological perspective on institutions. The major exception to that generalization would appear in the sociological literature on networks (Broadbent, 1989; Knoke and Burleigh, 1989) in which there is more than a little development of a theory of the manner in which organizations function within larger aggregations of organizations.[1] Even if there are no breakthroughs in institutional theory, these analyses do point to the ways in which these important components of the political system can be conceptualized through an institutional lens.

---

[1] This concern with the embeddedness of organizations reflects the "new institutionalism" in sociology. See Chapter 6.

The relationship between networks and institutions is particularly interesting in light of the argument that institutions and issue networks (and the related "policy communities") are alternative explanations for some of the same phenomena (Jordan, 1990; Richardson, 2000). The argument made is that the new institutionalism—at least in the normative version of March and Olsen—is too vague to provide any meaningful explanations for political phenomena and that a greater connection to empirical research is needed to demonstrate that there are meaningful ways of explaining policy choices.

Grant Jordan (1990, pp. 477–8) argues that the "extra-constitutional" structures that link state and society are indeed institutions. He points to the well-documented institutionalized relationships that exist between an increasing variety of organizations in society and government organizations in the United Kingdom and elsewhere. These relationships exist within individual policy sectors, rather than as relationships that span the range of government activities such as in corporatist politics. Despite that segmentation, within those individual domains these structural relationships are useful as means for explaining policy choices. Further, some manner of institutionalized relationships between state and society has been documented in virtually all national settings (Knoke et al., 1996) so that networks and their ilk present important possibilities for comparative research. Indeed, the relationships that exist in Anglo-American societies are among the least institutionalized of those in the industrialized democracies (see, for example, Sorensen and Torfing, 2000; Hermet, 2004).

We will point out below that Jordan is perhaps excessively optimistic about the utility of network analysis and its potential superiority as a form of institutional theory that can be used for these informal actors in the political system. In particular, he does not appear to be using more than a minimal definition of the term "institutional" as a regular pattern of behavior (Huntington, 1965). As we have pointed out already with respect to regime approaches in international politics (pp. 162–4) and the normative approach to institutions (pp. 25–8), this minimalist definition of institutions can describe any number of social and economic relationships, some of them being extremely minimal forms of connection among the participants. It is not clear, however, that all these regularized patterns of interaction should be considered "institutionalized," and certainly not in the sense of their having value for, and commitment of, the members. Still, Jordan assumes that this definition is adequate to argue for the existence of "institutionalized relationships" existing within a policy network or a policy community.

Jordan concentrates on the British and American versions of network analysis (and their differences) in his discussion of the institutional features of state–society relationships. There are also some important contributions from other national research traditions. For example, although not formally discussed as a network model, some French analysis of the sectorization of the State (Mueller, 1985; Le Gales and Thatcher, 1995; see also Baumgartner, 1989) is in some ways more directly institutional in its perspective on government than is the Anglo-American, pluralist tradition of studying interest groups as relatively autonomous actors.[2] There is also a very well-developed tradition of network analysis in Germany, Denmark, and the Netherlands (Bogason, 1991; 1996; Marin and Mayntz, 1991; Kickert et al., 1997) that again has clearer structural and institutional elements than that found in the typical Anglo-American approaches.

Parties and Party Systems

Political parties are examples of the dominant players in the political arena and, like any other organizations, can be conceptualized as institutions. Many political parties do have the persistence that one expects of an institution; the American Democratic and Republican parties have been the dominant parties for almost a century and a half, and in some ways the British Conservative party can trace its roots to a period well before the democratization of the political system. Those historical roots also have created a strong sense of path dependence in their behavior, with connections with the past and familiar political symbols being important for most parties.[3]

Political parties are also the carriers and promoters of ideological values and provide for their members, and for their society, if they are allowed by elections or other mechanisms for achieving office, a "logic of appropriateness" in the form of party policy statements and ideologies. Further, discursive models of institutionalism might be conceptualized to include the clash of different policy perspectives offered by political parties.

Political parties may differ, however, in the degree of institutionalization of their structures and in the extent to which they attempt to utilize rules to control the behavior of their members. At one extreme might be Communist, Fascist and other strongly ideological parties that attempt to mold the behavior of their members through formalized rules as well as through ideologies that could internalize those controlling values. At the other extreme would be found "caucus" parties such as American and British parties that have few operational rules or values other than to win elections if possible.[4] Parties, therefore, employ a variety of mechanisms to integrate themselves with their potential members. The more

---

[2] This is not least because of the rather minimal conceptualization of the state in this tradition (Dyson, 1980).

[3] This can often be seen in their conventions and rallies in which they invoke the successful leaders of the past, and recall their great victories and the strategies that produced those victories.

[4] The development of a clearer ideology, especially about social issues, has made the Republican Party into a very different party than the historical image of American parties. By imposing litmus tests, for example opposition to abortion or support of school prayer, this might change the nature of the party significantly. The Democratic Party retains much of its historical openness and lack of ideology, although it may be forced to become more programmatic if it is to be successful in coping with the more integrated Republicans.

ideological parties motivate their members through patterns of beliefs, while the caucus parties attempt to give their members, and especially their activists, the opportunity to gain office and to influence public policy by controlling government offices directly.

Given that political parties have extremely different aims and very different incentive structures, it should not be surprising that they would also have very different internal structures and institutional formats. Roberto Michels (1915), in one of the first organizational or institutional analyses of parties, argued that all political parties would tend toward oligopoly, but there are in fact marked organizational differences in party structures. Following from Michels's work there was a rich tradition of what might be termed "old institutionalists" who examined the structure of political parties and party systems, including scholars such as Duverger (1951), McKenzie (1963), and Ostrogowski (1964). These scholars focused primarily on the structural aspects of parties, and assumed that those formal characteristics would largely determine the behavior of the parties and their members.

The more rigid structure of ideological parties has now largely withered away, but the typical organizational format was hierarchical, with Communist parties, for example, using the concept of "democratic centralism" to combat potential factions within the party (Rodinov, 1988). These political parties also tended to create a large number of peripheral organizations for youth, women, sports, and so on in order to structure as much as possible of the lives of their adherents. Thus, as well as being an electoral organization, political parties in the Communist tradition attempted to be more "total institutions" (Goffman, 1961) that shaped all aspects of behavior. As such, these organizations are more comprehensible through the March and Olsen approach, for example, as propagating a "logic of appropriateness" than through rational choices views of institutions.

The loose organization of caucus parties such as those typical of political organization in the United States, Canada, and the United Kingdom is very different. The American comedian Will Rogers once commented that "I do not belong to any organized political group—I am a Democrat." Rogers may have overstated the point, but not by much.[5] Political parties operating in this pattern do not expect their central offices to exercise much power, and indeed they generally are more successful if they develop a strong grassroots basis of organization rather than a centralized structure. Still, they are an institution in most meanings of the term. As much as anything else, parties have a "logic of appropriateness" that may not be intersubjectively transmissible, but yet is very real to the members of the party. The party activists do know what it means to be a Republican, or to be a Progressive Conservative, and they generally know when one of their members is stepping outside the bounds of acceptable

[5] More recently Willie Brown, now mayor of San Francisco, defined a Democrat as anyone who voted Democratic.

political behavior (for an excellent account of the values of Conservative Party activists in Britain see Whiteley et al., 1994).

It is also clear that parties vary over time in their degree of institutionalization (see Panebianco, 1988). When the political conflicts and tensions are familiar, and are along the dimensions in which the parties were originally formed, political parties tend to be more capable of maintaining their institutional structures and values than when there are unexpected and unfamiliar challenges. For example, in the United States, the shift of major dimensions of political cleavage from economic policy to social and cultural issues (abortion, school prayer, etc.) has unhinged the party structures to some extent. Much of this ideological debate has been played out within the Republican Party, and that often vociferous debate had some impact on their presidential fortunes during the 1990s and the first part of the twenty-first century.[6]

The preceding discussion has concentrated on the level of institutionalization of more traditional political parties. The proportion of votes going to these parties has been declining in most political systems. Their appeal has to some extent been replaced by "flash parties" that are organized around a single issue or a single individual, and may not persist for more than one or two elections (Selb, 2010; Lago, 2011). These parties are unlikely to become institutionalized in any meaningful way, but rather respond to short-term opportunities.

The structure of individual parties is an interesting feature of the conduct of politics in virtually all countries, but it tells only part of the story. The individual parties function within party systems, and these systems also have some institutional features. Party systems tend to be structural and relatively stable, so that if an individual party ceases to exist for some reason, there may be a replacement that occupies the niche held by the failing party. In this way, party systems are not dissimilar to the "organizational ecologies" that are the center of population ecology models of organizations in sociological institutionalism and some studies of interest groups (Hannan and Freeman, 1989; Gray and Lowery, 1996a). That is, these ecologies define "niches" that provide opportunities for individual parties.

Further, the nature of the party system tends to define the limits of behavior of the individual members of the system. For example, a political party in an extreme multiparty system cannot act like a vote-maximizing, centripetal party typical of two party systems if it hopes to survive. Further, existing political parties and the structure of cleavages may create niches for certain types of parties, but not others, and the cooperation among some parties, but not others, in coalition governments also creates opportunities for the formation of new parties.

---

[6] It may be that a candidate who can be nominated by the party may not be able to win the general election, and vice versa, given the disparities between the views of Republican activists and the voting population in general. Republicans in Congress, on the other hand, tend to be very similar ideologically.

Finally, the party systems are to some extent determined by yet another institutional aspect of a political system—electoral laws. There is a well-established relationship between the way in which members of legislative bodies are elected and the number of parties that function within the system (Taagapera and Shugart, 1989; Reilly, 2001). Electoral laws can be manipulated and with the legal changes in the party system can produce desired outcomes in party systems. For example, the two-party system of New Zealand has been transformed into a multiparty system by a simple change in the electoral law in the mid-1990s (Denemark, 1997).

The way in which party systems do function as institutions can be seen by examining some of the major models of party systems. For example, Giovanni Sartori (1976) argued that party systems in Western democracies tended to come in three types: two-party, limited multiparty, and extreme multiparty. This classification was an extension of Maurice Duverger's earlier (1951) analysis that the only meaningful difference was between two-party and multiparty systems. Sartori instead argued that the dynamics and impacts of limited multiparty systems such as that of Sweden are significantly different from those of more extreme multiparty systems such as in the French Fourth Republic (Chapsal, 1969) or in post-war Italy (Farneti, 1985; Pridham, 1988). The moderate multiparty system has two poles (usually left–right), just as a two-party system does, so that the electoral contest is actually between two blocs: five or more parties engage in the campaign but the underlying dynamics of the party system are those of a two-party system (Lewin, 1988).

Richard Katz and Peter Mair (2009) have argued that many contemporary political party systems have become "cartel party" systems in which the parties become closely linked to the State. The argument is that because of the party funding coming directly from public sources, the parties become closely linked to State and may come to represent the interests of the State to the public, rather than vice versa.

Party systems do differ in their degrees of institutionalization. Some such as that of the United States have persisted for many decades with little or no change, while others have undergone significant transformations, for example Italy. Although some more fundamental political changes are reflected in the transformations of party systems, the relative ease of change may also reflect differences in electoral laws that may provide greater opportunities for new parties to break into the parliament and establish themselves as viable options for voters.

In summary, political parties themselves, as well as party systems, have many of the characteristics of institutions. The individual parties persist over time and they also create a "logic of appropriateness" for individuals within the party. Parties also are the loci of various attempts to use discourse to shape party platforms and their political strategies. Similarly, party systems also have a good degree of path dependence and affect the behavior of the parties that comprise them. These structures are perhaps not the first things we might think of political institutions but that does not prevent their actually being institutions.

Interest Intermediation

Political parties demonstrate a number of institutional characteristics, but the literature on interest intermediation, and the linkage of interest groups with the state, provides an even richer setting for a structural analysis of political organizations. There has been a rich Anglo-American literature dealing with relationship of groups with government institutions that extends back for decades (Finer, 1958; Freeman, 1965; Latham, 1965). Although not explicitly institutionalist, the traditional conceptualizations of interest group behavior did examine the structure of relationships between groups and government (see Baumgartner and Leech, 1998). Concepts such as "iron triangles" in that literature definitely implied a formal and persistent interaction of groups and government in making and implementing public policies that corresponded to the usual definitions of an institution.

More recently the literature on interest groups has been enlivened by the inclusion of the concept of corporatism (Schmitter, 1974; Molina and Rhodes, 2002), corporate pluralism (Rokkan, 1966; Heisler, 1979), and the numerous other characterizations of corporatism developed in the literature (Cawson, 1985; Williamson, 1985; Streeck, 1991). Again, although there was not an explicit institutional analysis contained within corporatism, there was clearly a structural relationship between government and interest organizations in the society that is central to the analysis. Schmitter's definition of corporatism, for example, included features such as "hierarchical" and "unitary" that posited a stable, formalized pattern of interaction between state and societal actors. Other characterizations, for example Stein Rokkan's descriptions (1966; see also Olsen, 1983) of corporate pluralism in Scandinavia, also demonstrate a stable pattern of interaction with mutual expectations about performance among the participants.

The pattern of state–society interactions within corporatism, and all its variants, could be interpreted through a variety of institutionalist perspectives. For example, given that the stable relationship between the groups and government could be seen to be rational for both sets of actors, this could be seen as a manifestation of rational choice, with rules and incentives developed to institutionalize the constraints on behavior. The stable pattern of interaction permits rational calculations by the participants, and (as in game-theoretic versions of institutions more generally) also creates mutual constraints on the possible behavior of the participants in the interactions so that defections from agreements are less likely.

There are also some elements of the normative version of institutionalism, given that the continued interaction of the "partners" may create some sense of appropriate forms of behavior in the relationships. Kvavik (1980), for example, described the pattern of behavioral expectations that existed in the advisory committees in Norwegian government—a major component of Norwegian corporate pluralism. Representatives of constituent organizations are expected to cooperate with other organizations and to work toward a general consensus, rather than defend their own interests at all costs. More recently, those values can be identified in the emergence of institutions analogous to corporatism in some post-communist systems. This "appropriate behavior" might well be in opposition to the apparent economic self-interest of these participants. That characterization, however, might hold only if the "game" were conceived of as a single iteration; building trust and cooperation over many iterations of the game may be a better long-term strategy.

Even more recently there has been a greater concern with the interrelationships among those interest groups themselves, and how groups of organizations interact to influence the public sector, in part as corporatism itself declines (Hermansson et al., 1997). The dominant conceptualization of the interrelationship between state and society has become that of "networks" (Knoke and Laumann, 1987; Rhodes, 1997; Sorensen and Torfing, 2007) or "communities" of various sorts (Sabatier, 1988; Haas, 1992; Thomas, 1997). In these ideas concerning the policy-making process, government organizations are only a few of the large number of relatively equal participants, rather than being the central actor in the drama.

The terms "network" and "community" are sometimes used interchangeably but there does appear to be some analytic utility in differentiating the terms. As usually discussed, the concept of a policy "community" appears analogous to normative institutionalism, with the possession of common values defining membership in the community. Likewise, the idea of an epistemic community appears closely related to discursive models of institutionalism. On the other hand, the idea of a network is often more mechanical defining membership through interactions. In the institutional terms being used here, this version of network analysis is more sociological, with structure being defined relationally and cognitively.

Especially in the sociological versions of network analysis the outcome of the interaction between public and private organizations is indeterminate, with public sector organizations enjoying little or no special position in these structures. Further, these interactions are definitely conceived of as structural relationships, with the several participants interacting on a predictable and regularized basis (Carrington et al., 2002). Indeed, the sociological interpretations of networks tend to utilize structural analogies very heavily, with mathematical models being used to represent the structural relationships among the actors involved in the network (Knoke, 1990).

What Is an Institution?

As we have noted above, these bodies of literature on parties and interest intermediation contain only limited original and independent theoretical perspectives on institutions and organizations. That having been said, however, there are some interesting questions that arise concerning the nature and definition of these entities as institutions. In the first place, there is the question of what sort of political organizations constitute a political party. The contrast between political parties and interest groups has been articulated for some time in terms of the difference between organizations that attempt to capture political office and those that only attempt to influence policy.

The growth of social movements from the 1970s onward has, however, made the distinction between parties and interest groups somewhat less clear (Della Porta and Diani, 2006). These organizations attempt to influence policy in the way that interest groups traditionally have, but they also at times will engage in electoral politics. The Greens in European politics, for example, have remained ideologically committed to goals beyond simply holding office while at the same time running candidates for elective office (Thaa, 1994).

The other interesting and crucial definitional question is the status of the more socially or theoretically constructed institutions, for example epistemic communities (see also p. 149) and policy networks (Galaskiewicz, 1985; Sorensen and Torfing, 2007). It is clear that individual interest groups and political parties can be conceptualized as institutions, or at least as organizations. It is much less obvious to the casual observer that amorphous entities that can be identified only by interviewing large numbers of their member organizations, or through monitoring patterns of interactions among organizations, and/or between interest organizations and government, can be said to comprise institutions in the usual meaning of the term.

It is possible, however, to make a strong case for the institutional status of networks and communities. First, there is substantial stability in their interactions, with the same groups tending to play their part in the same networks year after year. Second, there are patterns of expectation and predictability in this behavior; interest groups expect to be consulted and government organizations may even depend upon those organizations for information and advice in policy-making. Finally, there are some common values existing within many of these structures. "Epistemic communities" that tend to share common perspectives on policy, generally based on their common scientific expertise, are especially important for governments as a continuing source of advice, if sometimes also a source of irritation.

For political parties the construct of party systems also raises questions about the definition of an institution. In many cases these collections of political organizations are basically stable, even if the individual parties may come and go. For example, even in multiparty systems with substantial creations and dissolutions of parties, the number of "niches" for parties remains relatively constant. For example, the Danish party system has had a number of political parties at all times in the post-war period, and there have been a number of new parties formed, but the number of parties gaining representation has been roughly constant.

As with almost all the forms of institutions we have been discussing, there are differences among different structures in the extent to which they conform to definitions of institutions. For example, we would expect networks in policy areas that have been functioning for a longer time to be, everything else being equal, more likely to be "institutionalized" than those in newer policy areas. Take, for example, agriculture policy in almost every developed democracy. This policy area has long been a concern of government and given that the fundamental purpose of the industry and some of the basic technology (growing plants and animals) has not changed the patterns that have been built up over years can persist. If, however, we consider a policy area such as biotechnology that has to some extent evolved from agriculture, the level of institutionalization of the actors is substantially less. This is true for the official government actors as well as groups (see Rhinard, 2010).

Where Do Institutions Come From?

I will not take up the challenge of explaining the formation of individual interest groups here, there being a large and often contentious literature on that subject.[7] The question of importance here is, instead, how do groups that previously existed interact to form stable structural arrangements among themselves, as well as between government organizations and those aggregations of groups. This is in itself a formidable research task, and for some versions of network and community models the formation of stable collective structures remains a central research question (see Kickert et al., 1997).

The corporatist model offers several alternative models of formation, and this characteristic is central to the typification of the interactions between state and society. Schmitter (1974) distinguishes between "state" corporatism and "societal" corporatism. In the former model, typical of Iberian variants of corporate structures, the state initiates the process of forming corporate relationships, and encourages or demands that interest groups join with it to stabilize policy-making in an area. In the most extreme cases, the state may actually mandate the creation of an interest group to assist it in organizing that sector of society.[8] In this case interest groups have no meaningful autonomy from the state and are largely extensions of the public sector.

Network formation is usually conceptualized as a more autonomous process, to the extent that it is conceptualized at all (see Klijn, 2001). Most studies of networks begin in the middle and identify the nature of an existing network and how it functions with little or no concern about the origins of the structure. The policy community literature (again especially the epistemic community literature) has somewhat more to say about this issue. This is especially true given that it is based on common scientific or professional understanding and training, but even then the process of identification of common interests and developing interactions is largely left undiscussed in the theories.

We appear to be left largely with a literature on the formation of individual interest groups writ large, with the principal option offered being action by one or more

7 This literature is influenced heavily by Olson (1965) and the responses of Frohlich, Oppenheimer, and Young (1971).

8 This is not found only in state corporatism but also in pluralist regimes such as the United States where government has needed to regularize behavior in an area.

entrepreneurs to create a viable network. The creation and institutionalization of networks appears as a crucial theoretical and methodological challenge because it is necessary to be able to say when there is sufficient interaction and sufficient stability for the network to persist.

The major alternative to reliance on individual entrepreneurs for an explanation of the formation of networks is that the political dynamics of contemporary states are the source of the creation of those structures. The basic argument here is that states increasingly utilize the private sector, especially for the implementation of policy but also for policy formulation and policy advice (see, for example, Peters, 1997a). For example, many important public sector programs such as labor market policies, and many aspects of the personal social services, increasingly are delivered through private sector organizations (Salamon, 1995). This is to some degree a political necessity to reduce costs and the nominal size of the public sector, but it is also a recognition of the capacity of this type of organization to deliver services efficiently and effectively.

The increasing use of the private sector means to implement policy and to provide policy expertise means in turn that governments are often in the business of creating, or at least encouraging the creation of, interests groups and networks of groups (Walker, 1983). This may not be as overt, and certainly not as Draconian, as the process described above for state corporatism but there is a role for government in the process. In some cases, governments attempt to create pressure groups for segments of the society that have been difficult to organize. For example, a number of social programs have provided funding for the less affluent portions of the population to organize and participate in the policy process concerning their neighborhoods.

The literature on political parties is somewhat less clear about the formation of parties than is that on interest groups and their initial construction.[9] The assumption appears to be that of individual entrepreneurship or at least that the actions of a small group of people are crucial for the formation of parties. For example, in the United Kingdom the "Gang of Four"[10] was responsible for splitting off from the Labour Party and creating the Social Democratic Party in 1981. As political parties are being formed in the countries of the former Eastern bloc countries there are a number of examples of individuals promoting themselves through the creation of an institutionalized political party. At the extreme, individuals such as Jean Marie Le Pen in France, Pim Fortuyn in the Netherlands, and Mogens Glistrup have used a political party (or the shell of one) to promote their own highly personal views about politics.

---

9 A major book on how political parties organize (Katz and Mair, 1994), for example, hardly mentions the initial formation of parties but concentrates on change.

10 These were Ray Jenkins, Shirley Williams, David Owen, and Bill Rogers all of whom had held positions of responsibility in Labour governments. See Crewe and King (1995).

The alternative approach to explaining the creation of political parties appears to be one of opportunity structures (Kitschelt, 1989; Arzheimer and Carter, 2006). That is, the distribution of political cleavages and political views in a country may create an obvious opportunity for a political party to seize a share of the vote. This may occur even without major changes in the electoral system, as when the Labour Party replaced the Liberals as one of the two major parties after the end of World War I. Likewise, the rapid emergence of issues cross-cutting the existing party system creates opportunities for new parties to challenge existing parties. For example, in Denmark and several other countries, first resistance to taxation (Wickman, 1977) and later concerns over immigration produced a succession of new parties. Those two explanations for party formation are actually more complementary than they are contradictory. Even with adequate or even exceptional levels of entrepreneurship, there may be little possibility for development of enduring parties without the existence of political circumstances conducive to the survival of those parties. Likewise, political opportunities may not be able to generate enduring parties without strong leadership to seize the opportunity—Mogens Glistrup in the Danish example mentioned above. Party systems thus may have a substantial degree of persistence even in the face of major environmental change.

How Do Parties and Party Systems Change?

If the arguments concerning the formation of interest groups, and particularly political parties, are somewhat underdeveloped, there is a somewhat stronger body of literature on the change of these institutions. The change literature in the area of political parties and party systems is particularly well-developed. At one level individual parties change much as other organizations and institutions do. These organizations' change can be seen as changing as their internal "logic of appropriateness" changes; the rightward move of many parties of the political left during the 1980s and 1990s demonstrates that type of adaptation to environmental change (Bell and Criddle, 1988; Shaw, 1996). Similarly, from a more sociological perspective this can be seen as a reaction to a major transformation of the environment within which these institutions function.

As well as the individual parties' changes, entire systems of parties can change. The conventional wisdom has been (Dalton et al., 1984) that there has been substantial dealignment, and a good deal of realignment, in party systems in the industrialized democracies. More recently, Peter Mair (1997) has discussed a variety of approaches to change in the party systems of Western Europe. These changes connect the transformation of individual parties with changes in the aggregation of parties, and with changes in the socioeconomic cleavage system that supports the party system. Mair argues that most party systems have been characterized by greater stability of these systems. Indeed, his analysis points to an *institutionalization* of parties and cleavages. There are a number of flash parties that may last for one or two elections that appear to alter the nature of party systems, but the basic structures in fact have remained relatively stable.

Further, as we have been demonstrating throughout this analysis, other theoretical approaches to institutions that we have been discussing can be applied easily to the analysis of parties and interest groups. For example, groups and even more clearly political parties have logics of appropriateness that link the institutions with the behavior of their members. Most of those organizations do impart to their members a sense of what they should and should not believe in, and how they should behave politically.[11] Some varieties of interest groups also can be understood through this "logic of appropriateness," especially attitudinal groups that are based on agreement on values (e.g., ecology) rather than on economic interests.

Rational choice theory could also be applied to the analysis of parties and networks. For example, beginning with Anthony Downs's (1957) original application of rational choice analysis to American political parties there has been a growing body of literature using that approach (Strom, 1990b; Müller, 2000). This research has attempted to explain the behavior of individual parties, as well as the dynamics of party systems, in terms of the rational calculations of voters and party leaders. In the applications of these models in the American context they tend to focus on "median voters,"[12] and the attempts of parties to position themselves so as to align their position with that of that median voter. In the West European context there has been a greater emphasis on the matching of party positions with the numerous opportunities created by social cleavages (Lane and Ersson, 1994), but an almost identical rational choice logic has been applied (Galeotti, 1991).

Perspectives on changes within a constellation of interest groups also depend in part on the initial intellectual perspective adopted with respect to these organizations. For example, if the initial perspective is corporatism then change occurs through the interactions of the involved groups and actors in the public sector; this is a substantially more State-centric conception of these interactions than is found in many other approaches, for example pluralism. Likewise, if the perspective on interest groups being utilized is that of networks then change will be conceptualized as a result of the interactions of the various components of the network, both public and private. This view of change is more organic and depends upon the mutual adaptation of the members of the networks, without the validation of a state actor. One or more state organizations may be involved but they will be only (relatively) equal partners in the network.

---

[11] Some "catchall parties" that attempt to be sufficiently broad to take in a wide range of political beliefs in order to win elections do not so clearly impart such a sense of appropriateness.

[12] The argument is that the median voter defines the center of gravity of the electorate so that parties in a two-party system will attempt to develop policies that appeal to that voter.

Basic Social Mechanisms

Although political parties, party systems, and networks of interest groups do have some characteristics of institutions, as discussed above, there appears to be little distinctive in the dynamics of these institutions. Political parties are in many ways simply organizations, so that people may join them for the same reasons that people join other organizations. Similarly, these organizations may be able to create some meaning for their members and hence to institutionalize in a manner that will enable them to persist and transmit values.

The dynamics of networks and amorphous structures such as party systems, corporatism, and networks are somewhat more difficult to identify. However, a good deal of contemporary organization theory (Dimaggio and Powell, 1991; Gibbons, 2004) focuses on the impact of organizational fields on the behavior of the individual components of the field, and party systems and networks are certainly analogous to these patterns. Todd La Porte (1996) has, for example, developed a detailed analysis of the dynamics of networks, pointing out the variety of forms that the internal relationships of the actors may take and their impacts on the behavior of the actors.

The Good Institution

The notion of a good institution in this collection of institutional studies is rather similar to that found in the empirical studies of institutions. That is, a good institution is one that is effective in doing what it is supposed to do. In this case, however, the expectations are perhaps not as clear as they are for presidential or parliamentary governments. For political parties, for example, a good institution may be one which is capable of winning elections if that party is operating in a party system that permits one party actually capturing government. In party systems that contain more parties the good party may be one that is capable of sustaining the commitment of that portion of the distribution of voters that they have represented.

If we move from the level of the individual party to the performance of party systems then we should think of performance in terms of their representative function. How well does the party system translate the values and political preferences of the population into active political parties? In some ways two party systems perform this function rather poorly; the need to compromise so extensively within the individual parties may result in their being incapable of representing diverse social groups and ideas effectively. Of course, performing well on this criterion may make it impossible to perform the function of choosing and creating governments.

Peter Mair (1997) and Richard Katz (1990) have argued that in many contemporary political systems this apparent conflict between the representative and governmental roles of parties has resulted in the development of "cartel party" systems. In this model, the dominant parties have an interest in maintaining their positions and may have less real interest in responding to voters if that will hurt their position as members of the cartel. Further, parties to some extent, therefore, are co-opted by their role in State functions and cease being societal actors. Thus, for the parties themselves, success is their continuing membership in the "club."[13]

For networks of interest groups quality can be assessed in several ways. One measure of quality is the capacity of networks to aggregate the preferences of the individual groups forming the larger aggregation. One of the functions typically assigned to political parties is interest aggregation, or bringing together a variety of potentially competing interests into a mutually acceptable resolution of differences (Almond and Powell, 1967). Unfortunately, the literature on networks does not appear particularly successful at, or even interested in, explaining resolution of the conflicts that appear inevitable within these aggregations of numerous interest groups (see Dowding, 1995). Thus, it appears that although networks should be capable of providing some level of interest aggregation within networks it is more the exception than the rule in practice.

The corporatist model of interest intermediation provides a somewhat more effective, but also more restrictive, account of the aggregation problem, and potential, in politics. The tripartite bargaining characteristic of the conventional corporatist model (Schmitter, 1974) implies a smaller number of actors involved in bargaining, with government functioning as something of a lead player bringing together the conflicting views of the two economic actors. That role as "honest broker" may be undermined in situations in which the government of the day is identified closely with one of the economic actors, for example a Social Democratic party being allied with labor unions in most party systems. That having been said, however, corporatist arrangements tend to be characteristic of consensual political systems in which governments of the day do not maximize their own short-term gains but rather attempt to maintain some continuity in policies.

The final way in which this aggregative requirement for parties and networks could be met is through the "corporate pluralist" system, in which a larger array of interest groups are brought together to negotiate agreements among themselves and with government. As noted, this model is based on the experience of the Scandinavian countries in which the consensual norms of those countries often produce long negotiations before an agreement acceptable to all is reached. While this is model has been extremely effective in that context, it is not clear how general that experience can be. Relatively few countries have such inclusive norms, so that the more likely outcome would be closer to imposition than to consensus.

Summary and Conclusion

It is clear that political parties and interest groups are organizations and that their structural features are important for explaining their performance within the

[13] This logic bears some resemblance to Michels's famous "Iron Law of Oligarchy," although in this case the actors are parties rather than individuals within parties or other organizations.

political system. It appears reasonable, therefore, to discuss them in institutional terms, just as we have been doing for legislatures or public bureaucracies. The real question, however, is whether there is anything distinctive about the concepts utilized to analyze these structures, or whether they are better understood through the more general approaches such as normative institutionalism that we have used for other organizations.

The best answer to the above question is that both possibilities are true. On the one hand, there are some approaches (especially to interest groups) that are distinctive and that distinguish the study of these organizations for making inputs into the political system from other sets of organizations. For example, although the logic of network analysis is applicable to a range of issues it is largely applied to interest groups. Similarly, the concept of party systems is of little utility outside the study of parties, although it might be applied to some other populations of organizations.

On the other hand, it can be seen that these organizations are little different from others involved in government and politics. As Gatlin (1968) argued some time ago that ". . . a political theory of political parties can hardly be said to exist." There is a tradition of analyzing political parties in organizational terms, as Michels did rather early in the history of the study of political parties. Political parties have many of the characteristics of bureaucracies, and interest groups also can be conceptualized as rather conventional organizations that simply happen to be in the business of attempting to influence public policy. Some of the same logic of populations of organizations applies to these groups as they do to market organizations like newspapers and restaurants.

While discussing these organizations and sets of organizations, as institutions as institutions may appear to stretch the concept in a rather unconscionable manner, there is also good justification for this approach. It appears that there can be some conceptual gains from understanding these components of the political process through an institutional lens. That lens by no means answers all the questions about political parties and interest groups, but it does help to advance the inquiry.

CHAPTER 9

International Institutionalism

The final version of institutionalism we will discuss will be analyzed under the rubric of "international institutionalism." We argued at the outset of this book that institutional thinking is pervading the social sciences (particularly political science). It appears that a version of institutional analysis can be detected very clearly in the international relations literature. This area might have been the last place to expect such a development, given the apparent absence of enforceable rules, and the seeming absence of internalized "logics of appropriateness" that could guide and constrain actors in most situations. At the risk of raising the fearsome specter of realism[1] in international relations theory, it appeared easier to argue that actors would be guided by national interest in international politics rather than by more collective values. The alternative view that nation states would be steered by the structural constraints of international political life we have been discussing with respect to institutionalism in other parts of the political system often appears excessively optimistic.

Before the analysis becomes carried away with the apparent anarchy of international politics (Axelrod and Keohane, 1986; Lake, 2001), one should remember that there are indeed some formalized rules and structures that do shape interactions in this arena and that also help to provide some structure and interpretative meaning to this dimension of politics (see Snidal, 1994). All the discussion of globalization in the international system does not mean that the system that has emerged is not to some extent steered by international institutions and organizations (Goldstein et al., 2007).

These factors can be seen at work most readily at the level of regional political organizations. Organizations such as the European Union (and even the more loosely structured North American Free Trade Association (NAFTA) and Association of South-East Asian Nations (ASEAN)) function as the effective governments for at least some aspects of the lives of their member states, and for the individual citizens within those states (Aspinwall and Schneider, 1999; Väyrynen, 2003; Peters, 2010).

[1] The last thing I want to do is to engage in another sterile debate concerning realism (Morgenthau, 1948), neorealism (Waltz, 1979), and all their variations in international relations. This point is made simply because of the popularity of this theoretical view of the international system.

The growing power of the European Union has been especially apparent as it virtually assumed control over economic policy from member states such as Greece and Ireland after the economic crisis that began in 2008. These institutional arrangements then produce complex multilevel governance arrangements (Jachtenfuchs, 2001), which the individual actors may find difficult to control.

At an even more international level the increasing importance of the World Trade Organization (WTO) for the economic lives of almost all countries is further evidence of the existence of some variety of international framework for governance. In addition, the continuing power of the International Monetary Fund in monetary policy and the World Bank for many developing countries add to the importance of international institutions for governance. Although the power of the economic institutions is most apparent, there are also important international organizations (institutions) in many areas such as health (WHO), Agriculture (FAO), and education (UNESCO).

Even with the existence of a number of international organizations, does it really make sense to conceptualize international politics through a structural or institutional framework? I will be arguing that this is already being done, and has been done for some time (see Krasner, 1983; Keohane, 1989; Rittberger, 1993). The underlying logics of several approaches to international politics are perfectly compatible with the institutionalist thinking we have been reviewing to this point, in this book.

The major barrier to integrating the perspective more closely appears to be the different languages that are used to describe some of the same phenomena, the different intellectual roots of the different components of the discipline, and some resistance (as described above) to think of international politics as having the capacity for enforcement of rules thought essential to institutional analysis. Even given this general tendency of international relations scholars to utilize their own vocabulary, several of these scholars have begun to employ terms such as "institution" more freely, even when not discussing conventional international organizations and also to conceptualize international politics in more institutional terms (Young, 1991, 1994; Milner, 1993, p. 494; Pevehouse, 2002).

This chapter will be an attempt to point out the similarities in these different components of political science, and then to ask the same set of questions of the international relations version of institutionalism that has been asked of the other versions. The major burden of the chapter is to substantiate the argument that institutional logics are applicable and useful for analysis of international politics. The second major point to be considered is if and when the particular characteristics of international politics may require some modification and refinement of the basic modes of institutional analysis that have been developed for domestic politics.

The International System as Institution

Having made the rash assertion that some common perspectives on international politics could be integrated with the other versions of institutional analysis, I will now attempt to make the case more completely and convincingly. At a minimal level, I could easily argue that there are international organizations that possess all features of an organization, or an institution, existing at other levels of analysis. These institutions and organizations can be discussed effectively utilizing several of the approaches to institutions we have already discussed (Kratochwil and Ruggie, 1986; Keohane, 1988; Wendt, 1992). Thus, just as rational choice approaches and normative institutionalism can be applied to interest groups and political parties (pp. 118ff.), these same approaches can be applied to international organizations.

Even though we can visualize how the models would fit the institutional approach, skeptics would argue that the models really do not fit the approach adequately. The usual critique of international institutions is that their rules are not enforceable externally as are those of other government organizations. Short of the use of force there is almost no means to ensure that the rules or guidelines of an international organization are enforced. On the other hand, their internal rules are as viable as those promulgated by other structures, and the internal impact of rules tends to be the principal defining characteristic of institutions. Further, as international organizations have become more important in economic policy areas their rules can be enforced by the utilization of economic sanctions, without having to resort to using force.

Examining several international organizations can demonstrate how these theories could be applied. The International Monetary Fund (IMF), for example, can be seen as displaying a clearly articulated and internalized "logic of appropriateness" that it acts like a bank rather than an international aid organization, and therefore imposes rather tough-minded economic criteria on its would-be creditors (Clark, 1996; Pauly, 1997; Woods, 2004). Likewise, a game theorist could easily conceptualize the interactions of the IMF and national monetary policymakers as an iterative game, very much like the national budgeting games described above when discussing rational choice theory (pp. 58ff.). Policymakers at the national level realize that they must be completely open and frank with the representatives of the IMF when negotiating loans. The national policymakers may be able to extract desirable terms by less than complete openness one time, but institutional memories at the IMF are long and they might not be able to negotiate with the organization effectively in the future if they have been devious in the past.

Analyzing international organizations in an institutional framework does not present any overwhelmingly difficult intellectual challenges. It is, however, a greater challenge to think about the interaction of nation states operating in the international arena within the institutionalist framework. We will be arguing that some aspects of regime theory, and some aspects of cognitive approaches to international relations, can be made to correspond with the general framework of institutional analysis.

These theories of international politics assume that there is some continuing pattern of interaction among the participants in a regime, and they also assume that there is the development of some common patterns of meanings and interpretations among those actors (see Kratochwil and Ruggie, 1986, p. 767).[2] These actors may be in adversarial relationships with one another, as well as in cooperative arrangements. The actors in most game-theoretic models of institutions (see pp. 57ff.) also are assumed to be pursuing somewhat competitive goals; if they were not, there would be little reason for the game. Indeed, game theory is applied even more frequently in international relations, and some of the games developed in that research tradition themselves also appear to have many general properties of institutions (Zürn, 1993), for example stability and repetitive behavior.

As well as being continuous, interactions in the international arena also demonstrate the existence of some structure. Again, although the word "anarchic" is sometimes utilized to describe international politics, there is more cooperation, and there are more rules and more structure than is sometimes admitted or understood by people outside those operating within the international regimes (Oye, 1986; Cortrell and Davis, 2000). Some of those rules are imposed by international organizations and treaties, but other rules are imposed upon themselves by the states that participate.

The rules promulgated by regimes are accepted by states in order to reduce their own transaction costs, as well as the unpredictability that otherwise would plague interactions among sovereign states in the stereotypical world of international politics (Hasenclever et al., 1997, pp. 37ff.). National actors are willing to accept some constraints on their own behavior in order to ensure that there are equal constraints on their adversaries (or even their friends). The dance of diplomacy continues even when nation states are very much opposed to each other on some fundamental issues. Even more than in domestic politics, any breakdown of these patterned interactions may have significant negative consequences for the actors involved, so there are strong incentives to maintain the normative integration of international regimes even in the face of adversarial relations among the participants in the regime.

Regime Theory as Institutional Theory

The most obvious candidate for discussion as institutionalism in international relations is regime theory (Keohane and Nye, 1977; Keohane, 1989; Hasenclever et al., 1996). Regime theory has its roots in American international relations scholarship in the early 1980s. The underlying motivation was to develop a concept that would capture the patterned interactions that were increasingly observable in international politics. Several different concepts of the regime emerged at that time, and debate over the most appropriate conceptualization continues to flourish among international relations scholars (see Davis, 2009). There has, in fact, been a substantial debate over the nature of regimes with the American international relations community (Krasner, 1983), as well as between American scholars and their European

---

[2] There is also a substantial literature on urban regimes, using much of the same logic to describe the interaction of actors in local government settings (Stone, 1989; Pierre, 1991; Popadopoulos, 1996), including the development of common patterns of meaning.

counterparts (Mueller, 1993; Rittberger, 1993). We will now proceed to look at regime theory through the lens of the several questions we have been asking about all forms of institutionalism.

As we go through this discussion of regime theory, we will also be concerned with the extent to which this body as theory offers distinctive insights into political behavior. There are some elements of regime analysis that appear very similar to broader theoretical approaches in political science. Hasenclever, Mayer, and Rittberger (1997), for example, argue that regime theories can be classified as interest-based, power-based, and knowledge-based. Each of those broad categories also contains several versions of the approach. This classification is not dissimilar to classifications of sociological institutional theory.

The above classification of regimes also points to the ways in which regime theory is similar to the versions of institutionalism found in other areas of the discipline. For example, the emphasis on common values and understandings as the method for defining regimes could be considered simply an international version of the normative institutionalism of March and Olsen (see pp. 28ff.), and there are some conspicuous attempts to relate rational choice analysis to regime theory (Snidal, 1991; Kydd and Snidal, 1993). The cognitive approach to international regimes is not dissimilar to that already encountered in sociological institutionalism. Is there, therefore, a distinctive regime theory, or is international institutionalism just a manifestation of other versions of institutionalism, albeit operating at a different level of analysis?

What Is an Institution?

In this chapter "What is an institution?" means "What is a regime?" A second question is "Do the characteristics of a regime correspond to the variables used elsewhere to define a political institution of a more generic nature?" There are various definitions of a regime in the international relations literature. Puchala and Hopkins (1983) offered a minimalist definition, speaking of regimes as "patterned behavior." That definition almost certainly encompasses in too much territory; habitual war-making might well be patterned behavior, while the current thrust of regime theory appears to be to provide a means of conceptualizing international politics in a more cooperative manner than has been characteristic of this subdiscipline.

There are also definitions of international regimes based upon rules and the behavior of nations, definitions in many ways analogous to those found in rational choice versions of institutionalism. In particular, Robert Keohane (1989, p. 4) defines regimes as:

> . . . institutions with specific rules, agreed upon by governments, that pertain to particular sets of issues in international politics.

This is a much more demanding definition than that offered by Puchala and Hopkins. In particular, the demand that governments explicitly agree upon a set of rules is a condition that may not be satisfied in many policy areas that appear to have operational regimes. And even if its criteria are met, the rules may be understood and accepted only by the one segment of a government directly concerned with the policy, rather than government as a more collective entity. Modern states are segmented along policy lines and their relationships with international regimes and organizations—even the European Union—may also be segmented.

Probably the prevailing definition of an international regime was provided by Stephen Krasner (1983, p. 2). Krasner defines a regime as:

> . . . implicit or explicit principles norms, rules and decision-making procedures around which actors' expectations converge in a given area of international relations.

Like many definitions designed to mediate differences between pitched intellectual camps, this definition appears to raise as many questions as it settles. For example, how important is it that the rules that govern a regime be explicit? Or is it sufficient that we can say after the fact that rules of some sort appeared to be governing the behavior of states or other relevant actors involved in the putative regime? A concentration on explicit rules leads to excessive formalism, and acceptance of possibly meaningless rules as evidence that a regime is in place in the international arena.

On the other hand, too great an emphasis on the *ex post facto* interpretation of behavior makes falsification difficult. As Haggard and Simmons (1987) have pointed out, that sort of definition may merely be a tautology; we would define regimes by observed behavior and then later use the existence of a regime to explain the same behavior. Similarly, cognitive definitions relying upon shared understandings among the participants (see Kratochwil and Ruggie, 1986) encounter the same problems of circularity. Again, the existence of a common set of perceptions is used both to define and to explain behavior within a regime. These same problems arise in other versions of institutionalism that are built on rules (see pp. 52ff.), but appear somewhat more severe here because of the level of analysis. That is, assessing and measuring the behavior of a state in international politics is, *ceteris paribus*, more difficult than looking at that of the individual members of a single organization in the more constrained arena of national politics.

In addition, the number of influences on the behavior of a state in international politics may be greater than in conventional domestic politics, and therefore assigning causation to the influence of a rather amorphous set of regime values may be suspect. In a number of policy areas that are argued to be regimes, especially when defined as areas of public concern, observed patterns of uniform behavior may have more to do with economic conditions or professional domination than with the existence of a functioning international regime. The actual political dynamics in these settings may emanate from national level actors who desire to ensure the perpetuation of their own well-being rather through the rules of behavior created and imposed by a regime.

Although it does raise questions of causation, basing regime theory on particular policy areas may be a substantial contribution toward understanding the dynamics of regimes. Each policy area tends to be influenced by a set of professional and substantive norms that define what is good policy and good behavior in that regime. This is also true for institutions and organizations that may be defined by their ideas and by their connections with professional standards.

One of the more interesting approaches to understanding the formation and implementation of norms in international politics is the concept of "epistemic communities" (Adler, 1992; Haas, 1992; 1993). These communities are conceptualized as agreements on certain fundamental bodies of knowledge that can then function as a mechanism for pressing those professional and scientific views onto government. These structures (regimes?) are the rough equivalents of the policy communities and networks encountered in domestic politics, and already discussed in reference to the institutions of interest intermediation (see Chapter 8). The difference here is that there is agreement across countries among the participants so that there would be relatively common reactions of national governments. That common reaction depends in part, however, on the ability of scientists and other professionals to influence their national governments.

The definition of regimes as occurring within policy areas lowers some of the barriers to the creation and acceptance of international regimes. Rather than having to develop sweeping norms of behavior that would bind nations across a range of policy concerns, nations or even segments of governments, could (within the bounds of the theory) be components of a regime. Organizations in government might cooperate with components of the private sector in their policy area, and with components of subnational governments also working in that area. Some of the same coordination and cooperation could also exist with international organizations in areas such as health (WHO, Pan American Health Organization, PAHO, etc.), economic management (IMF, Organisation for Economic Co-operation and Development, OECD), or almost anything else that governments do. Thus, national governments become the means for "suturing" (Hirst and Thompson, 1996) together a series of actors within a regime, although the content of the regime may be deeply influenced by international actors as well as by domestic actors from the public and private sectors.

Other scholars have argued that governance within the international system should be conceptualized as occurring across policy areas as well as just within the individual areas (Rosenau, 1992). The concept of "international order" is used to describe a more encompassing structure of values and rules that coordinate the overall behavior of nations, perhaps especially in security policy, but also meshing security with a range of other international policy concerns (Ashley, 1989). Although perhaps more tenuously connected than the definitions of regimes, the concept of an international order also has some important institutional characteristics. This is especially true of the reliance on norms to regulate the behavior of its members.

Those norms may be less demonstrable, and perhaps less operational, than in regimes but they are nonetheless real.

For both the more specific and the more general conceptions of regimes in international politics some sense of common interest appears required. Even if there is a common policy activity and a common collection of policy ideas, if there are fundamental differences in goals and values then the likelihood of an effective regime being formed is low. For example, despite some general agreement among the industrialized democracies about the need for a regime for environmental policy, the differences in economic goals between them and the less developed countries make the formation of a regime in this area difficult. Likewise, differences in religious values make the formation of a regime in population policy perhaps even less likely at present (Crane, 1993).

Finally, the development of international entities such as the European Union raises particularly important boundary questions for regime theory. When do these regional associations cease to be regimes and becomes proto-states, or even real states? This distinction can be seen in the debate in the literature between the "intergovernmentalists" (Moravcsik, 1993) and "supranationalists" (Sandholz, 1993). Further, it is easy to argue that within the European Union there are a number of other organizations that can be considered as institutions in their own right, especially in the terms of the empirical institutionalism. How far does this approach, and institutionalism in general, permit the embedding of institutions within each other while still maintaining their own institutional character? If this is permitted, as it almost certainly must be,[3] then institutional analysis will be applicable at several levels.

Where Do Institutions Come From?

To some extent the definitional question concerning international institutions also address questions about the origins of those institutions. In order for a regime to come into existence there must be an acceptance of a common definition of a policy area or a repetitive pattern of interaction among the participants in a regime that is governed by rules (whether formal or informal). These two variables are of course closely related, as some affinity of ideas will generate greater interaction, and interaction will also tend to generate more agreement on policy definitions and policy values.

Thus, the question of becoming a regime involves defining some point at which behaviors become sufficiently common, and perhaps sufficiently governed by rules, for the regime to be said to exist. If there were a clear empirical measure of the behaviors that define regimes then this question might be a relatively simple one to answer.

[3] For example, a legislature would be considered an institution, but so too could the committees that operate within it be (see Shepsle and Weingast, 1995).

The trouble is that there are few if any measures of that sort agreed upon this body of literature, and regime theorists tend to rely on impressionistic evidence more than on "intersubjectively transmissible" evidence. In some policy areas, for example financial communities, there is some evidence about patterns of interaction and patterns of control, while in others the evidence is at best anecdotal.

The Design of Institutions

One view in most approaches to institutions is that they simply emerge from interaction, while in other views they can be the product of conscious design. The same is true of international institutions and regimes. The definitions advanced for regimes display those two options, with the minimalist Puchala and Hopkins definition implying that regimes emerge from the interactions of the actors, while the definitions by Krasner, and particularly Keohane, imply greater intentionality, and the construction of sets of rules to govern behavior. In more formal conceptions of international organizations the possibilities of design are greater (Duffield, 2003).

Even in the Keohane and Krasner definitions it is not clear exactly who the actors are, and this appears to be a major question in regime theory. Even when Keohane requires that the rules of a regime be accepted by government, it is not clear whether that acceptance is after those rules are negotiated elsewhere, or is a necessary condition for the creation of the regime. For example, in environmental politics the creation of rules may be the product of discussions, lobbying, and political pressure from interest groups, and then only later validated by government. In other areas such as taxation, governments may have to be involved in the negotiations from the beginning. In some cases, for example the formation of a regime (by almost any definition) around land mines, the impetus may be largely individual.

As well as a question about the nature of the actors involved in the design of an institution, there is a question of how to factor the level of compliance into design. This variable is important in defining and measuring the existence of a regime. It is also important for thinking about designing institutions simply because different thresholds of compliance open and close different options for design. If there is a low threshold of compliance, and substantial variation in behavior is acceptable within a regime, then it may be sensible to go for more demanding standards. If any failure to comply represents the negation of the regime then minimal designs are more appropriate.[4] Again, it seems crucial to differentiate regimes encountered in various policy areas, with those with lower compliance thresholds being more amenable to design than those demanding more complete compliance.

Duffield (2003) and other scholars have emphasized the importance of design for international organizations and institutions. Rosendorff and Milner (2001), for

[4] For example, regimes in nuclear arms may permit little deviations from standards, while one in education (e.g., Bologna in Europe) may permit substantial variance.

example, argue that designing international institutions is a more rational act for states than it might appear. In this view, then, institutions are perhaps more the creatures of their participants than they are autonomous actors. However, as with institutions composed of individuals, there are some interactions between the components of the institution and the institution itself.

How Do Individuals and Institutions Interact?

One of the questions we are asking about each version of institutional theory is how do individuals interact with institutions within the theory. For international institutions, meaning here especially international regimes, that question becomes how do national governments interact with the international institution, for example the regimes? Although given the level of analysis identifying the effects of regimes may be more difficult, the analytic question remains the same—how does the institution shape the behavior of its component parts (States) and how do those component parts shape the behavior of the larger system.

The definition of regimes discussed above provides a part of the answer to that question, at least for the effects of an institution on the component members. The assumption behind regime theories is that the "expectations" of the actors involved will converge through their interactions over time so that there will be substantially less variance in values and behavior when there is an operative regime than when there is not. As already noted there is a strong suspicion that this definition of a regime could be tautological; the presumed effect of a regime is also its definition.

Leaving the potential epistemological problems aside, the basic operational element here is very much the same as that contained in the normative version of institutionalism—the institution influences the values of the components and then the values influence behavior. The principal difference from the normative approach appears to be that domestic institutions tend to be more directly involved in the shaping of the individual values of its members.[5] In contrast, regimes tend to be associated with a convergence of values of the member states (or components thereof), a seemingly less hierarchical conceptualization of the pattern of influence.

In some instances, however, that apparently benign convergence may be brought about through coercion, as when international organizations coerce potential clients to behave in certain ways. Caiden and Wildavsky (1974) documented the role of international organizations in imposing "modern" budget standards on poorer countries, and more recently those same international organizations have imposed "modern" styles of administrative reform. The coercion here is that if the poorer countries want resources from organizations such as the IMF or the World Bank

[5] March and Olsen (1989) argue, for example, the norms of an institution, such as the logic of appropriateness, determine the behavior of the individuals involved.

they must comply with their demands.[6] That coercion is by no means a thing of the past, with these organizations (and perhaps especially the IMF) continuing to impose their own values on less-developed, or less fortunate, countries if those countries want to have the money from those organizations. The experiences of several of the "Little Tigers" of Asia in the late 1990s point to the extent of influence that these international organizations may have.

The other direction of influence in regime theory is somewhat less clearly articulated, although the notion that there is a convergence of values implies that there is at least some interaction among the component actors. This pattern may be analogous to that encountered in intergovernmental politics within nation states (Rhodes, 1988; Wright, 1988), in which there is a vertical interaction among the levels of government. This is not a hierarchical pattern of interaction but rather one of mutual influence and indeed mutual dependency. As with the discussion of epistemic communities above, this interaction often is conducted within individual policy areas that have shared orientations and values.

The shared values that are created facilitate moving the interactions from hierarchy to cooperation and mutual influence. There are agreed upon standards of proof and styles of argument in most policy areas that enable its members to interact effectively and to reach agreements on other than political grounds. Although broadly shared, there can be national differences so that politics and national interest may not be removed entirely from these interactions. Even in basic science there appear to be national styles and with that often substantial differences in interpreting the policy relevance of particular sets of facts (Zito, 2001), and sometimes even differences in what the facts are.

The most difficult of these interactions is attempting to determine how individual nations can shape or reshape regimes. This shaping may be relatively easy for powerful nations such as the United States but not for small and less influential countries.[7] Interestingly, however, the creation of the international regime on land mines appears to be more the product of nongovernmental actors, and not very powerful actors at that. In that case there were important values that those actors could manipulate in order to produce agreement, at least among countries with little to lose from joining, on the formation of the regime. Helen Milner (1997; see also Murphy, 2000) has made a more sophisticated argument about the influence of national governments on the nature of regimes. She argues that the structure of preferences within individual countries will influence the policies that regimes adopt,

[6] In fairness, some of the more affluent countries may also be coerced by international regimes. The United Kingdom, for example, was very clearly coerced by the IMF during the 1970s. Also, the Maastricht budget criteria for joining the EMU place a great deal of external pressure on national governments.

[7] One exception may be smaller countries that have large quantities of crucial materials such as oil or gold, or perhaps one that can make a particular moral claim in a policy area, as the Scandinavian countries have in some policy areas.

and their success in implementing those regimes. She uses a game-theoretic perspective, based upon Putnam's idea (1988) concept of "two level games" to model the interactions of States and regimes in a number of policy areas, arguing that domestic preferences do matter and limit the possible outcomes for a regime.

Thus, it appears that this aspect of the institutionalist puzzle can be answered readily for international regimes. There are ways in which the two sets of actors—nation states and regimes—can interact and can affect each other's values. The reification of regimes does, of course, remain a crucial problem in this analysis. Even that nagging problem may be resolvable when there are international organizations that appear to serve as a collective memory in the policy area. The International Labour Office for employment and labor policies, the World Health Organization for health policy, and the IMF for international financial affairs may all be seen as organizational manifestations of underlying regimes operating in those policy areas.

Change in International Regimes

Compared to the apparent permanence characterizing historical institutionalism, and often attributed to other forms of institutional analysis, international regimes appear to be relatively mutable. At the extreme, it appears that the defection of one major actor, for example the United States leaving UNESCO, can cripple a regime (Coate, 1988; Valderrama, 1995). Even in less extreme cases international regimes appear more fragile that other institutional structures. Even "epistemic" communities may not be stable over time as new approaches to scientific problems and differences in national styles of science create internal divisions within those communities based on agreements on common scientific principles. For example, differences between American and French scientists over the nature of AIDS (and who discovered what) threatened the early development of science and treatment in this budding international regime (Feldman, 1995). This fragility is especially marked for epistemic communities based on social scientific knowledge rather than "hard sciences" with their more agreed upon standards of evidence.

The real question is whether there is anything specific in regime theory that can distinguish change in these international models from change in other, more general, institutional theories. The language we have been utilizing in the above paragraph is that of normative institutionalism ("values") or game theories ("defection") rather than a specific conception of change coming from international relations. Likewise, the constructivist perspectives on institutions appear very much like discursive models of institutions (see Payne, 2001). We can also consider change through a process of "institutionalization," but again that characterization is just a version of another, broader sociological approach to institutions rather than any characteristic specific to international regime theories.

Perhaps the most important feature of change in international regimes is the fragility of international regimes. In most instances there are few binding, or even compelling, reasons for a national actor to remain a part of a regime. States will continue to play by the rules of the regime so long as it remains in their interest to do so, and will quickly withdraw from the regime (explicitly or implicitly) when it is no longer in their interest to do so. Again, however, there is the problem of a tautology in regime theory and the absence of any external referent against which to compare national interests and values in a regime. That is, the only way that we can know that the regime was no longer in the interest of the nation state was when it chooses to withdraw from the regime.

At the same time that an individual regime may be fragile, there has been a proliferation of international regimes. More and more policy areas are now influenced by international actions and by formal or informal organizations that cross national boundaries. Therefore, increasingly, the environment of each regime is becoming heavily populated with other regimes, and the interaction of these groups can in themselves further shape the behavior of the actors. These "regime complexes" (Raustiala and Victor, 2004) may further create serious problems of coordination and inconsistency in the policies being promulgated.

Knill and Lenschow (2001) have addressed the problem of change in international institutions through focusing on the structure-agency dimensions of change, as opposed to the usual method of identifying different ontologies of institutions, for example rational actor versus the more sociological approaches. The question for Knill and Lenschow is, therefore, perhaps more basic—the extent to which change occurs through the manipulation of structure or through the purposeful actions of individuals. While these differences may be difficult to identify in large and amorphous institutions such as regimes, they may be readily seen in more mundane and readily identifiable institutions.

The Good Institution

Finally, we must ask what constitutes a good institution within the context of an international regime. Again, at a very minimum, the good regime, or the successful regime, is one that survives. If we adopt the minimalist conception of regimes put forward by Puchala and Hopkins then the perpetuation of interactions and "patterned behavior" would be sufficient for success. For some regimes, where there is little agreement on basic values, the mere continuation of discussions may be all that is possible. This continued interaction may lead to success on the more demanding criteria, simply because continued interaction tends to create more bargaining and perhaps more mutual agreement on basic issues in the area.

As with the normative version of institutionalism, a good institution in this international version of institutional theory is one which is capable of inculcating its values into the behavior of its members. In many instances propagating those common values is not such a difficult task, given that the members of the regime may have initiated their interactions on the basis of common professional or scientific values. These actors within the incipient regime thus can initiate their search for a new regime with a good deal of collective understanding, and this creates the opportunity for using those common values as a foundation for common rules and mutual constraints on behavior.

Another way to think of the "good" institution in international regimes is as a regime that is successful in constraining the behavior of its members. This is, of course, somewhat related to the first conception of a good institution, given that acceptance of common values is also likely to constrain the behavior of the individual participants. Within the numerous conceptions of regimes based on enforceable rules, there are constraints on behavior even without agreement on fundamental values. These rules may be sufficient to create a successful regime with sufficient power to constrain action; recipient nations may not agree with the economic values of the IMF, but the international financial regime is sufficiently powerful to enforce its own principles on those nations. The IMF has been able to enforce its guidelines even over seemingly wealthy countries such as South Korea, and at one time even over the United Kingdom.

Summary and Conclusion

International relations is often seen as the domain of anarchy, rather than an arena in which stable institutions operate. The above description should demonstrate that it is not totally unreasonable to think of regimes as the analogues of institutions at the international level. They display some of the same characteristics of stability and predictability that are used to define institutions. These regimes also have some of the same effect of molding the behavior of the individual members (in this case the nation states). Finally, some of these also are able to promulgate a set of values that are accepted as "appropriate" for the participants in the regime.

Although the above arguments appear compelling to me, there are also some questions remaining. In particular, there are questions about the extent to which international regimes have sufficient capacity to produce changes in behavior of members to say that they are really comparable to other types of institutions such as public bureaucracies or even political parties. The most obvious concern is that there is little capacity to separate regimes from non-regimes in other than a matter that makes it difficult to assess independently the impact of a regime. That is, regimes can be said to exist if national actors behave in certain ways. This definition then assures that a researcher will find that regimes are effective, although that finding may then be virtually meaningless.

One principal advantage of conceptualizing international politics in regime and institutional terms is that it helps to move the debate in that subdiscipline away from power politics to thinking about consonance, at least within specific policy areas. This perspective is perhaps especially important after the end of the Cold War, and with the end of the bloc system a shift toward greater internationalization of most, if not all, policy areas. The world has not become a totally benign place, but the economic and social dimensions of international politics are of increasing importance, and those policy areas appear more amenable to regime analysis.

As well as making international politics appear more similar to domestic politics, the use of institutional modes of thinking in this field directs attention to the place of values. As noted already, power and conflict have tended to dominate thinking in the international arena, but there are also important values that operate in this arena. Some of these values may be specific to the epistemic communities but others, for example a preference for peace over war, may be more general. Whatever the generality, values do play a part in international politics and a focus on regimes helps to make that role clearer.

I believe the case has been made that it is reasonable to think about international politics in institutional theory terms. Institutionalism is by no means the only viable approach to international affairs, nor is the regime concept applicable to all facets of world politics. There are, however, certainly some policy areas in which regimes do exist, and for which institutional thinking is appropriate and indeed even essential. The theoretical and research task, therefore, is to differentiate both regime and non-regime circumstances and to develop further the conceptualization of regimes as institutions. That conceptual development may require much closer connection between international relations and other aspects of political science (especially comparative politics) than has been characteristic of either side of the discussion.

CHAPTER 10

Conclusion: One Institutionalism or Many?

To this point we have been operating very explicitly as if there were different versions of institutionalism in contemporary political science. This approach has been a useful exercise for explicating each of the individual theories. We need, however, to consider if despite the subtle, and even not so subtle, differences that exist among these approaches to institutions there may really be one fundamental perspective on political and social life, with a number of different variations on the same theme. Thus, is this body of theory like Elgar's *Enigma* with its apparently different versions all bound together by the basic theme, or is it really a series of interesting solo pieces with few real common themes?

There are points that could be made on either side of this argument (see Mulé, 1999). On the one hand, it appears that all these approaches to institutionalism stress the same fundamental analytic points. The most fundamental point is that scholars can achieve greater analytic leverage by beginning with institutions rather than with individuals. Further, all the approaches point to the role that structure plays in determining behavior, as well as its role in determining the outcomes of political processes. In addition, all the versions of institutionalism argue that institutions create greater regularities in human behavior than would be otherwise found. At a practical level institutions do have the capacity to mold individual behavior and to reduce (but not eliminate) the uncertainty that otherwise dominates much of social life. To the extent that the environment of one institution is composed largely of other institutions (and hence of somewhat lesser variability) that uncertainty can be reduced even further (Meyer and Rowan, 1977; DiMaggio and Powell, 1991; Pierre and Peters, 2009). For the social scientist this reduction of uncertainty makes prediction more feasible, and provides a better route for social explanation.

Finally, institutions are seen in all but perhaps the most extreme conceptualizations as the results of purposive human action, so that the fundamental paradox (Grafstein, 1992) of institutions being formed by human agents yet constraining those same actors arises in all versions of the new institutionalism. This paradox in turn requires that each of the approaches find some means of explaining why presumably autonomous actors accept the constraints of an institution. For some visions of institutions (game theory and regime theory) this may be in order to have their adversaries constrained, while for others it may be a more normative explanation that individuals expect values and roles to be provided to them by the institutions they join.

The above points of similarity can be counterbalanced by some fundamental differences among the approaches. One difference is the instrument through which constraint on the individual is exercised. In some approaches this constraint is exercised through values and norms, while in others it is performed through rules (whether intra- and inter-institutional). For example, in normative institutionalism and to some extent in historical institutionalism norms are the crucial constraints, while in rational choice versions formal rules are more significant.

Another fundamental difference among the approaches is the degree to which institutions are assumed to be mutable or relatively fixed. In some approaches the fundamental means of understanding institutions is their degree of fixity, while in others there is assumed that organizations enjoy a substantial capacity for change, planned or unplanned. To some extent all versions of institutionalism have been criticized for being too concerned with persistence and as paying inadequate attention to issues of design and change. That said, however, the historical institutionalism has been centered on ideas of persistence, while change is relatively easy in discursive models.

Finally, there are also differences in the extent to which institutions are conceptualized as concrete objects, as opposed to more intangible collections of norms and values that have their influence primarily through the perceptions of the members of the institutions. Empirical institutionalism is just that, and focuses on formal structures. Some other versions, however, are concerned with much more amorphous conceptions of institutions, and with institutions that exist primarily as analytic constructs. The institutional form of a regime, for example, may not exist in any tangible form.

I will now proceed to go through the above six points about institutions to describe more fully the similarities and differences among the approaches to institutionalism. There can perhaps be no definite solution to the question of whether there is one underlying approach or not, but this exercise should help to clarify the principal points about which there would be possible disagreement and similarity. Further, it may help clarify the extent to which the differences are so fundamental that they would prevent any amalgamation of approaches as a means of creating a more unified body of institutional theory for political science. There are, of course, differences or there would not be the different approaches; the question is: are those differences fatal for any integration?

Similarities in Institutional Analysis

The first and fundamental point of similarity for the approaches to institutions is their emphasis on institutions. This most basic, and blindingly obvious, point for all the approaches to institutional analysis is that institutional factors are the most appropriate points of departure for social analysis. This addresses a classic problem in social analysis—the relative importance of structure and agency in explanation

(Dessler, 1989; Sztompka, 1994; Hay, 1995; see also Archer, 1997)—encountered in a number of areas in the social sciences. That is, are outcomes in social processes determined, or best predicted by, structural factors or are they more predictable by the actions of human agents? We have pointed out that to at least one major social theorist, Anthony Giddens (1981; 1984), the structure–agency distinction is largely a false dichotomy. Giddens argues that there is a duality in all social relationships so that both factors are almost always in operation. Even if that is the case, the institutionalists would still argue that in the public sector social scientists can gain greater leverage by beginning an analysis with the structures and then thinking about the independent impacts of agency.

Given that these are all institutional theories it appears obvious that they all focus on the impact of structure on those outcomes. Zucker (1988, p. 27) argues, for example, that alone among social science theories institutionalism provides no place for individuals and their interests. Zucker's statement is almost certainly an overstatement, and some versions such as discourse do indeed place a good deal of emphasis on the actions of individuals. That said, however, all of these approaches begin with institutions of some sort or another, simply because their proponents believe that is the source of the greatest analytic leverage in the social sciences.

There are, however, still some important variations in the way in which these approaches deal with the central role of structure in the analysis (see Easton, 1990). For example, for the empirical institutionalists there appears to be little else other than structure available to provide the explanation; the only set of variables included in the analysis are structural, and even they are largely confined to differences between presidential and parliamentary regimes.[1] Also, the international version of institutionalism appears to allow little or no room for human agency. If, however, the nation state is used as the analogue of the individual, as an actor, then there is substantially more room for agency, and indeed the question of whether the regime exists at all is a question of whether there is something that distinguishes a regime from a non-regime.[2] Finally, the rational choice institutionalists appear to provide a good deal of latitude for human agency at the inception of an institution and in its design—but then there is almost no opportunity for individual action, with those being determined largely by the rules and incentives.

At the other end of the dimension within the institutional theories would lie the March and Olsen approach and the discursive approach. Interestingly for the seminal approach in the new institutionalism the "normative" institutional approach appears to depend more on human agency than any of the others discussed. Their conceptualization of an institution, with its emphasis on the development and transmission

---

1 Even here, however, individual presidents and prime ministers do help to shape their offices and to some degree alter the nature of the institutions more generally.

2 That approach runs the risk for reifying the State and treating it as a unitary actor. Given that regimes tend to be policy specific, the principal actors may be segments of a State structure rather than the State as a whole.

of norms among the members of the institution places much more emphasis on the way in which the members behave. In particular, it focuses on individual members of the institution as the unit of analysis, at least to the extent that their interpretations of the norms may vary. Thus, an objective outsider may identify a particular "logic of appropriateness" but the members of the institution may interpret the norms very differently. Also, given that the dominant discourse of an institution may emerge from the interaction of individuals, the discursive model also appears to place substantial emphasis on agency.

The degree of latitude for agency in the other approaches to institutional analysis lies somewhere between these two. Most interestingly the rational choice versions of institutionalism are somewhat ambiguous with respect to agency. On the one hand, the emphasis on choice and design appears to provide a good deal of latitude for human action, especially in the "individual" version of rational choice advocated by Keman (1996), Scharpf (1997), and their associates (Hertier, 1996). Further, the notion that individuals may defect in the game-theoretic version or that some actors may require external control within the principal–agent version implies a good deal of room for agency. On the other hand, there also appears to be little latitude for differential interpretation of rules within that one version of the approach. Thus, there appears to be a mixed score card for rational choice institutionalism here.

In summary, the approaches to institutional analysis all focus attention on the importance of structure in explaining political behavior. That having been said, they differ in the manner in which they posit that influence and the role which they allow for human agency. Indeed, for some approaches the role of institutions depends heavily on the actions of the members of the institution, and their perceptions of the rules of their institutions. For most approaches the structural characteristics of those institutions are the determining features.

Regularities

All forms of institutionalism also argue that institutions create greater regularity in individual behavior than would be found without the existence of those institutions. This is true even of amorphous institutions such as the market that also constrain the behavior of individuals, and therefore produce greater predictability than would be the case if individuals were not influenced by their rules and/or incentives. The same logic holds true of regimes in international relations theory, with the behavior of individual nations being constrained by their membership in the regime. If this constraint is indeed apparent then it represents a major accomplishment in the international arena presumably characterized by the actions of sovereign and autonomous actors.

This concern with commonality of behavior within institutions is analogous to the question of agency raised above. If there is a sizeable capacity for human agency then there will not be the degree of behavioral regularity that is expected from an institution, in any of the approaches. Although we will agree that there is some regularity in behavior, we still do not know how much regularity is sufficient to say that the institution exists. This points out, in a rather perverse way, one of the clearest commonalities in the literature—none of them provides any clear standards for reduction of variance in behavior as a means of determining the existence of the institution.

The real theoretical problem that arises here is that some of the approaches, for example rule-based rational choice, tend to define institutions by the creation of regularity, or by the acceptance of rules of behavior. As we have pointed out, these criteria for the existence of an institution appear to approach being tautological in some instances. In other cases, however, there is a clear acceptance of continued deviations from the dominant standards of behavior within the institution. For example, in the March and Olsen approach to the "logic of appropriateness" there is an assumption that members of the institution will behave in the "appropriate" manner, but the model is also capable of accepting that some, or even many, members of the institution will behave in inappropriate ways. There will still be an institution in that case, but it would not be as fully institutionalized as would one with greater uniformity of values.

In an empirical approach to institutions, we can also see that not all institutions require the same level of regularity in behavior. Some such as the military may demand rigid uniformity, and prisons (as examples of total institutions) take that demand to even greater extremes. Universities, on the other hand, tolerate or even encourage rather wide ranges of behavior, and most institutions fall between the extremes. Thus, again, it is difficult to determine exactly how much predictability is essential for there to be said to be an institution in place.

Measurement

A final commonality among the institutional theories, and a somewhat troubling one for any scholar advocating these theories, is the methodological problem of measurement and verification. We all know that institutions exist; our lives are influenced by them every day and in numerous ways. This is true for amorphous institutions such as the family and law as well as more tangible institutions such as a public bureaucracy. The problem we encounter, however, is one of defining those institutions in a way that is intersubjectively transmissible and that fits with the canons of contemporary social science. I argued earlier in this book that one thing that distinguishes the "new" institutionalism from the old is the more explicit concern with methods and theory. Unfortunately, that difference from old institutionalism is not as pronounced as it might be, and there are still major methodological problems in the new institutionalism.

Even here there are some important differences among the approaches. On one end of a dimension the sociological institutionalists appear to have made the most progress in measurement, in large part because of their close link with organization theory.[3] Almost by definition the empirical institutionalists have made some gains in measurement, but that is often at a simple nominal (presidential–parliamentary) level. At the other end of the spectrum the normative institutionalists and the discursive institutionalists appear to have made the least progress, given their reliance on relatively "soft," albeit significant, concepts such as norms and values. In all cases, however, there appears to be a great need for greater rigor in conceptualization and then measurement of the phenomena that are assumed to make up institutions.

The need to measure institutions is closely related to the ideas of institutionalization and deinstitutionalization. If we accept the general point that institutions are almost always changing and their level of institutionalization differs across time, then we need to have some ways of measuring those changes. There are some schemes for measurement (see Oliver, 1992; Ragsdale and Theis, 1997), but the schemes tend to be multidimensional and provide a rather vague and confusing picture of those changes. The purpose of measurement, of course, is to reduce that vagueness and therefore it appears there is a good deal to be done in order to assess levels of institutionalization, and therefore degrees of "institution-ness."

Differences among Institutional Theories: They Are Not All the Same

There are a number of common features in institutional theory, but there also appear to be a number of significant differences among these various approaches. None of the approaches stands out totally from the others, and one may align with others on some characteristics and with others on other characteristics. In general, however, the March and Olsen "values" approach to institutions appears relatively similar to the historical institutional approach. Also, given its intellectual roots and its substantive content the values version of institutions is also very close to the sociological version of the approach. Similarly, the rational choice approach to institutions appears very compatible with some aspects of the empirical approach, given the emphasis of both on the capacity to choose institutions. But are these similarities sufficient to define a common core in institutional theory?

Definitions of Institutions

The most basic differences among the approaches arise in the definitions of what is an institution, and the factors that operate to constrain individual behavior within the context of the organization. As we have been pointing out earlier, there are three types of answers to that question. The first is that values constrain individuals, and

[3] The sociological approach, given its greater emphasis on change and "institutionalization" may have greater demands for measurement than do the more static approaches coming largely from political science.

that the nature of institutions is largely normative. The assumption for this answer is that although individuals may import some values when they join an institution[4] they are willing, by virtue of joining, to allow institutional values to dominate at least this aspect of their lives.

An alternative answer is that institutions are defined by their rules, and that what constrains individual behavior within institutions are more formal statements of what a good member of the institution should and should not do. This type of answer is typical of the rational choice approach, although it should be broadened to include positive incentives as well as the more negative constraint of rules. In such a conception individuals may not feel constrained so much by their membership as they use the rules and incentives as means of achieving certain goals.

Finally, individual behavior may be constrained by the regularized patterns of interaction among individuals within institutions. This is a weak criterion and (like several other arguments in institutional theory) borders on the tautological. Institutions are defined in some approaches by their capacity to constrain behavior, yet here their capacity to constrain is being assessed as a relatively independent criterion. Thus, what may be a behavioral regularity in one version of institutionalism may be a constraint in other versions of these theories (see Diermeier and Krehbiel, 2003). And there is also the underlying question of whether constraints that are chosen voluntarily are really constraints.

Preferences

Another extremely fundamental difference among these approaches to institutionalism is the source of preferences in the theories (see Dowding and King, 1995, pp. 2–7). On the one hand in some versions of institutionalism preferences are external, or exogenous, to the theory. In these approaches preferences are assumed to be a product of the socialization of individuals and are brought by the individuals into their institutions. For example, in rational choice theory making the choices is basic, and the roots of those preferences are irrelevant. The real question for these theories is the structure of incentives and rules that will determine behavior. Indeed, in rational choice theories of institutions the preferences of the individuals are assumed to be almost uniform, especially the preference for maximizing personal utilities. This assumption in turn limits some of the utility of rational choice models of use in comparative political analysis.

Although much less explicit than in rational choice approaches, and also much less significant, preferences also are assumed to be exogenous in the empirical approaches to institutions. In these perspectives the basic preference is for a

[4] An individual probably would not select an institution unless its values were compatible with his or hers. The obvious exception would be Etzioni's "coercive" institutions over which the individual had no choice.

capacity to make decisions and to implement them efficiently. The often discussed differences among institutional structures such as presidential versus parliamentary regimes are phrased in terms of their capacity to govern effectively. There is little or no attention paid to the concerns of the individuals within the governing institutions, all of whom are assumed to share this concern with effective governance, and indeed assumed to share some common commitment to the particular institutions.

The discursive version of institutionalism may have a somewhat ambiguous answer to the question of the sources of preferences within institutions. On the one hand, there are multiple discourses involved in the creation and even maintenance of the institution. On the other hand, to the extent that some sort of equilibrium is reached within the institution the (relatively) common ideas within the institution become a source of endogenous preferences. Thus, the degree to which preferences in this model are endogenous may depend upon the level of institutionalization of the structure at any one time.

For all the other approaches to institutions preferences are endogenous, or the product of individual involvement with the institution. For the normative approach this endogeneity is most evident. March and Olsen argue that individuals do possess sets of basic values before they become involved with institutions but that their involvement also shapes preferences. In particular, involvement with the institution shapes those values that are specifically relevant to the functioning of that institution. Given the close connections between the normative approach and the sociological approach to institutions it is not surprising to find similar arguments about the endogeneity of preferences in these two approaches.

Although regime theory appears to argue that preferences and regimes emerge almost simultaneously, it does appear that preferences are better understood as endogenous. In particular, the need for sovereign states to negotiate among themselves to find an acceptable set of policies appears to argue strongly that preferences are endogenous. On the other hand, however, the importance of the "epistemic communities" (Zito, 2001; Campbell, 2002) in facilitating the formation of regimes points to some possible exogeneity of preferences in regimes. To some extent the degree of endogeneity in a regime may vary in different regimes, with those with a stronger technical or scientific basis having the greatest exogeneity.

As well as being important analytically, the source or preferences is also important for understanding the dynamics of institutions. We will discuss the role of change in institutional theories immediately below, but it is important to understand that if preferences are created externally, and also largely unchangeable, then the only way to generate change is to alter the structure of incentives and rules that exist within an institution. On the other hand, if preferences are conceptualized as mutable then transformations can be an ongoing process of remaking individual preferences through the operations of the institutions themselves. There have been notable attempts to integrate different conceptions of the nature of preferences (Katznelson and Weingast, 2005; Hilbink, 2009).

Change

The most important of the differences among approaches to institutions include their conceptions of change and the ways in which the different approaches consider change (see Kingston and Caballero, 2009). Most fundamentally, there is the question of whether or not change is recognized as an ordinary part of institutional life or as the exception to a rule of stability, and perhaps even hyperstability. We noted early in the discussion of institutional theory that one of the common ways of thinking about the structure–agency debate in social theory is to ascribe stability to structure, and hence to institutions. Indeed in some views of institutions, for example historical institutionalism, there is a judgment that institutions do not change readily. There is a fundamental assumption that institutions are in an equilibrium that will remain in place unless there is some major "punctuation" to move them off that equilibrium position (Krasner, 1984).

The alternative conception is that institutions are almost inherently nonequilibrium structures. The argument of William Riker (1980) and other scholars operating from very different assumptions (Grafstein, 1992) is that institutions and their rules are human constructions. Institutions, therefore, are subject to the whims of the very people (or at least people fulfilling the same functions) that created them in the first instance. In this view, rules are short-term constraints on behavior, at best, with rules to some extent always being renegotiated among the members of the institution, or perhaps among several institutions. In some societies (the United States) basic institutional rules such as constitutions can survive for a very long period of time, while in others (France perhaps) constitutions tend to be more periodical literature (Hayward, 1983). If we move down the level of generality then the framing rules of government tend to be even less stable.

All the various rational choice versions of institutionalism share some of the same nonequilibrium conceptions of institutions mentioned above.[5] The assumption of many rational choice theorists is that institutions are almost infinitely mutable, simply through the selection of rules or structures. This assumption makes the design of institutions a more viable activity than in other versions of institutionalism, but also makes any particular institutional choice subject to relatively easy revision and replacement. If institutions do not have values to constrain the behavior of individuals, and if the initial choices of those institutions do not tend to persist, then there can be little sense of equilibrium of institutions in this model.

We may talk about institutional change as a relatively undifferentiated whole, but different types of institutions may change differently. For example, Roland (2004) discusses the difference rates of change for formal institutions (my empirical institutionalism) which can change rapidly, and that for cultural institutions (normative institutions) which tend to change more slowly. This differential pace of change may

---

[5] This is true even though ironically the notion of structure-induced equilibrium is central to the arguments of many rational choice institutionalists such as Shepsle.

mean that the formal institutions may lack the cultural basis needed to support them and make them successful. On the other hand, if cultures are too sticky then it may suppress overall adaptation of governments and the society more broadly.

The capacity to provide meaningful conceptions of change in institutions is one of the most crucial elements of the development of institutional theory. Institutionalism has been developed in part to explain the persistence of institutions, but that strength has also been its weakness. The various approaches to change all contribute to the expansion of the theoretical relevance of institutional theory, but the absence of any clear logic to unify the approaches to some extent undermines the approach.

Individuals and Institutions

Another difference among the various theoretical approaches to institutions concerns the alternative ways in which individuals and institutions are hypothesized to interact to shape each other's behavior. In the first instance, there are differences in whether an approach emphasizes the capability of an institution to shape individual behavior, or whether it emphasizes more the capacity of individuals to shape institutional performance and choices. All versions of institutionalism have something to say about both directions of influence, but there are pronounced differences in the emphasis they attach to one direction or the other of influence.

At one extreme the empirical approach appears to assume that institutions will shape the values and/or behaviors of individuals, but that there is little reciprocal influence. For example, although there is some questioning of whether individual presidents and prime ministers can permanently transform the office (Rockman, 1984; Jones, 1991), the real question is how these types of regimes act as regimes to shape policy outcomes that affect society. Similarly, the application of institutional theories to political parties and interest groups appears to emphasize the influence that these structures have on the behavior of individuals, rather than the ways in which individual behavior shapes these institutions. For example, it appears that individual members of political parties are virtually irrelevant to the dynamics of party systems, with the number of parties and their characteristics tending to determine the nature of systems (see Downs, 1957). Further, as the parties become more linked to the State the variance in parties may also be reduced (Katz and Mair, 2009).

At the other extreme, regime theories and other international institutional approaches tend to assume a substantial level of influence of "individuals"—themselves collective actors—on the nature of the regime. As we argued above in relationship to preferences, regimes are sufficiently amorphous entities that they are greatly influenced by the actors taking part in them. Rational choice versions of institutionalism also tend to permit a great deal of influence for individual actors. The basic point is that institutions are the products of human agency and the structure of rules and incentives that is created to shape the behavior of the participants is a choice of the designers.

The normative approach to institutionalism falls somewhere between these two extremes. More than the other versions it permits, and in many ways is founded upon, the mutual influence of individuals and institutions. Given the central role assigned to collective norms and values in defining institutions in this approach, this might appear to be a misstatement. However, there is role for individual members of the institution in shaping those values that does remain in the theory. Part of the strength, and the weakness, of the normative approach is that institutions and their values are expected to continue to evolve, and much of that evolution comes about as a result of the somewhat disparate values of individuals who are recruited into the institution. The discursive model is in many ways an extreme version of the normative version, given that the institution is to be defined largely by the discourses of the members and the equilibria that develop among alternative sets of ideas.

Conclusion: Is There a New Institutionalism?

We now arrive at the end of the book, and a major question (or the major question) still remains: Is there sufficient commonality among the approaches to assert that there is a single, coherent "new institutionalism" in political science? It is clear that there are a number of contending approaches and conceptions about institutions, but is there enough of a central core to the approaches to argue for the existence of "A" new institutionalism, and can core explain the central phenomena of contemporary politics?

Even after going through all the various approaches and their important differences I will argue that there is a sufficient core to justify these approaches being considered one broad, if variegated, approach to politics. The fundamental issue holding all these various approaches, and their various components, together is simply that they consider institutions the central component of political life. In these theories institutions are the variables that explain political life in the most direct and parsimonious manner, and they are also the factors that themselves require explanation. The basic argument is that institutions do matter, and that they matter more than anything else that could be used to explain political decisions.

In all the approaches, something about institutions—their values, their rules, their incentives, or the pattern of interactions of the individuals within them—explains the decisions that governments make. Individuals remain as important actors in most of these theories, but the implicit or explicit argument is that there is substantially greater leverage to be gained through understanding the institutional frameworks within which they operate. Perhaps more than anything else, the individual element of policy-making comes into play as the members of the institution interpret what the rules and values of their institutions are.

Another indication of the extent of commonality among the perspectives on institutions is the number of times that a discussion of one of the approaches naturally led to a discussion of some aspect of another. It appeared in writing the book (and I hope in reading it) that these seemingly disparate groups of scholars were talking about many common questions, albeit from different angles and different intellectual perspectives. Some common problems of governing—implementation, forming governments, and making effective decisions—popped up whenever we began to think and write about institutions.

What the new institutionalism does less well is to explain the nature of the institutions themselves.[6] Some of the approaches contain some conceptions about where institutions come from and how they change, but the majority of them are more concerned with what impacts the institutions have on policy and other political choices. For both the historical institutionalists and the empirical institutionalists the existence of an institution is largely a given. One of the requirements for the future development of these theories is to concentrate more on the formation and transformation of structures. Likewise, few if any of the approaches are explicit about the internal dynamics of an institution and the underlying behavioral mechanisms that make them work.

Another of the future requirements will be to find better ways of testing institutional theory. We have noted several times that institutional approaches often run the risk of being nonfalsifiable. Institutional theories provide relatively few independent hypotheses that can be tested without the possibility of escaping by arguing that there was not really an institution in place. That is, if institutional norms are not followed it can be argued that either it was not a fully developed institution, or that any institution is permitted to have some deviations from established norms. Those statements may be accurate, but with those escapes it is difficult to disconfirm any hypotheses about the impacts of institutions on individual behavior, despite the importance of that linkage of the theories.

For all the problems that we can identify in institutional theory the approach still provides an important, and indeed I would argue essential, window on political life. Most political action of real consequence for society occurs within institutions, or is heavily influenced by institutions, so it is crucial to understand how these bodies act and how they influence the behavior of individuals working within them. The numerous strands of the new institutionalism carry us political scientists some distance in that understanding, although no one of the versions of institutionalism can provide a complete explanation of institutional behavior. Also, there are still a number of questions that require further exploration and further elaboration. Still, the discipline has moved forward, and continues to move forward, in addressing those questions as a result of the development of the "new institutionalism" as a fundamental perspective on politics and governing.

---

[6] This point was especially obvious for the "empirical institutionalists."

Bibliography

Abbott, K. W. (2008) Enriching Rational Choice Institutionalism for the Study of International Law, *University of Illinois Law Review*, 1.

Abdelal, R., M. Blyth and C. Parsons (2006) *Constructing the International Economy* (Ithaca, NY: Cornell University Press).

Aberbach, J. D., R. D. Putnam and B. A. Rockman (1981) *Bureaucrats and Politicians in Western Democracies* (Cambridge, MA: Harvard University Press).

Achen, C. H. and W. P. Shively (1995) *Cross-Level Inference* (Chicago: University of Chicago Press).

Adams, J. (1999) Culture in Rational Choice Theories of State Formation, in G. Steinmetz, ed., *State Formation after the Cultural Turn* (Ithaca, NY: Cornell University Press).

Adler, E. (1992) The Emergence of Cooperation: National Epistemic Communities and the International Evolution of the Idea of Arms Control, *International Organization* 46, 101–46.

Aldrich, H. (2007) *Organizations and Environments* (Palo Alto, CA: Stanford University Press).

Aldrich, J. H. and D. W. Rohde (1997) The Transition to Republican Rule in the House of Representatives: Implications for Theories of Congressional Politics, *Political Science Quarterly* 112, 541–68.

Alesina, A. and L. H. Summers (1993) Central Bank Independence and Economic Performance, *Journal of Money, Credit and Banking* 25, 151–62.

Alexander, E. R. (2005) Institutional Transformation and Planning: From Institutionalization Theory to Policy Design, *Planning Theory* 4, 209–33.

Alexander, G. (2001) Institutions, Path Dependence and Democratic Consolidation, *Journal of Theoretical Politics* 13, 249–69.

Aligica, P. D. And P. J. Boethke (2009) *Challenging Institutional Analysis and Development: The Bloomington School* (Abingdon: Routledge).

Almond, G. A. (1988) The Return to the State, *American Political Science Review* 82, 853–74.

— (1990) *A Discipline Divided: Schools and Sects in Political Science* (Beverly Hills, CA: Sage).

Almond, G. and J. S. Coleman (1960) *The Politics of Developing Areas* (Princeton, NJ: Princeton University Press).

Almond, G. and G. B. Powell (1966) *Comparative Politics: A Developmental Approach* (Boston: Little, Brown).

Almond G. and S. Verba (1965) *The Civic Culture* (Boston: Little, Brown).

Alston, L. J., T. Eggertsson and D. C. North (eds) (1996) *Empirical Studies of Organizational Change* (Cambridge: Cambridge University Press).

Altman, M. (2000) A Behavioral Model of Path Dependence: The Economics of Profitable Inefficiency and Market Failure, *Journal of Socio-Economics* 29, 127–36.

Apter, D. E. (1991) Institutionalism Reconsidered, *International Social Science Journal* 129, 453–81.

Archer, C. (2007) *International Organizations* (London: Routledge).

Archer, M. S. (1997) *Culture and Agency: The Place of Culture in Social Theory*, 2nd edn (Cambridge: Cambridge University Press).

Aristotle (1996) *The Politics and the Constitution of Athens*, ed. by S. Everson (Cambridge: Cambridge University Press).

Arrow, K. J. (1951) *Social Choice and Individual Values* (New York: Wiley).

— (1974) *The Limits of Organization* (New York: Norton).

Arthur, W. B. (1988) Self-Reinforcing Mechanisms in Economics, in P. W. Anderson and K. J. Arrow, eds, *The Economy as an Evolving Complex System* (Menlo Park, CA: Addison-Wesley).

Arzheimer, K. and E. Carter (2006) Political Opportunity Structures and Right-Wing Extremist Party Success, *European Journal of Political Research* 45, 419–43.

Ashley, R. K. (1989) Imposing International Purpose: Notes on a Problematic of Governance, in E.-O. Czempiel and J. N. Rosenau, eds, *Global Changes and Theoretical Challenges* (Lexington, MA: Lexington Books).

Aspinwall, M. D. and G. Schneider (1999) Same Menu, Separate Tables: The Institutionalist Turn in Political Science and the Study of the European Union, *European Journal of Political Research* 38, 1–36.

Axelrod, R. (1984) *The Evolution of Cooperation* (New York: Basic Books).

Axelrod, R. and R. O. Keohane (1986) Achieving Cooperation under Anarchy: Strategies and Institutions, in K. A. Oye, ed., *Cooperation Under Anarchy* (Princeton, NJ: Princeton University Press).

Bache, I. And M. Flinders (2004) *Multi-Level Governance* (Oxford: Oxford University Press).

Back, H. (2003) *Explaining Coalitions: Lessons Learned from Studying Coalitions in Swedish Local Government* (Uppsala: Acta Universitatis Uppsaliensis).

Bagehot, W. (1928) *The English Constitution* (London: Oxford University Press).

Banks, J. S. and B. R. Weingast (1992) The Political Control of Bureaucracies under Asymmetric Information, *American Journal of Political Science* 36, 509–24.

Bardach, E. (1998) Getting Agencies to Work Together: The Practice and Theory of Managerial Craftsmanship (Washington, DC: Brookings Institution).

Barnard, C. I. (1938) *The Functions of the Executive* (Cambridge, MA: Harvard University Press).

Bastian, S. and Luckham, R. (eds) (2003) *Can Democracy Be Designed? The Politics of Institutional Choice in Conflict-Torn Societies* (New York: Zed Books).

Bates, R. H. (1988) Contra Contractarianism: Some Reflections on the New Institutionalism, *Politics and Society* 16, 387–401.

Baumgartner, F. R. (1989) Independent and Politicized Policy Communities: Education and Nuclear Energy in France and the United States, *Governance* 2, 42–66.

Baumgartner, F. R. and B. D. Jones (1993) *Agendas and Instability in American Politics* (Chicago: University of Chicago Press).

Baumgartner, F. R. And B. L. Leech (1998) *Basic Interests: The Importance of Groups in Politics and Political Science* (Princeton, NJ: Princeton University Press).

Becker, G. S. (1986) *An Economic Analysis of the Family* (Dublin: Economic and Social Research Institute).

Bell, D.S. and B. Criddle (1988) *The French Socialist Party: The Emergence of a Party Government* (Oxford: Clarendon Press).

Bendix, R. (1960) *Max Weber: An Intellectual Portrait* (Garden City, NY: Doubleday).

Bendor, J. B. (1985) *Parallel Systems: Redundancy in Government* (Berkeley: University of California Press).

Berger, P. L. and T. Luckmann (1967) *The Social Construction of Reality: A Treatise on the Sociology of Knowledge* (Garden City, NY: Doubleday Anchor).

Berry, W. D., M. B. Berkman and S. Schneiderman (2000) Legislative Professionalism and Incumbent Reelection: The Development of Institutional Boundaries, *American Political Science Review* 94, 859–74.

Beyers, J. (2005) Multiple Embeddedness and Socialization in Europe: The Case of Council Officials, *International Organization* 59, 899–936.

Bicchieri, C. (2009) Do the Right Thing: But Only If Others Do So, *Journal of Behavioral Decision Making* 6, 235–48.

Blais, A. and S. Dion (1991) *The Budget-Maximizing Bureaucrat: Appraisals and Evidence* (Pittsburgh: University of Pittsburgh Press).

Blyth, M. (2003) Structures Do Not Come with an Instruction Sheet: Interests, Ideas, and Progress in Political Science, *Perspectives on Politics* 1, 695–706.

Boetke, P. J., C. J. Coyne and P. T. Leeson (2008) Institutional Stickiness and the New Development Economics, *American Journal of Economics and Sociology* 67, 331–58.

Bogason, P. (1991) Control for Whom?: Recent Adventures in Government Guidance and Control, *European Journal of Political Research* 20, 189–208.

— (1996) *New Modes of Local Political Organizing: Local Government Fragmentation in Scandinavia* (Commack, NY: Nova Science).

Bogdanor, V. (1994) Ministers, Civil Servants and the Constitution, *Government and Opposition* 29, 676–95.

Bohte, J. (1997) Critical Institutional Events and Agenda Setting: The Case of Welfare, Paper presented at annual meeting of the Midwest Political Science Association, Chicago, IL, April 9–13.

Boin, A. and P. 't Hart (2000) Institutional Crises and Reforms in the Public Sector, in H. Wagenaar, ed., *Government Institutions: Effects, Changes and Normative Foundations* (Dordrecht: Kluwer).

Borman, W. (1986) *Gandhi and Non-Violence* (Albany, NY: State University of New York).

Boston, J. (1991) The Theoretical Background of Reform, in Boston et al., *Reshaping the State: New Zealand's Bureaucratic Revolution* (Auckland: Oxford University Press).

— (1994) Purchasing Policy Advice: The Limits of Contracting Out, *Governance* 7, 1–30.

Bourdeaux, C. (2008) Politics and Professionalism: The Effect of Institutional Structure on Democratic Decision-Making in a Contest Policy Area, *Journal of Public Administration Research and Theory* 18, 349–73.

Bourdieu, P. (1998) *Acts of Resistance: Against the Tyranny of the Market* (New York: New Press).

Bowen, E. R. (1982) The Pressman-Wildavsky Paradox, *Journal of Public Policy* 2, 1–22.

Boxenbaum, B. and S. Jonsson (2008) Isomorphism, Diffusion and Decoupling, in R. Greenwood, C. Oliver, K. Sahlin and R. Suddaby, *The Sage Handbook of Organizational Institutionalism* (London: Sage).

Branch, T. (1988) *Parting the Waters: America in the King Years, 1954-1963* (New York: Simon and Schuster).

Braun, D. and A. Busch (1999) *Policy and Political Ideas* (Cheltenham: Edward Elgar).

Breton, A., G. Galeotti, P. Salamon and R. Wintrobe (1993) *Preferences and Democracy* (Dordrecht: Kluwer).

Broadbent, J. (1989) Strategies and Structural Contradictions: Growth Coalition Politics in Japan, *American Sociological Review* 54, 707–21.

Broderick, A. (1970) *The French Institutionalists: Maurice Hauriou, Georges Renard, Joseph T. Delos* (Cambridge, MA: Harvard University Press).

Brunsson, N. (1989) *The Organization of Hypocrisy: Talk, Decisions and Actions in Organizations* (Chichester: Wiley).

Brunsson, N. and J. P. Olsen (1993) *The Reforming Organization* (London: Routledge).

Brunsson, N., A. Forssell and H. Winberg (1989) *Reform som tradition* (Stockholm: EFI).

Buchanan, J. M. and G. Tullock (1962) *The Calculus of Consent: Logical Foundation of Constitutional Democracy* (Ann Arbor: University of Michigan Press).

Burton, M. G. and J. Higley (1987) *Elite Settlements* (Austin, TX: Center for Latin American Studies, University of Texas).

Busch, A. (1994) Central Bank Independence: An Option for Britain?, in H. Kastendick and R. Stinhoff, eds, *Changing Conceptions of Constitutional Government* (Bochum: Brockmeyer).

Caiden, N. and A. Wildavsky (1974) *Planning and Budgeting in Poor Countries* (New York: Wiley).

Callinicos, A. (1987) *Making History: Agency, Structure and Change in Social Theory* (Cambridge: Polity).

Calvert, R. L. (1995) The Rational Choice Theory of Institutions: Implications for Design, in D. Weimer, ed. *Institutional Design* (Dordrecht: Kluwer).

Cameron, C. M. (2000) *Veto Bargaining* (Cambridge: Cambridge University Press).

Camp, R. A. (1996) *Politics in Mexico*, 2nd edn (Oxford: Oxford University Press).

Campbell, A., P. C. Converse, W. E. Miller and D. Stokes (1960) *The American Voter* (New York: Wiley).

Campbell, J. L. (1997) Institutional Analysis and the Role of Ideas in Political Economy, Unpublished Paper, Department of Sociology, Dartmouth College.
— (2002) Ideas, Politics and Public Policy, *Annual of Sociology* 28, 21–38.
Campbell, J. L. and O. K. Pedersen (2001) *The Rise of Neoliberalism and Institutional Analysis* (Chicago: University of Chicago Press).
Canon, D. (1989) The Institutionalization of Leadership in the U.S. Congress, *Legislative Studies Quarterly* 14, 415–53.
Carpenter, D. (2001) The Political Foundations of Bureaucratic Autonomy, *Studies in American Political Development* 15, 113–22.
Carrington, P. J., J. Scott and S. Wasserman (2002) *Models and Methods in Social Network Analysis* (Cambridge: Cambridge University Press).
Carroll, G. R. (1984) Organizational Ecology, *Annual Review of Sociology* 10, 71–93.
Carstensen, M. B. (2011) Paradigm Man vs. the Bricoleur: Bricolage as an Alternative Vision of Agency in Ideational Change, *European Political Science Review* 3, 147–67.
Carter, G. M. and J .H. Herz (1962) *Major Foreign Powers* (New York: Harcourt, Brace and World).
Casstevens, T. W. (1984) The Population Dynamics of Government Bureaus, *UMAP Journal* 5, 178–99.
Castles, F. G. and R. Wildenmann (1986) *Visions and Realities of Party Government* (Berlin: DeGruyter).
Cawson, A. (1985) *Organized Interests and the State: Studies in Meso-Corporatism* (London: Sage).
Cerny, P.G. (1990) *The Changing Architecture of Politics: Structure, Agency and the Future of the State* (London: Sage).
Chapsal, J. (1969) *La vie politique en France depuis 1940*, 2nd edn (Paris: Presses universitaires de France).
Cheibub, J. A. and F. Limongi (2002) Democratic Institutions and Regime Survival: Parliamentary and Presidential Democracies Reconsidered, *Annual Review of Political Science* 5, 151–79.
Cheung, S. N. S. (1996) Roofs or Stars: The Stated Intents and Actual Effects of Rent Controls, in L. J. Alston, T. Eggertsson and D. C. North, eds, *Empirical Studies of Organizational Change* (Cambridge: Cambridge University Press).
Chia, R. (2000) Discourse Analysis as Organization Analysis, *Organization* 7, 513–18.
Chiva, C. (2007) The Institutionalization of Post-Communist Parliaments: Hungary and Romania in Comparative Perspective, *Parliamentary Affairs* 60, 197–211.
Christensen, J. G. (1997) Interpreting Administrative Change: Bureaucratic Self Interest and Institutional Inheritance in Government, *Governance* 10, 143–74.
Christensen, T. (2011) Bounded Rationality, in *International Encyclopedia of Political Science* (Thousand Oaks, CA: Sage).
Christensen, T. and K. A. Rovik (1999) The Ambiguity of Appropriateness, in M. Egeberg and P. Laegreid, eds, *Organizing Political Institutions* (Oslo: Scandinavian University Press).
Clark, D. (1996) Inside the IMF: Comparisons with Policy Making Organizations in Canadian Governments, *Canadian Public Administration* 39, 57–92.
Clegg, S. T. Hardy, W. W. Nord and T. Lawrence (2006) *Handbook of Organizational Studies* (London: Sage).
Clemens, E. S. and J. M. Cook (1999) Politics and Institutionalism: Explaining Durability and Change, *Annual Review of Sociology* 25, 441–66.
Clotfelter, J. and B. G. Peters (1976) Profession and Society: Young Military Officers Look Outward, *Journal of Political and Military Sociology* 4, 122–34.
Coase, R. (1937) The Nature of the Firm, *Economica* 4, 386–405.
Coate, R. A. (1988) *Unilateralism, Ideology and U. S. Foreign Policy: The United States In and Out of UNESCO* (Boulder, CO: Lynne Rienner).
Coen, D. and M. Thatcher (2005) The New Governance of Markets and Non-Majoritarian Regulators, *Governance* 19, 329–46.

Cohen, M., J. G. March and J. P. Olsen (1972) A Garbage Can Model of Organizational Choice, *Administrative Science Quarterly*, 17, 1–25.

Collier, D. and J. E. Mahon (1993) Conceptual "Stretching" Revisited: Adapting Categories in Comparative Analysis, American Political Science Review 87, 845–55.

Collier, R. B. and D. Collier (1991) Shaping the Political Arena: Critical Junctures, the Labor Movement, and Regime Dynamics in Latin America (Princeton, NJ: Princeton University Press).

Colomer, J. M. (2000) *Strategic Transitions: Game Theory and Democratization* (Baltimore, MD: Johns Hopkins University Press).

— (2001) Disequilibrium Institutions and Pluralist Democracy, *Journal of Theoretical Politics* 13, 235–47.

Committee on Armed Services, US Senate (1976) *Honor Codes at Service Academies* (Washington, DC: US Government Printing Office).

— (1994) *Honor Codes and Sexual Harassment at the Service Academies* (Washington, DC: US Government Printing Office).

Coneybeare, J. (1984) Bureaucracy, Monopoly and Competition: A Critical Analysis of the Budget Maximizing Model of Bureaucracy, *American Journal of Political Science* 28, 479–502.

Cook, B. and B. D. Wood (1989) Principal–Agent Models of Political Control of the Bureaucracy, *American Political Science Review* 83, 965–78.

Cook, T. D. and D. T. Campbell (1979) *Quasi-Experimentation: Design and Analysis for Field Situations* (Chicago: Rand-McNally).

Cooper, J. and D. W. Brady (1981) Toward a Diachronic Analysis of Congress, *American Political Science Review* 75, 988–1006.

Cortrell, A. P. and J. W. Davis (2000) Understanding the Domestic Impact of International Norms: A Research Agenda, *International Studies Review* 2, 65–87.

Cox, G. W. and M. D. McCubbins (2001) The Institutional Determinants of Economic Policy Outcomes, in S. Haggard and McCubbins, eds, *Presidents, Parliaments and Policy* (Cambridge: Cambridge University Press).

Crane, B. B. (1993) International Population Institutions: Adaptations to a Changing World, in P. M. Haas, R. O. Keohane and M. Levy, eds, *Institutions for the Earth: Sources of Effective International Environmental Protection* (Cambridge, MA: Harvard University Press).

Crewe, I. and A. King (1995) *SDP: The Birth, Life and Death of the Social Democratic Party* (Oxford: Oxford University Press).

Crouch, C. and H. Farrell (2004) Breaking the Path of Institutional Development? Alternatives to the New Determinism, *Rationality and Society* 16, 5–43.

Crozier, M. (1964) *The Bureaucratic Phenomenon* (Chicago: University of Chicago Press).

Cyert, R. and J. G. March (1963) *A Behavioral Theory of the Firm* (Englewood Cliffs, NJ: Prentice-Hall).

Dalton, R. J., S. C. Flanagan, and P. A. Beck (1984) *Electoral Change in Advanced Electoral Democracies* (Princeton, NJ: Princeton University Press).

Damaska, M. R. (1986) *The Faces of Justice and State Authority* (New Haven, CT: Yale University Press).

David, P. A. (1994) Why Are Institutions the "Carriers of History"? Notes on Path-dependence and the Evolution of Conventions, Organizations and Institutions, *Structural Change and Economic Dynamics* 5, 205–20.

Davies, G. (1997) Critics of Bank Independence Miss the Point, *The Independent* March 12.

Davis, C. (2009) Overlapping Institutions in Trade Policy, *Perspectives on Politics* 7, 25–31.

Davis, L. and D. C. North (1971) *Institutional Change and American Economic Growth* (New York: Cambridge University Press).

Della Porta, D. and M. Diani (2006) *Social Movements: An Introduction*, 2nd edn (Malden, MA: Blackwell).

Dempster, M. A. H and A. Wildavsky (1980) On Change: Or, There Is No Magic Size for an Increment, *Political Studies* 27, 371–89.

Denemark, D. (1997) Thinking Ahead to Mixed-Member Proportional Representation: Party Strategies and Electoral Campaigning Under New Zealand's New Electoral Law, *Party Politics* 2, 409–20.

Dequech, D. (2001) Bounded Rationality, Institutions and Uncertainty, *Journal of Economic Issues* 35, 911–28.
Derthick, M. and P. J. Quirk (1985) *The Politics of Deregulation* (Washington, DC: The Brookings Institution).
Dessler, D. (1989) What's at Stake in the Agent-Structure Debate?, *International Organization* 43, 441–73.
Deutsch, K. (1963) *The Nerves of Government: Models of Political Communication and Control* (New York: The Free Press).
Dewey, J. (1938) *Logic: The Theory of Inquiry* (New York: Holt)
Diermeier, D. and K. Krehbiel (2003) Institutionalism as Methodology, *Journal of Theoretical Politics* 15, 123–44.
DiMaggio, P. and W. Powell (1991) The Iron Cage Revisited: Institutional Isomorphism and Collective Rationality in Organizational Fields, *American Sociological Review* 48, 147–60.
Dimock, M. E. and G. O. Dimock (1963) *Public Administration* (New York: Rinehart).
Diskin, H. and A. Diskin (1995) The Politics of Electoral Reform in Israel, *International Political Science Review* 16, 31–45.
Djelic, M.-L. and S. Quack (2003) *Globalization and Institutions: Defining the Rules of the Economic Game* (London: Edward Elgar).
Doern, G. B., L. A. Pal and B. W. Tomlin (1996) *Border Crossings: The Internationalization of Canadian Public Policy* (Toronto: Oxford University Press).
Dogan, M. and D. Pelassey (1990) *How to Compare Nations: Strategies in Comparative Politics*, 2nd edn (Chatham, NJ: Chatham House).
Doig, J. (1983) "If I See a Murderous Fellow Sharpening a Knife Cleverly . . .": The Wilsonian Dichotomy and Public Authority, *Public Administration Review* 43, 292–304.
Doughty, R. A. (1985) *The Seeds of Disaster: The Development of French Army Doctrine, 1919-39* (Hamden, CT: Archon Books).
Douglas, M. (1982) Cultural Bias, in Douglas, ed., *In the Active Voice* (London: Routledge and Kegan Paul).
— (1987) *How Institutions Think* (London: Routledge and Kegan Paul).
Dowding, K. (1994) The Compatibility of Behaviouralism, Rational Choice and "New Institutionalism," *Journal of Theoretical Politics* 6, 105–17.
— (1995) Model or Metaphor?: A Critical Review of the Policy Networks Approach, *Political Studies* 43, 136–58.
Dowding, K. and D. S. King (1995) Introduction, in Dowding and King, eds, *Preferences, Institutions and Rational Choice* (Oxford: Clarendon Press).
Downs, A. (1957) *An Economic Theory of Democracy* (New York: Harper and Row).
— (1967) *Inside Bureaucracy* (Boston: Little, Brown).
Duffield, J. S. (2003) The Limits of "Rational Design," *International Organization* 57, 411–30.
Dunleavy, P. (1991) *Democracy, Bureaucracy and Public Choice* (Englewood Cliffs, NJ: Prentice Hall).
Duquech, D. (2001) Bounded Rationality, Institutions and Uncertainty, *Journal of Economic Issues* 35, 911–29.
Durant, R. F. (2006) Agency Evolution, New Institutionalism and "Hybrid" Policy Domains: Lessons from the "Greening" of the U. S. Miltary, *Policy Studies Journal* 34, 469–90.
Durkheim, E. (1922) *De la division du travail social* (Paris: F. Alcan).
— (1986) *Durkheim on Politics and the State*, ed. by A. Giddens (Cambridge: Polity).
— (1992) *Professional Ethics and Civic Morals*, trans. Cornelia Brookfield (London: Routledge).
Duverger, M. (1951) *Les partis politiques* (Paris: Armand Colin).
— (1980) A New Political System Model: Semi-Presidential Government, *European Journal for Political Research* 8, 165–87.
— (1987) *La cohabitation des francais* (Paris: Presses Universitaires de France).
— (1988) *Les regimes semi-presidentiels* (Paris: Presses Universitaires de France).

Dye, T. R. (1966) *Politics, Economics and the Public: Policy Outcomes in the American States* (Chicago: Rand McNally).
Dyson, K. H. F. (1980) *State Tradition in Western Europe: A Study of an Idea and Institution* (Oxford: Oxford University Press).
Easton, D. (1953) *The Political System: An Inquiry into the State of Political Science* (New York: Knopf).
— (1990) *The Analysis of Political Structure* (London: Routledge).
Eckstein, H. (1963) A Perspective on Comparative Politics, in H. Eckstein and D. Apter, eds, *Comparative Politics* (New York: Free Press).
Edelman, L. (1992) Legal Ambiguity and Symbolic Structures: Organizational Mediation of Civil Rights Law, *American Journal of Sociology* 97, 1531–76.
Edelman, M. J. (1964) *The Symbolic Uses of Politics* (Urbana: University of Illinois Press).
— (1988) *Constructing the Political Spectacle* (Chicago: University of Chicago Press).
Egeberg, M. (2003) in B. G. Peters and J. Pierre, eds, *Handbook of Public Administration* (London: Sage).
— (2004) An Organizational Approach to European Integration: Outline of a Complementary Perspective, *European Journal of Political Research* 43, 189–219.
Eggertsson, T. (1990) *Economic Behavior and Institutions* (Cambridge: Cambridge University Press).
— (1996) A Note on the Economics of Institutions, in L. J. Alston, T. Eggertsson and D. C. North, eds, *Empirical Studies in Institutional Change* (Cambridge: Cambridge University Press).
Eisenstadt, S. N. (1959) Bureaucracy, Bureaucratization and Debureaucratization, *Administrative Science Quarterly* 4, 302–20.
— (1963) *The Political Systems of Empires* (New York: Free Press).
— (1965) *Essays on Comparative Institutions* (New York: John Wiley).
Eisenstadt, S. N., R. Bar Yosef and C. Adler (1970) *Integration and Development in Israel* (New York: Praeger).
Eisner, M. A., J. Worsham and E. Ringquist (1996) Crossing the Organizational Void: The Limits of Agency Theory in the Analysis of Regulatory Control, *Governance* 9, 407–28.
Elgie, R. (2001) *Divided Government in Comparative Perspective* (Oxford: Oxford University Press).
Etzioni, A. (1963) *A Comparative Analysis of Complex Organizations: On Power, Involvement and Their Correlates*, rev. edn (New York: Free Press).
Eulau, H. (1963) *The Behavioral Persuasion in Politics* (New York: Random House).
Evans, P. B., D. Rueschmeyer and T. Skocpol (1985) *Bringing the State Back In* (Cambridge: Cambridge University Press).
Fairclough, N. (1992) *Discourse and Social Change* (Oxford: Polity).
Farneti, P. (1985) *The Italian Party System, 1945–1980* (New York: St. Martin's).
Feigenbaum, H., R. Samuels and R. K. Weaver (1993) Innovation, Coordination and Implementation in Energy Policy, in R. K. Weaver and B. A. Rockman, eds, *Do Institutions Matter?* (Washington, DC: The Brookings Institution).
Feldman, J. L. (1995) *Plague Doctors: Responding to the AIDS Epidemic in France and America* (Westport, CT: Bergin and Garvey).
Fenno, R. F. (1978) *Home Style: House Members in their Districts* (Boston: Little, Brown).
Finer, S. E. (1958) *Anonymous Empire: A Study of the Lobby in Great Britain* (London: Pall Mall).
— (1997) *The History of Government from the Earliest Times* (Oxford: Oxford University Press).
Finnemore, M. and K. Sikkink (1998) International Norm Dynamics and Political Change, *International Organization* 52, 887–917.
Fiorina, M. P. (1982) *Congress: Keystone of the Washington Establishment* (New Haven, CT: Yale University Press).
— (1987) *Congress: The Keystone of the Washington Establishment* (New Haven, CT: Yale University Press).
— (1992) Coalition Government, Divided Government and Electoral Theory, *Governance* 4, 236–49.
— (1996) *Divided Government*, 2nd edn (Boston: Allyn and Bacon).

Fligstein, N. (1990) *The Transformation of Corporate Control* (Cambridge, MA: Harvard University Press).
Foley, M. (1993) *The Rise of the British Presidency* (Manchester: University of Manchester Press).
Fontana, B. (1994) *The Invention of the Modern Republic* (Cambridge: Cambridge University Press).
Franklin, M. N. (1985) *The Decline of Class Voting in Britain: Changes in the Basis of Electoral Choice 1964–83* (Oxford: Clarendon Press).
Franzen, L. (2011) Why Do Private Governance Organizations Not Converge: A Politico-Institutional Analysis, *Governance* 24, 311–30.
Freeman, J. L. (1965) *The Political Process* (New York: Random House).
Frenkel, J. A. and M. Goldstein (1996) *Functioning of the International Monetary System* (Washington, DC: IMF).
Friedberg, E. (1998) En lisant Hall and Taylor: Néo-institutionalisme et ordres locaux, *Revue Francaise de science politique* 48, 507–14.
Friedrich, C. J. (1950) *Constitutional Government and Democracy: Theory and Practice in Europe and America* (Boston: Ginn).
Friedrich, C. J. and Z. K. Brzezinski (1956) *Totalitarian Dictatorship and Autocracy* (Cambridge, MA: Harvard University Press).
Frohlich, N., J. A. Oppenheimer and O. R. Young (1971) *Political Leadership and Collective Goods* (Princeton, NJ: Princeton University Press).
Frumkin, P. and J. Galaskiewicz (2004) Institutional Isomorphism and Public Sector Organizations, *Journal of Public Administration Research and Theory* 14, 283–307.
Galaskiewicz, J. (1985) Professional Networks and the Institutionalization of a Single Mind-Set, *American Sociological Review* 50, 639–58.
Galeotti, G. (1991) The Number of Parties and Political Competition, in A. Breton, G. Galeotti, P. Salamon and R. Wintrobe, eds, *The Competitive State* (Dordrecht: Kluwer).
Galton, R. J. and S. Weldon (2007) Partisanship and Party System Institutionalization, *Party Politics* 13, 179–96.
Gamble, A. (1994) *The Free Economy and the Strong State: The Politics of Thatcherism*, 2nd edn (Basingstoke: Macmillan).
— (1996) *Hayek: The Iron Cage of Liberty* (Boulder, CO: Westview Press).
Ganghof, S. (2003) Promises and Pitfalls of Veto Player Analysis, *Swiss Political Science Review* 9, 1–26.
Garrett, G. (1992) International Cooperation and Institutional Choice: The European Community's Internal Market, *International Organization* 46, 533–60.
Garrett, G. and G. Tsebelis (1996) An Institutional Critique of Intergovernmentalism, *International Organization* 50, 269–99.
Garud, R. and P. Karnøe (2001) *Path Dependence and Creation* (Mahwah, NJ: Lawrence Erlbaum).
Gatlin, D. (1968) Towards a Functionalist Theory of Political Parties, in W. Crotty, ed., *Approaches to the Study of Party Organization* (Boston: Allyn & Bacon).
Gauvreau, E. H. and L. Cohen (1942) *Billy Mitchell, Founder of Our Air Force and Prophet Without Honor* (New York: E. P. Dutton).
Geering, J. (2001) *Party Ideologies in America, 1828-1926* (Cambridge: Cambridge University Press).
Genschel, P. (1997) The Dynamics of Inertia: Institutional Persistence and Change in Telecommunications and Health Care, *Governance* 10, 43–66.
Gerlich, P. (1973) The Institutionalization of European Parliaments, in A. Kornberg, ed., *Legislatures in Comparative Perspective* (New York: David McKay).
Gerth, H. H. and C. W. Mills (1946) *From Max Weber: Essays in Sociology* (New York: Oxford University Press).
Gibbons, D. E. (2004) Network Structure and Innovation: Ambiguity Effects on Diffusion of Dynamic Organizational Fields, *Academy of Management Journal* 47, 938–51.
Gibbons, R. (2006) Four Formal(izable) Theories of the Firm, *Journal of Economic Behavior and Organization* 58, 200–45.

Giddens, A. (1979) *Central Problems in Social Theory* (Berkeley: University of California Press).
— (1981) *A Contemporary Critique of Historical Materialism*, Vol. 1: Power, Property and the State (London: Macmillan).
— (1984) *The Constitution of Society: Outline of the Theory of Structuration* (Cambridge: Cambridge University Press).
Gidron, B., R. M. Kramer and L. M. Salamon (1992) *Government and the Third Sector: Emerging Relationships in Welfare States* (San Francisco, CA: Jossey-Bass).
Gofas, A. and C. Hay (2008) *The Ideas Debate in International and European Studies: Towards a Cartography and Critical Assessment.* IBEI Working Paper.
— (2010) *The Role of Ideas in Political Analysis: A Portrait of Contemporary Debates* (London: Routledge).
Goffman, E. (1961) *Asylums: Essays on the Social Situation of Mental Patients and Other Inmates* (Garden City, NY: Anchor).
Goldman, K. (2005) Appropriateness and Consequences: The Logic of Neo-Institutionalism, *Governance* 18, 35–52.
Goldstein, J. and R. O. Keohane (eds) (1993) *Ideas in Foreign Policy: Beliefs, Institutions, and Political Change* (Ithaca, NY: Cornell University Press).
Goldstein, J. L., D. Rivers and M. Tomz (2007) Institutions in International Relations: Understanding the Effects of the GATT and the WTO in World Trade, *International Organization* 61, 37–67.
Goodin, R. E. (1995) *The Theory of Institutional Design* (Cambridge: Cambridge University Press).
Goodman, J. B. (1992) *Monetary Sovereignty: The Politics of Central Banking in Western Europe* (Ithaca, NY: Cornell University Press).
Gormley, W. T. (1989) *Taming the Bureaucracy: Muscles, Prayers and Other Strategies* (Princeton, NJ: Princeton University Press).
Gottweiss, H. (2006) Argumentative Policy Analysis, in B. G. Peters and J. Pierre, eds, *Handbook of Public Policy* (London: Sage).
Grafstein, R. (1992) *Institutional Realism* (New Haven, CT: Yale University Press).
Granovetter, M. (1985) Economic Action and Social Structure: The Problem of Embeddedness, *American Journal of Sociology* 91, 481–510.
— (1992) Economics Institutions as Social Constructions: A Framework for Analysis, *Acta Sociologica* 35, 3–12.
Gray, V. and D. Lowery (1996a) A Niche Theory of Interest Representation, *Journal of Politics* 58, 91–111.
— (1996b) *The Population Ecology of Interest Representation* (Ann Arbor: University of Michigan Press).
Green, D. P. and I. Shapiro (1994) *Pathologies of Rational Choice Theory: A Critique of Applications in Political Science* (New Haven, CT: Yale University Press).
Greenwood, R. and C. R. Hinnings (1993) Understanding Strategic Change: The Contribution of Archetypes, *Academy of Management Journal* 36, 1052–81.
— (1996) Understanding Radical Organizational Change: Bringing Together the Old and New Institutionalism, *Academy of Management Review* 21, 1022–54.
Greif, A. and D. D. Laitin (2004), A Theory of Endogenous Institutional Change, *American Political Science Review* 98, 633–52.
Grendstad, G. and P. Selle (1995) Cultural Theory and the New Institutionalism, *Journal of Theoretical Politics* 7, 5–27.
Grilli, V., D. Masciandaro and G. Tabellini (1991) Political and Monetary Institutions and Public Financial Policies in the Industrial Countries, *Economic Policy* 13, 341–78.
Gyimah-Boadi, E. (1996) Civil Society in Africa, *Journal of Democracy* 7, 118–32.
Haas, P. M. (1992) Introduction: Epistemic Communities and International Policy Coordination, *International Organization* 46, 1–35.

— (1993) Epistemic Communities and the Dynamics of International Environmental Cooperation, in V. Rittberger and P. Mayer, eds, *Regime Theory in International Relations* (Oxford: Clarendon Press).
Habermas, J. (1984) *The Theory of Communicative Action: Reason and Rationalization in Society* (London: Heinneman).
— (1989) *The Structural Transformation of the Public Sphere* (Cambridge, MA: MIT Press).
— (1996) *Between Facts and Norms: Contributions to a Discourse Theory* (Cambridge: Polity).
Hacker, J. (2005) Policy Drift: The Hidden Politics of US Welfare State Retrenchment, in K. Thelen and W. Streeck, eds, *Beyond Continuity: Explorations in the Dynamics of Advanced Political Economies* (Oxford: Oxford University Press).
Haggard, S. and B. A. Simmons (1987) Theories of International Regimes, *International Organization* 41, 491–517.
Hajer, M. A. and H. Wagenaar (2003) *Deliberative Policy Analysis: Understanding Governance in a Network Society* (Cambridge: Cambridge University Press).
Hall, P. A. (1986) *Governing the Economy: The Politics of State Intervention in Britain and France* (New York: Oxford University Press).
— (1989) *The Power of Economic Ideas* (Princeton, NJ: Princeton University Press).
— (1992) The Movement from Keynesianism to Monetarism: Institutional Analysis and British Economic Policy in the 1970s, in S. Steinmo, K. Thelen and F. Longstreth, eds, *Structuring Politics* (Cambridge: Cambridge University Press).
— (1993) Policy Paradigms, Social Learning and the State: The Case of Economic Policy-making in Britain, *Comparative Politics* 25, 275–96.
Hall, P. A. and D. Soskice (eds) (2001) *Varieties of Capitalism: The Institutional Foundations of Comparative Advantage* (New York: Oxford University Press).
Hall, P. A. and R. C. R. Taylor (1996) Political Science and the Three New Institutionalisms, *Political Studies* 44, 952–73.
Hallerberg, M. (2003) *Domestic Budgets in an United Europe: Fiscal Governance from the End of Bretton Woods to the EMU* (Ithaca, NY: Cornell University Press).
Hammond, T. (1986) Agenda Control, Organizational Structure and Bureaucratic Politics, *American Journal of Political Science* 30, 379–98.
Hammond, T., C. W. Bonneau and R. S. Sheehan (2005) *Strategic Behavior and Policy Choice on the U. S. Supreme Court* (Palo Alto, CA: Stanford University Press).
Hannan, M.T. and J. Freeman (1989) *Organizational Ecology* (Cambridge, MA: Harvard University Press).
Hardin, J. and J. Baden (1977) *Managing the Commons* (San Francisco, CA: W. H. Freeman).
Hardy, C. and S. Maguire (2008) Institutional Entrepreneurship, in R. Greenwood, C. Oliver, K. Sahlin and R. Suddaby, eds, *The Sage Handbook of Organizational Institutionalism* (London: Sage).
Hart, O. (1995) An Economist's Perspective on the Theory of the Firm, in O. E. Williamson, ed., *Organization Theory* (Oxford: Oxford University Press).
Hasenclever, A., P. Mayer and V. Rittberger (1996) Interests, Power, Knowledge: The Study of International Regimes, *Mershon International Studies Review* 40, 177–228.
— (1997) *Theories of International Regimes* (Cambridge: Cambridge University Press).
Hathaway, O. A. (2001) Path Dependence and the Law: The Course and Pattern of Legal Change in a Common Law System, *The Iowa Law Review* 86, 101–65.
Haveman, H. A. and R. H. Rao (1997) Structuring a Theory of Moral Sentiments: Institutional and Organizational Coevolution in the Early Thrift Industry, *American Journal of Sociology* 102, 1606–51.
Hay, C. (1995) Structure and Agency, in D. Marsh and G. Stoker, eds, *Theory and Methods in Political Science* (New York: St. Martins).
— (2001) The "Crisis" of Keynesianism and the Rise of Neoliberalism in Britain, in J. L. Campbell and O. K. Pedersen, eds, *The Rise of Neoliberalism and Institutional Analysis* (Princeton, NJ: Princeton University Press).

— (2006) Constructivist Institutionalism, in R. A. W. Rhodes, S. A. Binder and B. A. Rockman, eds, *Oxford Handbook of Political Institutions* (Oxford: Oxford University Press).
Hayek, F. A. von (1967) A Note on the Evolution of Systems of Rules of Conduct, in Hayek, ed. *Studies in Philosophy, Politics and Economics* (Chicago: University of Chicago Press).
— (1973) *Economic Freedom and Representative Government* (London: Institute of Economic Affairs).
Hayes, M. T. (1992) *Incrementalism and Public Policy* (New York: Longman).
Hayward, J. E. S. (1983) *Governing France: The One and Indivisible Republic*, 2nd edn (London: Weidenfeld and Nicolson).
Hechter, M. (1990) The Emergence of Cooperative Social Institutions, in M. Hechter, K.-D. Opp and R. Wippler, eds, *Social Institutions* (New York: Aldine de Gruyter).
Hechter, M. and S. Kanazawa (1997) Sociological Rational Choice Theory, *Annual Review of Sociology* 23, 191–214.
Heclo, H. (1974) *Modern Social Politics in Britain and Sweden: From Relief to Income Maintenance* (New Haven, CT: Yale University Press).
— (2008) *Thinking Institutionally* (Boulder, CO: Paradigm).
Heclo, H. and A. Wildavsky (1974) *The Private Government of Public Money* (Berkeley: University of California Press).
Heidenheimer, A. J., M. Johnston and V. T. Levine (1989) *Political Corruption: A Handbook* (New Brunswick, NJ: Transaction).
Heisler, M. O. (1979) Corporate Pluralism; Where Is the Theory?, *Scandinavian Political Studies* 2 (n.s.), 277–98.
Helms, L. (2000) "Politische Fuhrung" als politikwissenshaftliches Problem. *Poltiische Vierteiljahrrschrift* 51, 411–34.
Hermansson, J., T. Svensson and P. O. Oberg (1997) Vad blev det av den svenska korporativismen, *Politica* 29, 365–84.
Hermesen, H. (1991) *Votes and Policy Preferences: Equilibria in Party Systems* (Amsterdam: Thesis Publishers).
Hermet, G. (2004) Un regime de pluralisme limite?: A propos de la gouvernance democratique, *Revue française de science politique* 54, 159–78.
Hertier, A. (1996) Institutions, Interests and Political Choice, in R. Czada, A. Hertier and H. Keman, eds, *Institutions and Political Choice: On the Limits of Rationality* (Amsterdam: VU University Press).
Herzberg, R. Q. (1996) Unity versus Division: The Effect of Divided Government on Policy Development, in P. F. Galdarisi, R. Q. Herzberg and P. McNamara, eds, *Divided Government* (New York: Rowman and Littlefield).
Hibbing, J. R. (1988) Legislative Institutionalization with Illustrations from the British House of Commons, *American Journal of Political Science* 32, 681–712.
Higley, J. and R. Gunther (1992) *Elites and Democratic Consolidation in Latin America and Southern Europe* (Cambridge: Cambridge University Press).
Hilbink, L. (2009) The Constituted Nature of Constituents' Interests, *Political Research Quarterly* 62, 781–97.
Himmelfarb, G. (1984) *The Idea of Poverty: England in the Industrial Age* (New York: Knopf).
Hindness, B. (1989) *Political Choice and Social Structure* (Cheltenham: Edward Elgar).
Hirsch, P. M. (1997) Sociology without Social Structure: Neoinstitutional Theory Meets Brave New World, *American Journal of Sociology* 102, 1702–23.
Hirschman, A. O. (1970) *Exit, Voice and Loyalty* (Cambridge, MA: Harvard University Press).
Hirst, P. and G. Thompson (1996) *Globalization in Question* (Cambridge: Polity Press).
Hjern, B. and D. O. Porter (1981) Implementation Structures: A New Unit of Administrative Analysis, *Organization Studies* 2, 211–27.
Hofstader, R. (1963) *The Progressive Movement, 1916-70* (Englewood Cliffs, NJ: Prentice-Hall).
Hogwood, B. W. and L. A. Gunn (1984) *Policy Analysis for the Real World* (Oxford: Oxford University Press).

Hogwood, B. W. and B. G. Peters (1983) *Policy Dynamics* (Brighton: Wheatsheaf).
Holmes, O. W. (1909) *The Common Law* (Boston: Little, Brown).
Hood, C. (1976) *The Limits of Administration* (New York: Wiley).
— (1999) The Garbage Can Model of Organizations: Describing a Condition or Prescriptive Design Principle, in M. Egeberg and P. Laegreid, eds, *Organizing Political Institutions: Essays for Johan P. Olsen* (Oslo: Universitetsforlaget).
Hood, C., M. Huby and A. Dunsire (1984) Bureaucrats and Budgeting Benefits: How Do British Central Government Departments Shape Up?, *Journal of Public Policy* 4, 163–79.
Hoogenboom, A. A. and O. Hoogenboom (1976) *The History of the ICC: From Panacea to Palliative* (New York: Norton).
Hooker, R. (1965) *Of the Laws of the Ecclesiastical Polity* (London: J. W. Dent) [original 1594–7].
Horn, M. (1995) *The Political Economy of Public Administration* (Cambridge: Cambridge University Press).
Horn, M. and K. Shepsle (1989) Commentary on "Administrative Arrangements and the Political Control of Agencies": Administrative Process and Organizational Form as Legislative Responses to Agency Costs, *Virginia Law Review* 77, 499–508.
Howarth, D. R., A. J. Norval and Y. Stavrakakis (eds) (2000) *Discourse Theory and Political Analysis: Identities, Hegemonies and Social Change* (Manchester: Manchester University Press).
Howorth, J. (2004) Discourse, Ideas, and Epistemic Communities in European Security and Defence Policy, *West European Politics* 27, 211–34.
Huber, E. and J. D. Stephens (2001) *Development and Crisis of the Welfare State* (Chicago: University of Chicago Press).
Huber, J. D. and C. R. Shipan (2002) *Deliberate Discretion?: The Institutional Foundation of Bureaucratic Authority* (Cambridge: Cambridge University Press).
Hueglin, T. and A. Fenna (2005) *Comparative Federalism* (Peterborough, ONT: Broadview).
Hughes, J. R. T. (1993) *The Governmental Habit Redux: Economic Controls from Colonial Times to the Present*, 2nd edn (Princeton, NJ: Princeton University Press).
Huntington, S. P. (1965) Political Development and Political Decay, *World Politics* 17, 386–430.
— (1968) *Political Order in Changing Societies* (New Haven, CT: Yale University Press).
Ikenberry, G. J. (1988) Conclusion: An Institutional Approach to American Foreign Economic Policy, in G. J. Ikenberry, D. A. Lake and M. Mastanduno, eds, *The State and American Foreign Economic Policy* (Ithaca, NY: Cornell University Press).
Immergut, E. (1990) Institutions, Veto Points, and Policy Results: A Comparative Analysis of Health Care, *Journal of Public Policy* 10, 391–416.
— (1992a) *Health Care Politics: Ideas and Institutions in Western Europe* (Cambridge: Cambridge University Press).
— (1992b) The Rules of the Game: The Logic of Health Policy-making in France, Switzerland and Sweden, in S. Steinmo, K. Thelen and F. Lonstreth, eds, *Structuring Politics: Historical Institutionalism in Comparative Politics* (Cambridge: Cambridge University Press).
— (1997) The Normative Roots of the New Institutionalism and Comparative Policy Studies, in A. Benz and W. Siebel, eds, *Theorieentwicklung in der Politikwissenschaft: Ein Zwischenbilanz* (Baden-Baden: Nomos).
Inglehart, R. (1990) *Culture Shift in Advanced Industrial Societies* (Princeton, NJ: Princeton University Press).
Inglehart, R. and P. Abramson (1994) Economic Security and Value Change, 1970-1993, *American Political Science Review* 88, 336–54.
Ingram, H. and A. B. Schneider (1990) Improving Implementation Through Framing Smarter Statutes, *Journal of Public Policy* 10, 67–87.
Jabko, N. (2006) *Playing the Market: A Political Strategy for Uniting Europe 1985-2005* (Ithaca, NY: Cornell University Press).
Jachtenfuchs, M. (2001) The Governance Approach to European Integration, *Journal of Common Market Studies* 39, 245–64.

Janda, K. (2011) *Party Systems and Country Governance* (Boulder, CO: Paradigm).

Jepperson, R. L. (1991) Institutions, Institutional Effects and Institutionalization, in W. W. Powell and P. J. Dimaggio, eds, *The New Institutionalism in Organizational Analysis* (Chicago: University of Chicago Press).

Jessop, B. (2003) Institutions and Rules, *Research Papers in Institutional Theory* 11, 1–11.

Jobert, B. (1989) The Normative Frameworks of Public Policy, *Political Studies* 37, 376–86.

Johnson, R. N. and G. D. Libecap (1994) *The Federal Civil Service System and the Problem of Bureaucracy* (Chicago: University of Chicago Press).

Johnston, M. and A. J. Heidenheimer (1989) *Political Corruption: A Handbook* (New Brunswick, NJ: Transaction Press).

Jones, B. D. (2001) *Politics and the Architecture of Choice* (Chicago: University of Chicago Press).

— (2003) Bounded Rationality and Political Science: Lessons from Public Administration and Public Policy, *Journal of Public Administration and Policy* 13, 395–412.

Jones, C. O. (1995) *Separate but Equal Branches: Congress and the Presidency* (Chatham, NJ: Chatham House).

Jones, G. (1991) Presidentialization in a Parliamentary System, in C. Campbell and M. J. Wyszomirski, eds, *Executive Leadership in Anglo-American Systems* (Pittsburgh: University of Pittsburgh Press).

Jordan, A. G. (1990) Policy Community Realism versus "New Institutionalism" Ambiguity, *Political Studies* 38, 470–84.

Joyal, S. (2005) *Protecting Canadian Democracy: The Senate You Never Knew* (Montreal: McGill-Queens University Press).

Judge, D. (2003) Legislative Institutionalization: A Bent Analytic Arrow, *Government and Opposition* 38, 497–516.

Kaiser, A. (1997) Types of Democracy: From Classical to New Institutionalism, *Journal of Theoretical Politics* 9, 419–44.

Kaplan, A. (1965) *The Conduct of Inquiry* (San Francisco, CA: Chandler).

Kato, J. (1996) Review Article: Institutions and Rationality in Politics—Three Varieties of Neo-Institutionalists, *British Journal of Political Science* 26, 553–82.

Katz, D. and R. L. Kahn (1978) *The Social Psychology of Organizations*, 2nd edn (New York: John Wiley).

Katz, E. and S. N. Eisenstadt (1960) Some Sociological Observations on the Response of Israeli Organizations to New Immigrants, *Administrative Science Quarterly* 5, 113–33.

Katz, R. (1990) Party as Linkage: A Vestigial Function?, *European Journal of Political Research* 18, 143–61.

Katz, R. S. and P. Mair (1994) *How Parties Organize: Change and Adaptation in Party Organizations in Western Democracies* (London: Sage).

— (2009) The Cartel Party Thesis: A Restatement, *Perspectives on Politics* 7, 753–66.

Katznelson, I. and B. Weingast (2005) *Preferences and Situations: Points of Intersection between Historical and Rational Choice Institutionalism* (New York: Russell Sage).

Kaufman, H. (1960) *The Forest Ranger: A Study in Administrative Behavior* (Baltimore, MD: Johns Hopkins University Press).

Keck, O. (1991) Der neue Institutionalismus in der Theorie der Internationalen Politik, *Politische Vierteiljahrsschrift* 32, 635–53.

Kelly, S. A. (1993) Research Note: Divided We Govern? A Reassessment, *Polity* 25, 475–84.

Kelman, S. (1988) *Making Public Policy: A Hopeful View of American Government* (New York: Basic Books).

Keman, H. (1996a) Konkordanzdemokratie und Korporatismus aus der Perspektive eines rationalen Institutionalismus, *Politische Vierteiljahrschrift* 37, 271–81.

— (1996b) Political Institutions and Public Governance, in R. Czada, A. Hertier and H. Keman, eds, *Institutions and Political Choice: The Limits of Rationality* (Amsterdam: VU Press).

Keohane, R. O. (1988) International Institutions: Two Approaches, *International Studies Quarterly* 32, 379–96.
— (1989) Neoliberal Institutionalism: A Perspective on World Politics, in Keohane, ed., *International Institutions and State Power: Essays in International Relations Theory* (Boulder, CO: Westview Press).
Keohane, R. O. and J. S. Nye (1977) *Power and Interdependence: World Politics in Transition* (Boston: Little, Brown).
Khalil, E. L. (1995) Organizations versus Institutions, *Journal of Institutional and Theoretical Economics* 151, 445–66.
Kickert, W. J. M., E.-H. Klijn and J. F. M. Koppenjan (1997) *Managing Complex Networks: Strategies for the Public Sector* (London: Sage).
King, D. S. (1995) *Actively Seeking Work: The Politics of Unemployment and Welfare Policy in the United States* (Chicago: University of Chicago Press).
King, G. (1995) Replication, Replication, *PS* 28, 444–9.
Kingdon, J. (2003) *Agendas, Alternatives and Public Policies*, 2nd edn (Boston: Little, Brown).
Kingston, C. and G. Caballero (2009) Comparing Theories of Institutional Change, *Journal of Institutional Economics* 5, 151–80.
Kiser, L. and E. Ostrom (1982) The Three Worlds of Action: A Metatheoretical Synthesis of Institutional Approaches, in E. Ostrom, ed., *Strategies of Political Inquiry* (Beverly Hills, CA: Sage).
Kitschelt, H. (1989) *The Logics of Party Formation: Ecological Politics in Belgium and West Germany* (Ithaca, NY: Cornell University Press).
Kjaer, P. and O. K. Pedersen (2001) Translating Liberalism: Neoliberalism in the Danish Negotiated Economy, in J. L. Campbell and O. K. Pedersen, eds, *The Rise of Neoliberalism and Institutional Analysis* (Chicago: University of Chicago Press).
Kliemt, H. (1990) The Costs of Organizing Social Cooperation, in M. Hechter, K.-D. Opp and R. Wippler, eds, *Social Institutions* (New York: Aldine de Gruyter).
Klijn, E.-H. (2001) Rules as Institutional Context for Decision-Making in Networks, *Administration & Society* 33, 133–64.
Knight, J. (1992) *Institutions and Social Conflict* (Cambridge: Cambridge University Press).
— (1998) Models, Interpretations and Theories: Constructing Models of Institutional Emergence and Change, in J. Knight and I. Sened, eds, *Explaining Social Institutions* (Ann Arbor: University of Michigan Press).
Knill, C. and A. Lenschow (2001) "Seek and Ye Shall Find!": Linking Different Perspectives on Institutional Change, *Comparative Political Studies* 34, 187–215.
Knoke, D. (1990) *Political Networks: The Structural Perspective* (Cambridge: Cambridge University Press).
Knoke, D. and F. Burleigh (1989) Collective Action in National Policy Domains: Constraints, Cleavages and Policy Outcomes, *Research in Political Sociology* 4, 187–208.
Knoke, D. and E. O. Laumann (1987) *The Organizational State* (Madison: University of Wisconsin Press).
Knoke, D., F. U. Pappi and Y. Tsujinaka (1996) *Comparing Policy Networks: Labor Politics in the U.S., Germany and Japan* (Cambridge: Cambridge University Press).
Konig. K. (1993) Bureaucratic Integration by Elite Transfer: The Case of the Former GDR, *Governance* 6, 386–96.
Kraan, D.-J. (1996) *Budgetary Decisions: A Public Choice Approach* (Cambridge: Cambridge University Press).
Krasner, S. (1983) *International Regimes* (Ithaca, NY: Cornell University Press).
— (1984) Approaches to the State: Alternative Conceptions and Historical Dynamics, *Comparative Politics* 16, 223–46.
— (1988) Sovereignty: An Institutional Perspective, *Comparative Political Studies* 21, 66–94.

Kratochwil, F. (2009) Toward a Post-Secular Political Order, *European Political Science Review* 1, 317–40.

Kratochwil, F. and J. G. Ruggie (1986) International Organization: The State of the Art on the Art of the State, *International Organization* 40, 753–75.

Krehbiel, K. (1991) *Information and Legislative Organization* (Ann Arbor: University of Michigan Press).

— (1996) Institutional and Partisan Sources of Gridlock: A Theory of Divided and Unified Government, *Journal of Theoretical Politics* 8, 7–40.

Kreppel, A. (2003) *The European Parliament and the Supranational Party System* (Cambridge: Cambridge University Press).

Kreuger, A. O. (1996) The Political Economy of Controls: American Sugar, in L. J. Alston, T. Eggertsson and D. C. North, eds, *Empirical Studies of Institutional Change* (Cambridge: Cambridge University Press).

Kriek, D. J. (1995) David Easton and the Analysis of Political Structure, *Journal of Theoretical Politics* 7, 29–39.

Kvavik, R. B. (1980) *Interest Groups in Norwegian Politics* (Oslo: Universitetsforlaget).

Kydd, A. and D. Snidal (1993) Progress in Game-Theoretic Analysis of International Regimes, in V. Rittberger, ed., *Regime Theory and International Relations* (Oxford: Clarendon Press).

Lachmann, L. M. (1971) *The Legacy of Max Weber* (Berkeley, CA: Glendessary Press).

Lago, I. (2011) Why New Parties?, *Party Politics* 17, 3–20.

Lake, D. A. (2001) Beyond Anarchy: The Importance of Security Institutions, *International Security* 26, 129–60.

Landau, M. (1969) Redundancy, Rationality and the Problem of Duplication and Overlap, *Public Administration Review* 29, 346–50.

Lane, J. E. (1981) The Concept of Implementation, *Statsvetenskapliga Tidskrift* 86, 17–40.

Lane, J.-E. and S. Ersson (1994) *Politics and Society in Western Europe*, 3rd edn (London: Sage).

LaPalombara, J. (1968) Macro-theories and Micro-applications: A Widening Chasm, *Comparative Politics* 1, 52–78.

La Porte, T. (1996) Shifting Vantage and Conceptual Puzzles in Understanding Public Organization Networks, *Journal of Public Administration Research and Theory*, 6, 49–74.

Latham, E. (1965) *The Group Basis of Politics: A Study of Basing-Point Legislation* (New York: Octagon Books).

Laughlin, R. C. (1991) Environmental Disturbances and Organizational Transitions and Transformations: Some Alternative Models, *Organization Studies* 12, 209–32.

Laver, M. and W. B. Hunt (1992) *Policy and Party Competition* (London: Routledge).

Laver, M. and N. Schofield (1990) *Multiparty Government: The Politics of Coalition in Europe* (Oxford: Oxford University Press).

Laver, M. and K. A. Shepsle (1995) *Making and Breaking Governments: Cabinets and legitimacy in Parliamentary Democracies* (Cambridge: Cambridge University Press).

Le Gales, P. and M. Thatcher (1995) *Les reseaux de politique publique: Debat autour des policy networks* (Paris: L'Harmattan).

Levi, M. (1997) A Model, a Method and a Map: Rational Choice in Comparative and Historical Analysis, in M. I. Lichbach and A. S. Zuckerman, eds, *Comparative Politics: Rationality, Culture and Structure* (Cambridge: Cambridge University Press).

Levinthal, D. A. and J. G. March (1994) The Myopia of Learning, *Strategic Management Journal* 14, 95–112.

Levitt, B. and J. G. March (1988) Organizational Learning, *Annual Review of Sociology* 19, 319–40.

Lewin, L. (1988) *Ideology and Strategy: A Century of Swedish Politics* (Cambridge: Cambridge University Press).

Lijphart, A. (1984) *Democracies: Patterns of Majoritarian and Consensus Government in Twenty-One Countries* (New Haven, CT: Yale University Press).

— (1994) Democracies: Forms, Performance and Constitutional Engineering, *European Journal of Political Research* 25, 1–17.
Lin, J. (1991) *The Red Guard's Path to Violence: Political, Educational and Psychological Factors* (New York: Praeger).
Lindahl, H. (2001) Sovereignty and the Institutionalization of Normative Order, *Oxford Journal of Legal Studies* 21, 165–80.
Lindblom, C. E. (1965) *The Intelligence of Democracy* (New York: Free Press).
Linder, S. H. and B. G. Peters (1989) Implementation as a Guide for Policy Formulation: A Question of "When" Rather than "Whether," *International Review of Administrative Sciences* 55, 631–52.
Linder, W. (1997) *The Swiss Political System* (Bern: Peter Lang).
Linz, J. J. (1990) The Perils of Presidentialism, *Journal of Democracy* 1, 51–69.
— (1994) Presidential or Parliamentary Democracy: Does it Make a Difference?, in J. J. Linz and A. Valenzuela, eds, *The Failure of Presidential Democracy* (Baltimore, MD: Johns Hopkins University Press).
Lipset, S. M. and S. Rokkan (1967) *Party Systems and Voter Alignments* (New York: Free Press).
Loewenberg, G. (1973) The Institutionalization of Parliament and Public Orientations to the Political System, in A. Kornberg, ed., *Legislatures in Comparative Perspective* (New York: David McKay).
Lowndes, V. (1996) Varieties of New Institutionalism: A Critical Appraisal, *Public Administration* 74, 181–97.
Luhmann, N. (1990) *Essays on Self-Reference* (New York: Columbia University Press).
Luong, P. J. (2002) *Institutional Change and Continuity in Post-Soviet Central Asia* (Cambridge: Cambridge University Press).
Lupia, A. and M. D. McCubbins (1994) Learning from Oversight: Fire Alarms and Police Patrols Reconstructed, *Journal of Law, Economics, and Organization* 10, 96–125.
Macdonald, L. (1983) *Somme* (London: M. Joseph).
Macridis, R. C. (1955) *The Study of Comparative Government* (New York: Random House).
Mahoney, J. (2000) Path Dependence in Historical Sociology, *Theory and Society* 29, 507–48.
Mahoney, J. and K. Thelen (eds) (2010) A Theory of Gradual Institutional Change, in J. Mahoney and K. Thelen, eds, *Explaining Institutional Change: Ambiguity, Agency, and Power* (Cambridge: Cambridge University Press).
Mainwaring, S. (1991) Politicians, Parties and Electoral Systems: Brazil in Comparative Perspective, *Comparative Politics* 24, 21–43.
Mainwaring, S. and M. S. Shugart (1997) *Presidentialism and Democracy in Latin America* (Cambridge: Cambridge University Press).
Mair, P. (1997) *Party System Change: Approaches and Interpretations* (Oxford: Clarendon Press).
Mair, P., W. Müller and F. Plasser (2004) *Political Parties and Electoral Change: Party Responses to Electoral Markets* (London: Sage).
Majone, G. (2001) Nonmajoritarian Institutions and the Limits of Democratic Governance: A Political Transaction-Cost Approach, *Journal of Institutional and Theoretical Economics* 157, 57–78.
Mann, M. (1997) Has Globalization Ended the Rise and Rise of the Nation State?, *Review of International Political Economy* 4, 477–96.
Manoilesco, M. (1934) *Le siecle du corporatisme* (Paris: Librairie Felix Alcan).
March, J. G. and J. P. Olsen (1984) The New Institutionalism: Organizational Factors in Political Life, *American Political Science Review* 78, 738–49.
— (1989) *Rediscovering Institutions* (New York: Free Press).
— (1995) *Democratic Governance* (New York: Free Press).
— (1996) Institutional Perspectives on Political Institutions, *Governance* 9, 247–64.
March, J. G. and H. A. Simon (1957) *Organizations* (New York: Wiley).
Marin, B. and R. Mayntz (1991) *Policy Networks: Empirical Evidence and Theoretical Considerations* (Boulder, CO: Westview).

Marsh, D. and R. A. W. Rhodes (1992a) *Implementing Thatcherite Policies: Audit of an Era* (Buckingham: Open University Press).
— (1992b) *Policy Networks in British Government* (Oxford: Clarendon Press).
Marshall, G. (1989) *Ministerial Responsibility* (Oxford: Oxford University Press).
Martin, J. and C. Siehl (1983) Organizational Culture and Counterculture: An Uneasy Symbiosis, *Organizational Dynamics* 12, 52–64.
Matthews, D. R. (1973) *U.S. Senators and Their World* (New York: Norton).
Mayhew, D. (1991) *Divided We Govern* (New Haven, CT: Yale University Press).
Mayntz, R. (2002) *Akteure, Mechanismen, Modelle: Zur Theoriefähigkeit makro-sozialer Analysen* (Frankfurt/New York: Campus Verlag).
McCubbins, M. and T. Schwartz (1984) Congressional Oversight Overlooked: Police Patrols versus Fire Alarms, *American Journal of Political Science* 28, 16–79.
McCubbins, M. D. and T. Sullivan (1987) *Congress: Structure and Policy* (Cambridge: Cambridge University Press).
McCubbins, M. D., R. G. Noll and B. R. Weingast (1987) Administrative Procedures as Instruments of Political Control, *Journal of Law, Economics and Organization* 3, 243–77.
McKenzie, R. T. (1963) *British Political Parties: The Distribution of Power within the Conservative and Labour Parties*, 2nd edn (New York: Praeger).
Mechanic, D. (1996) Changing Medical Organization and the Erosion of Trust, *The Milbank Quarterly* 74, 171–88.
Melo, M. A. (2007) The Majoritarian Bias in Comparative Politics: Accountability, Institutional Design and Democratic Quality, *Revista Brasileira de Ciencias Socials* 22, 163–87.
Meyer, J. and B. Rowan (1977) Institutionalizing Organizations: Formal Structure as Myth and Ceremony, *American Journal of Sociology* 83, 340–63.
Michels, R. (1915) *Political Parties* (London: Jarrold and Sons).
Milgrom, P. and J. Roberts (1988) Economic Theories of the Firm: Past, Present and Future, *Canadian Journal of Economics* 21, 444–58.
Miller, G. (2000) Rational Choice and Dysfunctional Institutions, *Governance* 13, 535–47.
Miller, H. T. and C. J. Fox (2001) The Epistemic Community, *Administration & Society* 32, 668–85.
Mills, C. W. (1940) Situated Actors and Vocabularies of Motives, *American Sociological Review* 5, 904–13.
Milner, H. V. (1993) International Regimes and World Politics: Comments on the Articles by Smouts, de Senarclens and Jonsson, *International Social Science Journal* 45, 491–7.
— (1997) *Interests, Institutions and Information: Domestic Politics and International Relations* (Princeton, NJ: Princeton University Press).
Moe, T. M. (1984) The New Economics of Organizations, *American Journal of Political Science* 28, 739–77.
— (1990) Political Institutions: The Neglected Side of the Story, *Journal of Law, Economics and Organizations* 6, 215–53.
— (2005) Power and Political Institutions, *Perspectives on Politics* 3, 215–33.
— (2006) Political Control and the Power of the Agent, *Journal of Law, Economics and Organization* 22, 1–29.
Moe, T. and M. Caldwell (1994) The Institutional Foundations of Democratic Government: A Comparison of Presidential and Parliamentary Systems, *Journal of Institutional and Theoretical Economics* 150, 171–95.
Mohr, L. B. (1982) *Explaining Organizational Behavior* (San Francisco, CA: Jossey-Bass).
Molina, O. and M. Rhodes (2002) Corporatism: The Past, the Present and the Future of a Concept, *Annual Review of Political* Science 5, 305–31.
Montesquieu, C. de S. (1989) *The Spirit of the Laws*, trans. A. M. Cohler et al. (Cambridge: Cambridge University Press).

Moravcsik, A. (1993) Preferences and Power in the European Community: A Liberal Intergovernmentalist Approach, *Journal of Common Market Studies* 31, 473–523.
Morgan, G. (1997) *Images of Organizations* (Thousand Oaks, CA: Sage).
Morgenthau, H. J. (1948) *Politics among Nations: The Struggle for Power and Peace* (New York: A. A. Knopf).
Mueller, H. (1993) *The Internationalization of Principles, Norms and Rules by Governments: The Case of Security Regimes* (Oxford: Oxford University Press).
Mueller, P. (1985) Un schema d'analyse des politiques sectorielles, *Revue francaise de science politique* 35, 165–88.
Mulé, R. (1999) New Institutionalism: Distilling Some "Hard Core" Propositions from the Works of Williamson and March and Olsen, *Politics* 19, 145–51.
Mulford, C. L. and D. L. Rogers (1982) Definitions and Models, in D. L. Rogers and D. A. Whetten, eds, *Inter-organizational Coordination: Theory, Research and Implementation* (Ames: Iowa State University Press).
Müller, W. (2000) Political Parties in Parliamentary Democracies: Making Delegation and Accountability Work, *European Journal of Political Research* 37, 309–33.
Murphy, C. N. (2000) Global Governance: Poorly Done and Poorly Understood, *International Affairs* 76, 789–804.
Niskanen, W. A. (1971), *Bureaucracy and Representative Government* (Chicago: Aldine/Atherton).
Nooteboom, B. (2007) Governance of Transactions: A Strategic Process Model, in G. Hodgson, ed., *The Evolution of Economic Institutions: A Critical Reader* (Cheltenham: Edward Elgar).
Norris, P. (2004) *Electoral Engineering: Voting Rules and Political Behavior* (Cambridge: Cambridge University Press).
North, D. C. (1990) *Institutions, Institutional Change, and Economic Performance* (Cambridge: Cambridge University Press).
— (1998) Five propositions about Institutional Change, in J. Knight and I. Sened, eds, *Explaining Social Institutions* (Ann Arbor: University of Michigan Press).
Nousiainen, J. (1988) Bureaucratic Tradition: Semi-Presidential Rule and Parliamentary Government: The Case of Finland, *European Journal for Political Research*, 16, 221–49.
Nugent, N. (1994) *The Government and Politics of the European Union* (Durham, NC: Duke University Press).
Oliver, C. (1991) Strategic Responses to Institutional Processes, *Academy of Management Review*, 16, 145–79.
— (1992) The Antecedents of Deinstitutionalization, *Organization Studies* 13, 563–88.
Olsen, J. P. (1983) *Organized Democracy* (Oslo: Universitetsforlaget).
— (1988) Administrative Reform and Theories of Organization, in C. E. Campbell and B. G. Peters, eds, *Organizing Government, Government Organizations* (Pittsburgh: University of Pittsburgh Press).
— (1996) Political Science and Organization Theory: Parallel Agendas but Mutual Disregard, in R. Czada, A. Hertier and H. Keman, eds, *Institutions and Political Choice: On the Limits of Rationality* (Amsterdam: VU University Press).
— (2006) Maybe It Is Time to Rediscover Bureaucracy, *Journal of Public Administration Research and Theory* 16, 1–24.
— (2009) Change and Continuity: An Institutional Approach to Institutions of Democratic Governance, *European Political Science Review* 1, 3–32.
Olsen, J. P. and B. G. Peters (1996) Introduction: Learning from Experience?, in J. P. Olsen and B. G. Peters, eds, *Lessons from Experience: Experiential Learning from Administrative Reform in Eight Democracies* (Oslo: Scandinavian University Press).
Olson, M. (1965) *The Logic of Collective Action: Public Goods and the Theory of Groups* (Cambridge, MA: Harvard University Press).

Opello, W. C. (1986) Portugal's Parliament: An Organizational Analysis of Legislative Performance, *Legislative Studies Quarterly* 11, 291–320.

Orren, K. and S. Skowronek (2004) *The Search for American Political Development* (Cambridge: Cambridge University Press).

Orru, M., N. W. Biggart and G. G. Hamilton (1991) Institutional Isomorphism in East Asia, in W. W. Powell and P. J. DiMaggio, eds, *The New Institutionalism in Organizational Analysis* (Chicago: University of Chicago Press).

Ostrogowski, M. (1964) *Democracy and the Organization of Political Parties* (Chicago: Quadrangle Books).

Ostrom, E. (1986) An Agenda for the Study of Institutions, *Public Choice* 48, 3–25.

— (1990) *Governing the Commons: The Evolution of Institutions of Collective Action* (Cambridge: Cambridge University Press).

— (2005) *Understanding Institutional Diversity* (Princeton, NJ: Princeton University Press).

— (2007), Challenges and Growth: The Development of the Interdisciplinary Field of Institutional Analysis, *Journal of Institutional Economics* 3, 239–64.

Ostrom, E., R. Gardner and J. Walker (1994) *Rules, Games and Common-Pool Resources* (Ann Arbor: University of Michigan Press).

Ostrom, E., J. Walker and R. Gardner (1992) Covenants with and without a Sword: Self-Governance Is Possible, *American Political Science Review* 86, 404–17.

Ott, J. (1989) *The Organizational Culture Perspective* (Pacific Grove, CA: Brooks-Cole).

Oye, K. (1986) *Cooperation under Anarchy* (Princeton, NJ: Princeton University Press).

Padgett, J. F. and C. Ansell (1993) Robust Action and the Rise of the Medici, 1400–1434, *American Journal of Sociology* 98, 1259–319.

Pagano, U. (2007) Bounded Rationality and Institutionalism, in G. M. Hodgson, ed., *The Evolution of Economic Institutions: A Critical Reader* (Cheltenham: Edward Elgar).

Page, E.C. (1992) *Political Authority and Bureaucratic Power: A Comparative Analysis*, 2nd edn (London: Harvester Wheatsheaf).

Panebianco, A. (1988) *Political Parties: Organization and Power* (Cambridge: Cambridge University Press).

Parsons, T. (1951) *The Social System* (New York: Free Press).

— (1960) A Sociological Approach to the Theory of Organizations, in Parsons, ed., *Structure and Process in Modern Societies* (Glencoe, IL: Free Press).

Pasquino, G. (1997) Semi-presidentialism: A Political Model at Work, *European Journal of Political Research* 31, 128–37.

Pauly, L. W. (1997) *Who Elected the Bankers?: Surveillance and Control in the World Economy* (Ithaca, NY: Cornell University Press).

Payne, R. A. (2001) Persuasion, Frames and Norm Construction, *European Journal of International Relations* 7, 137–61.

Pedersen, O. K. (1991) Nine Questions to a Neo-Institutional Theory in Political Science, *Scandinavian Political Studies* 14, 125–48.

Perez-Diaz, V. (1994) *The Return of Civil Society: The Emergence of a Democratic Spain* (Cambridge: Harvard University Press).

Perez-Linan, A. (2001) Neoinstitutional Accounts of Voter Turnout: Moving Beyond Industrial Democracies, *Electoral Studies* 20, 261–97.

— (2007) *Presidential Impeachment and the New Political Instability in Latin America* (Cambridge: Cambridge University Press).

Peters, B. G. (1996) Institutionalism Old and New, in R. E. Goodin and H.-D. Klingenmann, eds, *A New Handbook of Political Science* (Oxford: Oxford University Press).

— (1997a) Escaping the Joint Decision Trap: Policy Segmentation and Iterative Games, *West European Politics* 22 (2), 22–36.

— (1997b) *The Policy Capacity of Government* (Ottawa: Canadian Centre for Management Development).
— (1998) *Comparative Politics: Theory and Methods* (Basingstoke: Macmillan).
— (2010) The Governance Turn Keeps Turning, Working Paper, Swedish Institute of International Studies (Stockholm: UI).
Peters, B. G. and B. W. Hogwood (1988) Births, Deaths and Metamorphoses in the U.S. Federal Bureaucracy, 1933-83, *The American Review of Public Administration* 18, 119–34.
— (1991) Applying Population Ecology Models to Public Organizations, *Research in Public Administration* (Westport, CT: JAI Press).
Peters, B. G., J. Pierre and D. S. King (2005) The Politics of Path Dependency: Political Conflict in Historical Institutionalism, *Journal of Politics* 67, 1275–300.
Peters, B. G., R. A. W. Rhodes and V. Wright (1998) *Administering the Summit: Services for Presidents and Prime Ministers* (London: Macmillan).
Peters, T. J. and R. H. Waterman (1982) *In Search of Excellence: Lessons from America's Best-Run Companies* (New York: Harper and Row).
Pevehouse, J. C. (2002) Democracy from the Outside-In? International Organizations and Democratization, *International Organization* 56, 515–49.
Pfeffer, J. and G. Salanick (1978) *The External Control of Organizations* (New York: Harper and Row).
Pierce, R. (1991) The Executive Divided against Itself: Cohabitation in France, 1986-1988, *Governance* 4, 270–94.
Pierre, J. (1991) *Den Lokala Staten* (Stockholm: Almqvist & Wiksell).
— (1998) *Partnerships in Urban Governance: European and American Experiences* (London: Macmillan).
— (2009), Post Hoc, Ergo Propter Hoc?: Path Dependency and Punctuated Equilibria in European Aviation Safety Regulation, *Critical Policy Studies* 3, 105–20.
Pierre, J. and B. G. Peters (2009), From a Club to a Bureaucracy: JAA, EASA, and European Aviation Regulation, *Journal of European Public Policy* 16, 337–55.
Pierson, P. (1996) The Path to European Integration: A Historical Institutionalist Perspective, *Comparative Political Studies* 29, 123–63.
— (2000) Increasing Returns, Path Dependence, and the Study of Politics, *American Political Science Review* 94, 251–67.
Pierson, P. and T. Skocpol (2002) Historical Institutionalism in Contemporary Political Science, in I. Katznelson and H. V. Milner, eds, *Political Science: State of the Discipline* (New York: Norton).
Pollack. M. A. (2007), Rational Choice and EU Politics, in K. E. Jorgensen, M. A. Pollack and B. Rosamond, *Handbook of European Union Politics* (London: Sage).
Polsby, N. (1968) The Institutionalization of the U.S. House of Representative, *American Political Science Review* 62, 144–68.
— (1975) Legislatures, in F. I. Greenstein and N. Polsby, eds, *The Handbook of Political Science*, Vol. 5 (Reading, MA: Addison-Wesley).
Popadopoulos, A. G. (1996) *Urban Regimes and Strategies* (Chicago: University of Chicago Press).
Popper, K. R. (1959) *The Logic of Scientific Discovery* (New York: Basic Books).
— (1963) *Conjectures and Refutations: The Growth of Scientific Knowledge* (London: Routledge).
Posner, R. A. (1980) The Theory of Primitive Society, with Special Reference of Law, *Journal of Law and Economics* 23, 1–53.
— (1986) *The Economics of Law* (Boston: Little, Brown).
— (1993) The New Institutional Economics Meets Law and Economics, *Journal of Law, Economics and Organization* 149, 73–87.
Power, T. J. and M. J. Gasiorowski (1997) Institutional Design and Democratic Consolidation in the Third World, *Comparative Political Studies* 30, 123–55.
Pressman, J. L. and A. Wildavsky (1974) *Implementation* (Berkeley: University of California Press).

Preuss, U. K. (1991) The Politics of Constitution-Making: Transforming Politics into Constitutions, *Law and Policy* 13, 107–23.
Pridham, G. (1988) *Political Parties and Coalitional Behavior in Italy* (London: Routledge).
Przeworski, A. and H. Teune (1970) *The Logic of Comparative Social Inquiry* (New York: Wiley-Interscience).
Puchala, D. J. and R. F. Hopkins (1983) International Regimes: Lessons from Inductive Analysis, in S. D. Krasner, ed., *International Regimes* (Ithaca, NY: Cornell University Press).
Putnam, R. D. (1988) Diplomacy and Domestic Politics: The Logic of Two-Level Games, *International Organization* 42, 427–60.
— (1995) Bowling Along: America's Declining Social Capital, *Journal of Democracy* 6, 65–79.
Putnam, R. D., with R. Leonardi and R. V. Nanetti (1993) *Making Democracy Work: Civic Tradition in Modern Italy* (Princeton, NJ: Princeton University Press).
Ragsdale, L. and J. J. Theis, III (1997) The Institutionalization of the American Presidency 1924-92, *American Journal of Political Science* 41, 1280–318.
Randall, V. and L. Svåsand (2002) Party Institutionalization in New democracies, *Party Politics* 8, 5–29.
Raustiala, K. and D. G. Victor (2004) The Regime Complex for Plant Genetic Resources, *International Organization* 58, 277–310.
Rawls, J. (1970) *A Theory of Justice* (Cambridge: Harvard University Press).
Rees-Mogg, W. (1997) Don't Bank on the Bank, *The Times* (London) May 8.
Reich, R. (1990) *The Power of Public Ideas* (Cambridge, MA: Harvard University Press).
Reilly, B. (2001) *Democracy in Divided Societies: Electoral Engineering for Conflict Management* (Cambridge: Cambridge University Press).
Rein, M. (1998) *Social Science and Public Policy* (New York: Penguin).
Remmer, K. L. (1997) Theoretical Decay and Theoretical Development: The Resurgence of Institutional Analysis, *World Politics* 50, 34–61.
Rhinard, M. (2010) *Framing Europe: The Policy Shaping Strategies of the European Commission* (Dordrecht: Republic of Letters Publishing).
Rhodes, R. A. W. (1988) *Beyond Westminster and Whitehall* (London: Unwin Hyman).
— (1997) *Understanding Governance: Policy Networks, Governance, Reflexivity and Accountability* (Buckingham: Open University Press).
Rice, B. R. (1977) *Progressive Cities: The Commission Government Movement in America, 1901-20* (Austin: University of Texas Press).
Richard, C. (2001) New Approaches to Public Administration, in K. Konig and H. Siedentopf, eds, *Public Administration in Germany* (Baden-Baden: Nomos).
Richardson, J. J. (2000) Government, Interest Groups and Public Policy, *Political Studies* 48, 1006–25.
Riggs, F. W. (1988) The Survival of Presidentialism in America: Para-constitutional Practices, *International Political Science Review* 9, 247–78.
Riker, W. H. (1962) *The Theory of Political Coalitions* (New Haven, CT: Yale University Press).
— (1980) Implications from the Disequilibrium of Majority Rule for the Study of Institutions, *American Political Science Review* 74, 432–46.
Riker, W. H. and P. C. Ordeshook (1973) *An Introduction to Positive Political Theory* (Englewood Cliffs, NJ: Prentice-Hall).
Rittberger, V. (1993) *Regime Theory and International Relations* (Oxford: Clarendon Press).
Robinson, G. O. (1991) *American Bureaucracy: Public Choice and Public Law* (Ann Arbor: University of Michigan Press).
Rockman, B. A. (1984) *The Leadership Question and the American System* (New York: Praeger).
— (1993) The New Institutionalism and Old Institutions, in L. C. Dodd and C. Jillson, eds, *Governing Processes and Political Change Dynamics of American Politics* (Boulder, CO: Westview).
Rodinov, P. A. (1988) *What Is Democratic Centralism?* (Moscow: Progress Publishers).
Rohde, D. W. (1991) *Parties and Leaders on the Post-Reform Congress* (Chicago: University of Chicago Press).

Rohr, J. A. (1995) *Founding Republics in France and America: A Study of Constitutional Governance* (Lawrence: University of Kansas Press).
Rokkan, S. (1966) Votes Count but Resources Decide, in R. A. Dahl, ed., *Political Oppositions in Western Democracies* (New Haven, CT: Yale University Press).
Roland, G. (2004) Understanding Institutional Change: Fast-Moving and Slow-Moving Institutions, *Studies in International and Comparative Development* 38, 109–31.
Rose, R. (1974) *The Problem of Party Government* (London: Macmillan).
Rose, R. and P. Davies (1994) *Inheritance in Public Policy* (New Haven, CT: Yale University Press).
Rosenau, J. N. (1992) Governance, Order and Change in World Politics, in J. N. Rosenau and E.-O. Czempiel, eds, *Governance without Government: Order and Change in World Politics* (Cambridge: Cambridge University Press).
Rosendorff, B. P. and H. Milner (2001) The Optimal Design of International Institutions: Uncertainty and Escape, *International Organization* 55, 829–57.
Roth, P. A. (1987) *Meaning and Method in the Social Sciences: A Case for Methodological Pluralism* (Ithaca, NY: Cornell University Press).
Rothstein, B. (1996) *The Social Democratic State* (Pittsburgh: University of Pittsburgh Press).
Ruiter, D. W. P. (1994) Economic and Legal Institutionalism: What Can They Learn from Each Other?, *Constitutional Political Economy* 5, 99–115.
Sabatier, P. A. (1986) "Top Down" and "Bottom-Up" Approaches to Implementation Research, *Journal of Public Policy* 6, 21–48.
— (1988) An Advocacy-Coalition Model of Policy Change and the Role of Policy-Oriented Learning Therein, *Policy Sciences* 21, 129–68.
Sabatier, P. A. and H. Jenkins-Smith (1993) *Policy Change and Learning: An Advocacy-Coalition Approach* (Boulder, CO: Westview Press).
Salamon, L. M. (1995) *Partners in Public Service: Government-Nonprofit Relations in the Modern Welfare State* (Baltimore, MD: Johns Hopkins University Press).
Samuels, D. J. and M. S. Shugart (2010) *Presidents, Parties and Prime Ministers* (Cambridge: Cambridge University Press).
Sanders, E. (1999) *Roots of Reform: Farmers, Workers and the American State, 1877-1917* (Chicago: University of Chicago Press).
Sandholz, W. (1993) Choosing Monetary Union: Monetary Politics and Maastricht, *International Organization* 47, 1–40.
Sartori, G. (1976) *Parties and Party Systems: A Framework for Analysis* (Cambridge: Cambridge University Press).
— (1997) *Comparative Constitutional Engineering: An Inquiry into Structures, Incentives and Outcomes* (Washington Square, NY: New York University Press).
Sbragia, A. M. (1996) *Debt Wish: Entrepreneurial Cities, U.S. Federalism, and Economic Development* (Pittsburgh: University of Pittsburgh Press).
Scharpf, F. W. (1988) The Joint Decision Trap: Lessons from German Federalism and European Integration, *Public Administration* 66, 239–78.
— (1993) *Games in Hierarchies and Networks* (Boulder, CO: Westview).
— (1997) *Games Real Actors Play: Actor-Centered Institutionalism in Policy Research* (Boulder, CO: Westview).
— (2000) Institutions in Comparative Policy Research, *Comparative Political Studies* 33, 762–90.
Schickler, E. (2002) *Disjointed Pluralism: Institutional Innovation and Development in the US Congress* (Princeton, NJ: Princeton University Press).
Schmidt, V. A. (2008) Discursive Institutionalism: The Explanatory Power of Ideas and Discourse, *Annual Review of Political Science* 11, 303–26.
— (2010) Taking Ideas and Discourse Seriously: Explaining Change through Discursive Institutionalism as the Fourth New Institutionalism, *European Political Science Review* 2, 1–25.
Schmitter, P. C. (1974) Still the Century of Corporatism?, *Review of Politics* 36, 85–131.

Schmitthenner, H. and H.-J. Urban (1999) *Sozialstaat als Reformprojekt: Optionen fur eine andere Politik* (Berlin: VSA Verlag).
Schon, D. A. and M. Rein (2000) *Frame Reflection: Solving Intractable Policy Issues*, rev. edn (Cambridge, MA: MIT Press).
Schubert, G. A. (1965) *The Judicial Mind: The Attitudes and Ideologies of Supreme Court Justices, 1946-1963* (Evanston, IL: Northwestern University Press).
Scott, W. R. (1987) The Adolescence of Institutional Theory, *Administrative Science Quarterly* 32, 493–511.
— (1992) *Organizations: Rational, Natural and Open Systems*, 3rd edn (Englewood Cliffs, NJ: Prentice-Hall).
— (1994) Institutions and Organizations: Toward a Theoretical Synthesis, in W. R. Scott and J. W. Meyer, eds, *Institutional Environments and Organizations* (Thousand Oaks, CA: Sage).
— (1995a) *Institutions and Organizations* (Thousand Oaks, CA: Sage).
— (1995b) Symbols and Organizations: From Barnard to the Institutionalists, in O. E. Williamson, ed., *Organization Theory*, exp. edn (Oxford: Oxford University Press).
— (2008) *Institutions and Organizations: Ideas and Interests* (Thousand Oaks, CA: Sage).
Searing, D. D. (1991) Roles, Rules and Rationality in the New Institutionalism, *American Political Science Review* 85, 1239–55.
Selb, P. (2010) Methodological Issues in the Study of New Parties' Entry and Electoral Success, *Party Politics* 10, 147–70.
Self, P. (1995) *Government by the Market?: Public Choice* (Boulder, CO: Westview Press).
Selznick, P. (1949) *TVA and the Grass Roots* (Berkeley: University of California Press).
— (1952) *The Organizational Weapon* (New York: McGraw-Hill).
— (1957) *Leadership in Administration* (New York: Harper and Row).
— (1996) Institutionalism "Old" and "New," *Administrative Science Quarterly* 41, 270–7.
Sending, O. J. (2002), Constitution, Choice and Change: Problems with the "Logic of Appropriateness" and Its Use in Constructivist Theory, *European Journal of International Relations* 8, 443–70.
Sened, I. (1991) Contemporary Theory of Institutions in Perspective, *Journal of Theoretical Politics*, 3, 379–402.
Sewell, W. H. (1992) A Theory of Structure: Duality, Agency and Transformation, *American Journal of Sociology*, 98, 1–29.
Sharkansky, I. (1968) *Spending in the American States* (Chicago: Rand McNally).
— (1997) *Policy Making in Israel: Routines for Simple Problems and Coping for the Complex* (Pittsburgh: University of Pittsburgh Press).
Shaw, E. (1996) *The Labour Party Since 1945: Old Labour, New Labour* (Oxford: Blackwell).
Shepsle, K. A. (1986) Institutional Equilibrium and Equilibrium Institutions, in H. Weisberg, ed., *Political Science: The Science of Politics* (New York: Agathon).
— (1989) Studying Institutions: Lessons from the Rational Choice Approach, *Journal of Theoretical Politics* 1, 131–47.
— (2006) Rational Choice Institutionalism, in R. A. W. Rhodes, S. Binder and B. Rockman, eds, *Oxford Handbook of Political Institutions* (Oxford: Oxford University Press).
Shepsle, K. A. and B. R. Weingast (1995) *Positive Theories of Congressional Institutions* (Ann Arbor: University of Michigan Press).
Shugart, M. S. (2005) Semi-Presidential Systems: Dual Executives and Mixed Authority Patterns, *French Politics* 3, 323–51.
Silverman, D. (1971) *The Theory of Organizations: A Sociological Framework* (New York: Basic Books).
Simon, H. A. (1947) *Administrative Behavior* (New York: Free Press).
Singh, J. V. (1990) Future Directions in Organizational Evolution, in Singh, ed., *Organizational Evolution* (Newbury Park, CA: Sage).
Skocpol, T. (1992) *Protecting Soldiers and Mothers: The Political Origins of Social Policy in the United States* (Cambridge: Cambridge University Press).

Skowronek, S. (1982) *Building a New American State* (Cambridge: Cambridge University Press).
Smith, R. M. (1988) Political Jurisprudence, "The New Institutionalism," and the Future of Public Law, *American Political Science Review* 82, 89–108.
Snidal, D. (1991) Relative Gains and the Pattern of International Cooperation, *American Political Science Review* 85, 701–26.
— (1994) The Politics of Scope: Endogenous Actors, Heterogeneity and Institutions, *Journal of Theoretical Politics* 6, 449–72.
Sorensen, E. and J. Torfing (2000) Development in the Future Skills Needs in Light of New Societal Megatrends (Research paper; 4). Roskilde: Roskilde University.
— (2002) Network Politics, Political Capital and Democracy, *International Journal of Public Administration* 26, 609–34.
— (2007) *Theories of Democratic Network Governance* (Basingstoke: Palgrave Macmillan).
Squire, P. (1992) The Theory of Legislative Institutionalization and the California Assembly, *Journal of Politics* 54, 1026–54.
Stearns, M. L. (2002) *Constitutional Processes: A Social Choice Analysis of Supreme Court Decision-Making* (Ann Arbor: University of Michigan Press).
Steinmo, S. (1993) *Taxation and Democracy: Swedish, British and American Approaches to Financing the Modern State* (New Haven, CT: Yale University Press).
Steinmo, S. and C. J. Tolbert (1998) Do Institutions Really Matter? Taxation in Industrial Democracy, *Comparative Political Studies* 31, 165–87.
Steinmo, S., K. Thelen and F. Longstreth (1992) *Structuring Politics: Historical Institutionalism in Comparative Analysis* (Cambridge: Cambridge University Press).
Stepan, A. and C. Skach (1993) Constitutional Frameworks and Democratic Consolidations, *World Politics* 46, 1–22.
Steunenberg, B. (2000) Constitutional Change in the European Union, in H. Wagenaar, ed., *Government Institutions: Effects, Changes and Normative Foundations* (Dordrecht: Kluwer).
Stillman, R. J. (1991) *Preface to Public Administration: A Search for Themes and Directions* (New York: St. Martin's).
Stinchcombe, A. (1997) On the Virtues of the Old Institutionalism, *Annual Review of Sociology* 23, 1–18.
Stone, C. N. (1989) *Regime Politics: Governing Atlanta 1946-1988* (Lawrence: University of Kansas Press).
Storing, H. J. (1962) *Essays on the Scientific Study of Politics* (New York: Holt, Rinehart and Winston).
Strang, D. (1994) The New Institutionalism as a Form of Structural Analysis, in C. Prendergast and J. D. Knottnerus, eds, *Recent Developments in the Theory of Social Structure* (Greenwich, CT: JAI Press).
Streeck, W. (1991) *From National Corporatism to Transnational Pluralism* (South Bend, IN: Kellogg Center, Notre Dame University).
Streeck, W. and Thelen, K. (eds) (2005) *Beyond Continuity: Explorations in the Dynamics of Advanced Political Economies* (Oxford: Oxford University Press).
Strom, K. (1990a) *Minority Government and Majority Rule* (Cambridge: Cambridge University Press).
— (1990b) A Behavioral Theory of Competitive Political Parties, *American Journal of Political Science* 34, 565–98.
Strom, K. And W. Müller (2008) *Cabinets and Coalition-Building: The Democratic Life-Cycle in Western Europe* (Oxford: Oxford University Press).
Sturm, R. (2001) Divided Government in Germany: The Case of the Bundesrat, in R. Elgie, ed., *Divided Government in Comparative Perspective* (Oxford: Oxford University Press).
Sugden, R. (1986) *The Economics of Rights, Cooperation and Welfare* (Oxford: Basil Blackwell).
Sundquist, J. L. (1988) Needed: A Political Theory for the New Era of Coalition Government in the United States, *Political Science Quarterly* 103, 613–35.
— (1992) *Constitutional Reform and Effective Government* (Washington, DC: The Brookings Institution).

Susser, B. (1989) Parliadential Politics: A Proposed Constitution for Israel, *Parliamentary Affairs* 42, 112–22.

Sutherland, S. L. (1991a) Responsible Government and Ministerial Responsibility: Every Reform Has Its Own Problem, *Canadian Journal of Political Science* 24, 91–120.

— (1991b) The Al-Mashat Affair: Administrative Accountability in Parliamentary Institutions, *Canadian Public Administration* 34, 573–604.

Sykes, R. (1998) Italian Public Policy and the "Southern Question": Policy Disaster or Political Disaster, in P. Gray and P. 't Hart, eds, *Understanding Policy Disasters* (London: Routledge).

Sztompka, P. (1994) *Agency and Structure: Reorienting Social Theory* (Yverdon, Switzerland: Gordon and Breach).

Taagapera, R. and M. S. Shugart (1989) *Seats and Votes: The Effects and Determinants of Electoral Systems* (New Haven, CT: Yale University Press).

Teubner, G. (1986) *Dilemmas of Law in the Welfare State* (Berlin: De Gruyter).

Thaa, W. (1994) *Grune an der Macht: Widerstrande und Chancen grunalternativer Regierungsbeteilungen* (Cologne: Bund Verlag).

Thatcher, M. (2002) Theory and Practice of Delegation to Non-majoritarian Institutions, *West European Politics* 25, 1–22.

Thaysen, U. (1994) *The Bundesrat, the Lander, and German Federalism* (Washington, DC: American Institute for Contemporary German Studies).

Thelen, K. (1999) Historical Institutionalism in Comparative Politics, *Annual Review of Political Science* 2, 369–404.

— (2004) *How Institutions Evolve: The Political Economy of Skills in Britain, Germany, the United States and Japan* (Cambridge: Cambridge University Press).

Thelen, K. and S. Steinmo (1992) Historical Institutionalism in Comparative Politics, in S. Steinmo, K. Thelen and F. Longstreth, eds, *Structuring Politics: Historical Institutionalism in Comparative Analysis* (Cambridge: Cambridge University Press).

Thomas, C. W. (1997) Public Management as Interagency Cooperation: Testing Epistemic Community Theory at the Domestic Level, *Journal of Public Administration Research and Theory* 7, 221–46.

Thurber, J. A. (1991) *Divided Democracy: Cooperation and Conflict between the President and Congress* (Washington, DC: CQ Press).

Tolbert, P. S. and L. G. Zucker (1996) The Institutionalization of Institutional Theory, in S. Clegg, C. Hardy and W. R. Nord, eds, *Handbook of Organization Studies* (Thousand Oaks, CA: Sage).

Torfing, J. (1999) *New Theories of Discourse* (Oxford: Blackwell).

Tsebelis, G. (1990) *Nested Games: Rational Choice in Comparative Politics* (Berkeley: University of California Press).

— (1995) Decision-Making in Political Systems: Veto Players in Presidentialism, Parliamentarianism, Multicameralism and Multipartyism, *British Journal of Political Science* 25, 289–326.

— (2002) *Veto Players: How Political Institutions Work* (Princeton, NJ: Princeton University Press).

Tsebelis, G. and J. Money (1997) *Bicameralism* (Cambridge: Cambridge University Press).

Tuma, N. B. and M. T. Hannan (1984) *Social Dynamics: Models and Methods* (Orlando, FL: Academic Press).

Tuohy, C. J. (1992) *Policy and Politics in Canada: Institutionalized Ambivalence* (Philadelphia: Temple University Press).

Valderrama, F. (1995) *A History of UNESCO* (Paris: UNESCO Publishing).

Väyrynen, R. (2003) Regionalism: Old and New, *International Studies Review* 5, 25–51.

Vibert, F. (2007) *The Rise of the Unelected: Democracy and the New Separation of Powers* (Cambridge: Cambridge University Press).

Volden, C. and C. J. Carrubba (2004) The Formation of Oversized Coalitions in Parliamentary Democracies, *American Journal of Political Science* 48, 521–37.

Von Mettenheim, K. (1996) *Presidential Institutions and Democratic Politics* (Baltimore, MD: Johns Hopkins University Press).

Wahlke, J. C., H. Eulau, W. Buchanan, and L. C. Ferguson (1962) *The Legislative System: Explorations in Legislative Behavior* (New York: Wiley).
Walker, J. (1983) The Origin and Maintenance of Interest Groups in America, *American Political Science Review* 77, 390–406.
Waltz, K. N. (1979) *Theory of International Relations* (Reading, MA: Addison-Wesley).
Weaver, R. K. (1992) Political Institutions and Canada's Constitutional Crisis, in Weaver, ed., *The Collapse of Canada?* (Washington, DC: The Brookings Institution).
Weaver, R. K. and B. A. Rockman (1993) *Do Institutions Matter?: Government Capabilities in the United States and Abroad* (Washington, DC: The Brookings Institution).
Weber, M. (1949) *The Methodology of the Social Sciences*, trans. E. Shils and H. A. Finch (Glencoe, IL: Free Press).
— (1976) *Wirtschaft und Gesellschaft*, ed. J. Winklemann (Tubingen: Mohr).
Weimer, D. L. (1995) *Institutional Design* (Dordrecht: Kluwer).
Weingast, B. (1996) Political Institutions, Rational Choice Perspectives, in R. E. Goodin and H.-D. Klingemann, *A New Handbook of Political Science* (Oxford: Oxford University Press).
Weingast, B. R. (2002) Rational Choice Institutionalism, in I. Katznelson and H. V. Milner, eds, *Political Science: State of the Discipline* (New York: Norton).
Wendt, A. (1987) The Agent-Structure Problem in International Relations Theory, *International Organization* 41, 335–70.
— (1992) Anarchy Is What States Make of It: The Social Construction of Power Politics, *International Organization* 46, 391–425.
White, L. D. (1958) *The Republican Era, 1869-1901: A Study in Administrative History* (New York: Macmillan).
White, L. T. (1989) *Policies of Chaos: The Organizational Causes of Violence in China's Cultural Revolution* (Princeton, NJ: Princeton University Press).
Whiteley, P., P. Seyd and J. J. Richardson (1994) *True Blues: The Politics of Conservative Party Membership* (Oxford: Oxford University Press).
Whitley, R. and P. H. Kristensen (1997) *Governance at Work: The Social Regulation of Economic Relations* (Oxford: Oxford University Press).
Wiarda, H. J. (1991) Political Development Reconsidered—and Its Alternatives, in D. A. Rustow and K. P. Erickson, eds, *Comparative Political Dynamics* (New York: Harper-Collins).
— (1997) *Corporatism and Comparative Politics: The Other Great "Ism"* (Armonk, NY: M.E. Sharpe).
Wickman, J. (1977) *Fremskridtpartiet: Hvem og Hvofor?* (Copenhagen: Akademisk Forlag).
Wildavsky, A. (1979) Policy as Its Own Cause, in A. Wildavsky, *Speaking Truth to Power* (Boston: Little, Brown).
— (1987) Choosing Preferences by Constructing Institutions: A Cultural Theory of Preference Formation, *American Political Science Review* 81, 3–22.
— (1992) *The New Politics of the Budgetary Process*, 2nd edn (New York: Harper-Collins).
Williamson, O. E. (1985) *The Economic Institutions of Capitalism* (New York: Free Press).
— (1993) Transaction Cost Economics Meets Posnerian Law and Economics, *Journal of Institutional and Theoretical Economics* 149, 99–118.
— (1996) *The Mechanisms of Governance* (Oxford: Oxford University Press).
Williamson, P. J. (1985) *Varieties of Corporatism: A Conceptual Discussion* (Cambridge: Cambridge University Press).
Wilson, W. (1884) Committee or Cabinet Government?, *Overland Monthly* 3, 17–33.
— (1887) The Study of Administration, *Political Science Quarterly* 2, 207–22.
— (1898) *The State: Elements of Historical and Practical Politics* (Boston: D. C. Heath).
— (1956) *Congressional Government: A Study in American Politics* (Cleveland, OH: World Publishing).
Winter, S. (2003) The Implementation Perspective, in B. G. Peters and J. Pierre, eds, *The Handbook of Public Administration* (London: Sage).

Winterton, G. (1983) *Parliament, the Executive and the Governor-General: A Constitutional Analysis* (Carlton: Melbourne University Press).
Wittfogel, K. A. (1957) *Oriental Despotism: A Comparative Study of Total Power* (New Haven, CT: Yale University Press).
Wood, B. D. and J. Bohte (2004) Political Transaction Costs and the Politics of Administrative Design, *Journal of Politics* 66, 178–202.
Wood, L. A. and R. O. Kroger (2000), *Doing Discourse Analysis: Methods for Studying Action in Talk and Text* (Thousand Oaks, CA: Sage Publications).
Woods, N. (2004) *The Globalizers: The IMF, the World Bank and Their Borrowers* (Ithaca, NY: Cornell University Press).
Woolley, J. T. (1984) *Monetary Politics: The Federal Reserve and the Politics of Monetary Policy* (Cambridge: Cambridge University Press).
— (1994) The Politics of Monetary Policy: A Critical Review, *Journal of Public Policy* 14, 57–85.
Woolsey, T. D. (1893) *Political Science: Or the State Theoretically and Practically Considered* (New York: C. Scribners and Sons).
Wright, D. S. (1988) *Understanding Intergovernmental Relations*, 3rd edn (Monterey, CA: Brooks/Cole).
Young, O. (1991) Political Leadership and Regime Formation: On the Development of Institutions in International Society, *International Organization* 45, 281–308.
— (1994) *International Governance: Protecting the Environment in a Stateless Society* (Ithaca, NY: Cornell University Press).
Zald, M. N. and P. Denton (1967) From Evangelism to General Service: The Transformation of the YMCA, *Administrative Science Quarterly* 8, 513–28.
Zito, A. R. (2001) Epistemic Communities, Collective Entrepreneurship and European Integration, *Journal of European Public Policy* 8, 585–603.
Zucker, L. (1977) The Role of Institutionalization in Cultural Persistence, *American Sociological Review* 42, 726–43.
— (1987) Institutional Theories of Organizations, *Annual Review of Sociology* 13, 443–64.
— (1988) Where Do Institutional Patterns Come From?: Organizations as Actors in Social Systems, in Zucker, ed., *Institutional Patterns and Organizations* (Cambridge, MA: Ballinger).
Zürn, M. (1993) Problematic Social Situations and International Institutions: On the Use of Game Theory in International Relations, in F. R. Pfetsch, ed., *International Relations and Pan-Europe* (Munster: Lit Verlag).

Index

actor-centered institutionalism 48
adaptation 27, 36, 49, 63, 73, 79, 81, 82, 85, 107, 130, 140, 141, 154, 155, 183
advocacy coalition theory 117
agenda
  control 73
  formation of 36
  -setting 79
aggregative organization 27–8, 39
  see also organizations
AIDS 170
Alexander, E. R. 73
Almond, G. A. 25
Althusius 3
Altman, M. 71
American Political Development 73
Ansell, C. 77
anti-normative bias, of behavioralism 13–14
anti-trust law 41
appropriateness, logic of 7, 20, 27, 29–36, 38, 43, 44, 46, 75, 114, 122, 131, 145, 146, 148, 154, 155, 159, 161, 168, 177, 178
Arrow, K. 54
Arrow Problem 51
Association of South-East Asian Nations (ASEAN) 159
Austria
  divided government 97
autopoesis 64
Axelrod, R. 58

Bagehot, W. 18
Balladur, E. 96
Bank of England 78, 79, 102
  see also United Kingdom
Barnard, C. 28
behavioral revolution
  anti-normative bias 13–14
  inputism 15–16
  methodological individualism 14–15
  theory and methodology 12–13
  see also behavioralism
behavioralism 1, 2, 10, 74
Belgium 53
Berkman, M. B. 100
Berry, W. D. 100
biological ecology model 132
Bismarckian laws 10
bricolage approach 119–20
Britain *see* United Kingdom
Brown, G. 78
Brown, W. 146
Brownlow, L. 5
Brunsson, N. 37
Bryce, J. 3
Buchanan, J. 54
budgeting 55, 56, 66, 76, 161, 168, 169
Bundesbank 79, 102
  see also Germany
Bundesrepublik 97
  see also Germany
bureaucracy(ies) 4, 9, 10, 13, 15, 19, 35, 39, 47, 52, 55, 56, 66, 68, 75, 79, 99, 101, 129, 131, 134, 141, 143, 158, 172, 178

cabinets 47, 97, 98, 104, 109
Caiden, N. 168
Canada
  divided government 96
  federal government 99
  political organization in 146
Canadian Mounted Police 75
cartel party systems 148, 156
  see also party systems
Carter, G. 3
catchall parties 155
central banks 78, 79, 102–3
Central Europe 67, 93, 108
change 76
  bricoleur version of *see* bricolage approach
  institutional 36–7, 62–3, 77–83, 106–7, 119–20, 139–40, 170–1, 182–3
China, cultural revolution in 38

Chirac, J. 96
Chisholm, S. 41
Christensen, J. G. 75
Christensen, T. 33
civic culture 14
civil society 103
clearance points 87–8, 102
Clinton, B. 109
coalition government 93–4, 96
  see also government
Coase, R. A. 48, 71
coercive institutions 180
  see also institution(s)
Commons, J. R. 22
communicative discourse 116–17, 119
community(ies) 143, 162
  epistemic 117, 150–2, 165, 169, 170, 173, 181
  financial 167
  medical 117
  policy 144, 150, 152, 165
comparative politics 5, 8, 9, 12, 17, 55, 67, 73, 173
compliance 33, 39, 41, 51, 52, 57, 58, 84, 167
consensual government 94, 98
  see also government
consequentiality, logic of 30, 37, 38
consociationalism 8
constitutional choices 108
constructivist institutionalism 75, 112–26
  affinity with international institutionalism 114–15
  individuals, within institutions 121
  and institutional change 119–20
  and institutions 116–18
    formation of 118–19
    good 123–4
    operation of 122–3
  and normative institutionalism
    comparisons 113–14
    similarities 114
  problems in 124–5
contextualism 16
contingent nature, of institutions 121
conversion 81–2, 86
cooperation 58, 104, 147, 150, 165
coordinative discourse 116, 118, 122
corporate pluralism 21, 149, 157
  see also pluralism
corporatism 8, 21, 149–50, 153, 155, 156
  state versus societal 152
corruption 31, 59
courts 47, 57, 68
critical junctures 78

de Gaulle, C. 39
decision points 21
decision rules 54–5, 61
  see also rules
decision-making 15–17, 32, 35, 36, 41, 51, 55, 64, 73, 94, 98, 108
democratic centralism 146
Democratic Party 145
democratization 67, 93, 103, 104, 145
Dempster, M. A. H. 76
Denmark 145, 154
deus ex machina 83
Deutsch, K. 140
DiMaggio, P. 134
discourse theory 75, 117
discursive institutionalism 75, 87, 112–26, 136, 181
  affinity with international institutionalism 114–15
  individuals, within institutions 121
  and institutional change 119–20
  and institutions 116–18
    formation of 118–19
    good 123–4
    operation of 122–3
  and normative institutionalism
    comparisons 113–14
    similarities 114
  problems in 124–5
displacement 81
divided government 4, 95–7, 109
  see also government
Dowding, K. 43
Downs, A. 13, 17, 55, 117, 155
drift 81, 86
Duffield, J. S. 167
Dunleavy, D. 48
Durkheim, E. 27, 129
Duverger, M. 146, 148

Eastern Europe 67, 93, 108
Eckstein, H. 5
economic policies, development of 71–2
Edelman, L. 138, 139
Eisenstadt, S. N. 130, 131, 136
electoral laws 74, 148
empirical institutionalism 90–111, 143, 175
  building 91–2
  development of 103–4
  divided government 95–7
  implementation of 101–2
  individuals, within institutions 109–10
  and institutions 104–7
    change in 106–7
    design of 107–8
    formation of 105–6
    good 110
  legislative institutionalization 99–101
  multilevel governance 98–9
  parliamentary government 92–5
  presidential government 92–5
entrepreneurs 62, 76, 116, 120, 153
epistemic communities 117, 150–2, 165, 169, 170, 173, 181
  see also community(ies)
equilibrium
  in institutions 17, 51, 54, 58, 61, 63, 73, 76, 77, 91, 118, 120, 121, 136, 181
  punctuated 78, 80, 81, 83, 135
  structure-induced 51, 182
Etzioni, A. 27, 137
Eulau, H. 1
European approaches to institutions 5–6
European Monetary System 53
European Monetary Union 102
European Union 47, 53, 58, 66, 72–3, 99, 159, 160, 164, 166
experimental design 90, 103

falsification 69, 88, 164
federal government 55, 91, 95, 98–9, 108–9
  see also government
Federal Reserve Bank 91, 102
  see also United States
financial communities 167
  see also community(ies)
Finer, H. 3
Finer, S. 3
Finland
  semi-presidentialist system 93, 104
Fiorina, M. P. 58
flash parties 147
Food and Agriculture Organization (FAO) 160
Ford, H. 10
formalism 9, 34, 164
Fortuyn, P. 153
framing 115, 134, 137, 140
France 86
  divided government 96, 97
  economic policy, development of 71
  legalism 7
  semi-presidentialist system 90, 93, 104
free riding 50
Friedrich, C. 3, 8
Frohlich, N. 152
functionalism 17–18, 130

game theory 51, 57–8, 61, 66, 71, 149, 162, 170, 177
Gandhi, M. K. 39
garbage can approach 36, 63
Gatlin, D. 158
Geering, J. 73
Gerlich, P. 99
Germany 10, 13, 145
  Bundesbank 79, 102
  Bundesrepublik 97
  federal government 98
  Justimonopol 6
  legalism 7
  presidential government 93
  Ressortsprinzip 98
  Staatswissenschaft 6
Giddens, A. 30, 118, 139, 175
Glistrup, M. 153, 154
Goffman, E. 137
good institution 44–5, 63, 67–9, 85–6, 110, 140–1, 156–7, 171–2
  see also institution(s)
governance 1, 7, 20, 21, 48, 94, 97, 104, 120, 125, 165, 181
  multilevel 98–9, 160

government
  coalition 93–4, 96
  consensual 94, 98
  divided 95–7
  federal 55, 91, 95, 98–9, 108–9
  majoritarian 94–5, 96, 98
  parliamentary 92–5, 97–8, 107, 108
  presidential 92–5, 107, 108
  Third World 93
  unitary 98–9
Greece 160
Greif, A. 71

habitualization 139
Haggard, S. 164
Hall, P. A. 71, 72, 74, 75, 86, 112, 128
Hasenclever, A. 163
Hay, C. 75, 112
Hayek, F. A. von 61
Heclo, H. 79
Hibbing, J. R. 99
historical analysis, of old institutionalism 10–11
historical institutionalism 20–1, 70–89, 116, 118, 126, 175
  critique against 119
  individuals, within institutions 83–4
  and institutions 74–88
    change in 77–83
    design of 84–5
    formation of 76–7
    good 85–6
  limits of 86–8
Hjern, B. 101
Hobbes, T. 3
holism 9–10
Holmes, O. W. 7
Hopkins, R. F. 163
human relations management 28
Hunt, W. B. 17
Huntington, S. P. 103

Ikenberry, G. J. 74
Immergut, E. 74, 84, 87, 101
immigration 154
implementation 36, 48, 87, 88, 153, 165
  structure of 101–2, 105–6
incentives 20, 32, 48, 50–3, 57, 65, 67, 69, 75, 91, 111, 141, 146, 149, 162, 176, 177, 180, 181, 183
  types of 27
incremental adjustment 80
individual maximization 50, 68
individuals, within institutions 19, 22, 26, 27, 37–41, 55–6, 63–5, 83–4, 109–10, 138–9, 168–70, 183–4
inputism 15–16
institution(s)
  coercive 180
  contingent nature of 121
  defined 29–34, 59–60, 74–5, 104–5, 137–8, 150–2, 163–6, 179–80
  design of 42, 65–7, 84–5, 107–9, 167–8
  development of 103–4
  empirical theory of, building 91–2
  as entities 127
  formation of 34–6, 76–7, 105–6
  game-theoretic version of 51, 57–8, 61, 66, 71, 149, 162, 170, 177
  good 63, 67–9, 85–6, 110, 140–1, 156–7, 171–2
  individuals within 63–5, 83–4, 109–10, 138–9, 168–70, 183–4
  of interest representation 143–58
  international system as 160–2
  mutability of 19, 91, 170, 175, 181, 182
  nonconformity in 39–40
  operation of 41–2
  origin of 152–4, 166–7
  political 3, 7, 8, 15, 30, 32, 35, 42, 45, 47, 54, 60, 68, 78, 94, 127, 143, 163
  rational 129
  rationality of 50, 53, 129
  as rules 52–3
  separated *see* divided government
  total 31, 137, 146, 178
institutional analysis
  measurement 178–9
  regularities in 177–8
  similarities in 175–7
institutional change 36–7, 62–3, 77–83, 106–7, 119–20, 139–40, 170–1, 182–3
  conversion 81–2, 86
  displacement 81

drift 81, 86
gradual 80–3
layering 81
major 78–80
see also change
institutional dynamics 65
institutional theories 18–21, 47–69
differences among 179–84
questions about 58–67
institutionalization 23, 35, 38, 44, 60–2, 72, 78, 119, 120, 127, 130, 131, 137, 139–40, 145, 147, 148, 152–4, 170, 179, 181
isomorphism and 133–4
legislative 99–101, 103, 105, 107
instrumentalism 18
integrative organization 27–8
see also organizations
interest intermediation 149–50
corporatist model of 157
interest representation, institutions of 143–58
basic social mechanisms 156
good institution 156–7
interest intermediation 149–50
party systems 145–8
change in 154–5
international institutionalism 21, 159–73
affinity with discursive institutionalism 114–15
change in regimes 170–1
defined 163–6
design of 167–8
good institution 171–2
individuals, within institutions 168–70
origin of 166–7
regime theory, as institutional theory 162–3
International Labour Office 170
International Monetary Fund (IMF) 21, 161, 165, 168–70, 172
international order 165–6
international system, as institution 160–2
Ireland 160
iron cage 134
"Iron Law of Oligarchy" 157
iron triangles 122, 149
isomorphism 133–4, 141
Israel
organizations, bureaucratic values of 131
semi-presidentialist system 90
Italy 53
central banks, control of 102
party systems in 148
social capital in 103

Jabko, N. 112
Janda, K. 94
Jenkins, R. 153
Jepperson, R. L. 137
Jordan, G. 144
Justimonopol 6

Kanzlerdemokratie (Chancellor democracy) 97
Katz, R. 148, 156
Katznelson, I. 77
Kaufman, H. 133
Kelman, S. 94
Keman, H. 48, 177
Keohane, R. 163
Keynesianism 75
King, D. S. 73, 76, 80, 82
King, M. L. 40
Kingdon, J. 36
Knight, J. 61, 80
Knill, C. 171
Krasner, S. 164
Krehbiel, K. 96
Kvavik, R. B. 149

La Porte, T. 156
Labour Party 102, 153, 154
Laitin, D. 71
Latin America 79, 81, 93
presidentialism in 108
Laver, M. 17
Law of Anticipated Reactions 8
layering 81, 135
leadership 40
learning, in organizations 49, 63
legalism 7
legislative institutionalization 99–101
see also institutionalization

legislatures 9, 14, 41, 47, 56, 66, 74, 75, 94, 99–101, 105, 107, 143, 158, 166
  arena 101
  transformative 101
Lenschow, A. 171
Lijphart, A. 94, 97
Linz, J. J. 107
Little Tigers 169
Locke, J. 4
Loewenberg, G. 99
Longstreth, F. 70

Mahoney, J. 81
Mair, P. 148, 154, 156
Majone, G. 48, 87
majoritarian government 94–5, 96, 98
  see also government
March of Dimes 81
March, J. G. 17, 18, 20, 27, 29, 30, 35, 36, 71, 114, 131, 168
Marie, J. 153
Matthews, D. 28
Mayer, P. 163
Mayhew, D. 95
McKenzie, R. T. 146
Merriam, C. 5
metaphor 78
methodological individualism 1, 14–15, 65
Mexico, presidentialism in 104
Meyer, J. 138
Michels, R. 146
military organizations 35, 39, 40, 45, 75, 178
  see also organizations
Mills, C. W. 31
Milner, H. 167, 169
Mitchell, B. 39
Mitterrand, F. 96
Moe, T. 61
Mohr, L. 127
monetarism 75
Montesquieu, C. de S. 4
multilevel governance 98–9, 160
  see also governance
mutability, of institutions 19, 91, 170, 175, 181, 182
mutual constitution of agency and structure 118

narrative institutionalism 26
Netherlands, the 94, 145
New Deal 5
New Zealand
  civil service system, reform of 66
  two-party system of 148
niches 132, 147, 151
Niskanen, W. A. 55, 56
nonconformity, in institutions 39–40
normative institutionalism 11, 25–46, 56, 61, 76, 77, 85, 113, 114, 121, 138, 143, 161, 163, 170, 175, 176, 181
  appropriateness, logic of 7, 20, 27, 29–36, 38, 43, 44, 46, 75, 114, 122, 131, 145, 146, 148, 154, 155, 161, 168, 177, 178
  consequentiality, logic of 30, 37, 38
  and discursive institutionalism
    comparisons 113–14
    similarities 114
  distinguished from sociological institutionalism 128
  individuals, within institutions 37–41
  and institutions 29–45
    change in 36–7
    design of 42
    formation of 34–6
    good 44–5
    operation of 41–2
  limits of 42–3
norms 6, 11, 17, 19, 20, 26, 30, 32, 34, 35, 38, 39, 41, 44, 46, 48, 49, 61, 67, 84, 88, 109, 111, 113, 114, 123, 139, 157, 165, 166, 168, 175, 177, 179, 184, 185
North American Free Trade Association (NAFTA) 53, 159
North, D. 22, 48, 52, 71
Norway 104
  corporate pluralism in 149
  divided government 97

objectivication 139
old institutionalism 3–11
  as background for New Institutionalism 16–18
  historical analysis of 10–11
  holism 9–10
  legalism 7

normative analysis of 11
proto-theory in 6–11
structuralism 8–9
Olsen, J. P. 17, 18, 20, 27, 29, 30, 33, 35, 36, 71, 79, 114, 131, 168
Olson, M. 53, 152
Opello, W. C. 99
Oppenheimer, J. A. 152
Ordeshook, P.C. 1
Organisation for Economic Co-operation and Development (OECD) 165
organizational archetypes 135–6
organizational culture 28, 32, 39
organizational leadership 130
organizational myths 26
organizational theory 114, 128
organizations
individuals within 55–6
integrative versus aggregative 27–8
military 35, 39, 40, 45, 75, 178
population ecology models of 131–3
Ostrogowski, M. 146
Ostrom, E. 52
Owen, D. 153

Padgett, J. F. 77
Pagano, U. 56
Pan American Health Organization (PAHO) 165
parliamentary government 92–5, 107, 108
variations within 97–8
see also government
Parsons, T. 129
partisanship 2, 4, 6, 12, 81, 96, 97
party systems 93, 143, 145–8, 151, 154–8, 183
cartel 156
change in 154–5
models of 18, 148
path dependency 20, 61, 70–4, 76, 77, 145, 148
Pedersen, O. K. 34, 91
Peters, B. G. 58, 79, 80
Peters, T. J. 39
Pierre, J. 80
Pierson, P. 72, 77, 80, 85
pluralism 155
corporate 21, 149, 157
policy(ies)
change 78, 81, 120
choices 15, 20, 55, 70–3, 77, 79, 83–5, 87, 91, 92, 94, 95, 98, 125, 144
entrepreneurs 126
formation 80
learning 79
networks 144, 150–3
policy-making 71–2, 97, 101, 116, 117, 150–2, 184
regulatory 57
political institution 3, 7, 8, 15, 30, 32, 35, 42, 45, 47, 54, 60, 68, 78, 94, 127, 143, 163
see also institution(s)
political parties 10, 73, 94–7, 143, 145–51, 153–8, 161, 172, 183
change in 154–5
Polsby, N. 99
Popper, K. R. 88
population ecology models, of organizations 131–3, 140, 141
see also organizations
Porter, D. 101
Posner, R. A. 71
Powell, W. 134
preferences 16, 26, 49, 51, 54–6, 62–4, 68, 69, 77, 81, 92, 109, 119, 122, 125, 156, 157, 169, 170, 173, 180–1, 183
congealed 91
formation of 27
presidential government 92–5, 107, 108
see also government
Pressman, J. L. 87, 101
prime ministers 32, 40, 95–7, 105, 109, 176, 183
principal–agent models 51, 56–7, 60, 66, 68, 177
Prisoners' Dilemma 58
see also game theory
Progressive Movement 4–5
Przeworski, A. 91
Public Administration Clearing House 5
Puchala, D. J. 163
punctuated equilibrium 78, 80, 81, 83, 135
see also equilibrium
Putnam, R. D. 103, 170

rational choice 1, 2, 9, 32, 36, 74, 77, 91, 107, 143, 155, 161, 178
as background for New Institutionalism 16–18
institutionalists 20
revolution of 12–16
as science 17
theory 47–69
varieties of 51–2
rationality of institutions 50, 53, 129
see also institution(s)
Rawls, J. 17
realism (international politics) 159
reductionism 17
reframing 79, 115, 117
regime(s)
change in 170–1
defined 163–6
design of 167–8
origin of 166–7
theory, as institutional theory 162–3
Reich, R. 87
Rein, M. 87, 117
Remmer, K. 106
Republican Party 145, 147
Ressortsprinzip 98
see also Germany
Riggs, F. W. 107
Riker, W.H. 1, 54, 63, 91, 182
Rittberger, V. 163
Rockman, B. A. 93
Rogers, B. 153
Rogers, W. 146
Rokkan, S. 149
Roland, G. 182
role crystallization 131
role theory 32, 43, 131
Rosendorff, B. P. H. 167
Roth, P. A. 2
Rovik, K. A. 33
Rowan, B. 138
rules 32, 48, 49, 51–5, 72, 75, 91, 92, 141, 149, 161, 162, 164, 167, 176–8, 180–3
decision 54–5, 61
institutions as 52–3
Sabatier, P. 79
Sartori, G. 148
Scandinavia, corporate pluralism in 149
Scharpf, F. W. 48, 177
Schmidt, V. A. 112, 119, 121
Schmitter, P. C. 152
Schneiderman, S. 100
Schon, D. A. 117
Scott, W. R. 51, 137
sedimentation 72, 80, 134–5, 139
Selznick, P. 2, 3, 27, 35, 44, 119, 130
semi-presidentialism 90, 93, 104
Sened, I. 62
separated institutions *see* divided government
separation of powers 4
Sewell, W. H. 30
Shepsle, K. A. 48, 51, 54
shirking 50
Simmons, B. A. 164
Simon, H. 5, 29, 56
Skocpol, T. 5, 70, 80
social capital 103
social class 74
Social Democratic Party 153, 157
societal institutionalism 21
sociological institutionalism 61, 127–42, 163
contemporary 131
discursive institutionalism 136
distinguished from normative institutionalism 128
individuals, within institutions 138–9
and institutions
change in 139–40
good 140–1
isomorphism 133–4
organizational archetypes 135–6
population ecology models, of organizations 131–3, 140, 141
questions about 136–8
roots of 129–31
sedimentation 134–5
sociology 22–3
historical 22
organizational 22
South Korea 172

sovereignty 98
Squire, P. 99, 100
Staatswissenschaft 6
Standard Operating Procedures 72
State 5–7, 10, 13, 16
  behavior of, in international politics 164
  corporatism and societal corporatism, link between 152
  nation 171, 176
  and political party system, link between 148
  power of 61
  Prussian 7
  sectorization of 144
  and society, relationship between 21, 144, 148–50, 152
  welfare 76, 125
Steinmo, S. 70, 86
Steunenberg, B. 66
Streeck, W. 80
structural analysis 2
structural-functionalism 12, 13
structuralism 8–9
structure–agency distinction 38, 43, 45, 80, 83, 121–2, 171, 176, 182
structure-induced equilibrium 51, 182
  see also equilibrium
sui generis 9
supranationalists 166
Sweden 86
  commune governments in 109
  federal government 99
  institutional change in 79
  policy-making in 101
Switzerland, policy-making in 101
symbols 27–9, 123, 129, 131, 133, 135, 136, 138, 145

tabula rasa 52
tax(ation)
  policy 86
  resistance to 154
Taylor, R. C. A. 128
Teune, H. 91
Thatcher, M. 40, 109
Thelen, K. 70, 80, 81
Third World 93
  see also government
total institutions 31, 137, 146, 178
  see also institution(s)
tragedy of the commons 53
transaction costs economic theory 48
Tugwell, R. G. 22
Tullock, G. 54
two level games 170

unitary government 98–9
  see also government
United Kingdom 86, 169, 172
  Bank of England 78, 79, 102
  central banks, control of 102
  Conservative Party 145
  divided government 97
  economic policy, development of 71
  election 1997 105
  federal government 99
  House of Commons 100
  institutional change in 77, 79
  institutionalized relationships in 144
  Labour Party 102, 153, 154
  political organization in 146–7
  presidential government 93, 95
  social and economic policies, differences between 90
  Social Democratic Party 153
  welfare politics, development of 76
United Nations 21
United Nations Educational, Scientific and Cultural Organization (UNESCO) 160, 170
United States 1, 57, 152, 169
  Anti-Trust Division (ATD) 41
  Congress 40
  Constitution of 62
  Democratic Party 145
  divided government 95–6
  federal government 99
  Federal Reserve Bank 91, 102
  Federal Trade Commission 41
  Forest Service 75, 133
  House of Representatives 99
  institutional change in 79

Naval Academy 38
political organization in 146, 147
presidential government 93, 95
Republican Party 145, 147
social and economic policies, differences between 90
societal institutionalism in 21
welfare politics, development of 76
utilitarianism 17
utility maximization 14, 20, 25, 26, 47, 49, 50, 60, 68, 125

values 6, 11, 17, 18, 20, 25–31, 35–41, 43–5, 49, 51, 52, 58, 79, 84, 90–2, 94, 100, 103, 104, 106, 107, 109, 113, 114, 117, 120–2, 124, 125, 127–31, 135–7, 139, 141, 145, 147, 149–51, 155, 156, 159, 163–6, 168–75, 178–84
Veblen, T. 22
veto
players 55, 75
power 104
points 21, 55, 66, 75, 78, 87–8, 101, 103
voting behavior 12

Waterman, R. H. 39
Weaver, R. K. 93
Weber, M. 27, 129, 134, 135
Weingast, B. 77
welfare politics, development of 76
welfare state 76, 125
see also State
Westminster system 96–7, 104
White, Leonard 5
Wildavsky, A. 76, 87, 101, 168
Williams, S. 153
Williamson, O. E. 48, 71
Wilson, W. 4–6, 8, 13, 92–3
Congressional Government 4
Progressive Movement 4–5
World Bank 168
World Health Organization (WHO) 160, 165, 170
World Trade Organization (WTO) 160

YMCA 81
Young, O. R. 152

Zucker, L. G. 176

Lightning Source UK Ltd.
Milton Keynes UK
UKOW06f1807150116

266472UK00011B/164/P

9 781441 13042